‘AZĪZ NASAFĪ

CURZON SUFI SERIES

Series editor: Ian Richard Netton

Professor of Arabic and
Middle Eastern Studies,
University of Leeds

The Curzon Sufi Series attempts to provide short introductions to a variety of facets of the subject, which are accessible both to the general reader and the student and scholar in the field. Each book will be either a synthesis of existing knowledge or a distinct contribution to, and extension of, knowledge of the particular topic. The two major under-lying principles of the Series are sound scholarship and readability.

BEYOND FAITH AND INFIDELITY
The Sufi Poetry and Teachings of Mahmud Shabistari
Leonard Lewisohn

AL-HALLAJ
Herbert W. Mason

RUZBIHAN BAQLI
Mysticism and the Rhetoric of Sainthood in Persian Sufism
Carl W. Ernst

ABDULLAH ANSARI OF HERAT
An Early Sufi Master
A.G. Ravan Farhadi

PERSIAN SUFI POETRY
An Introduction to the Mysticaql Use of Classical Persian Poetry
J.T.P. de Bruijn

THE CONCEPT OF SAINTHOOD IN EARLY ISLAMIC MYSTICISM
Bernd Radtke and John O'Kane

SUHRAWARDI AND THE SCHOOL OF ILLUMINATION
Mehdi Amin Razavi

‘AZĪZ NASAFĪ

Lloyd V. J. Ridgeon

CURZON

First Published in 1998
by Curzon Press
15 The Quadrant, Richmond
Surrey, TW9 1BP

Typeset in Sabon by LaserScript Ltd, Mitcham, Surrey
Printed and bound in Great Britain by
Biddles Limited, Guildford and King's Lynn

British Library Cataloguing in Publication Data
A catalogue record of this book is available from the British Library

Library of Congress Cataloguing in Publication Data
A catalog record for this book has been requested

ISBN 0–7007–1013–2 (Hbk)
ISBN 0–7007–1014–0 (Pbk)

For Evie, Barbara and Fiona

I am as My servant imagines Me. I am with him when he thinks of Me. If he thinks of Me inwardly, I think of him inwardly; if he mentions Me in company, I mention him in a superior company. If a man approaches Me by a foot, I shall approach him by a yard; if he approaches Me by a yard, I shall approach him by a furlong. If he comes to Me walking, I shall go to him running.

Ḥadīth, see W. Graham, *Divine Word and Prophetic Word in Early Islam* (The Hague: Mouton, 1977), p. 130.

Contents

Introduction

If Sufism in its beginnings had been an "outspoken elitist form of religion,"[1] then it had matured by the middle of the twelfth century by means of the establishment of orders in to a mass movement which had penetrated all sections of society in the Middle East and North Africa and had made great inroads into Central Asia and India. The thirteenth century was indeed a vibrant age for Sufism and one cannot speak of a uniform version of Islamic mysticism because its manifestations differed in terms of form and understanding. The myriad forms were exemplified in the voluminous speculative thought of Ibn 'Arabī (1165–1240), the poetic subtleties of Jalāl al-Dīn Rūmī (d. 1273) and the manuals interpreting visions of light by Najm al-Dīn Kubrā (d. 1221). With regard to the understanding of "reality", one need only look at the various interpretations of existence offered by 'Azīz Nasafī (see chapter two).[2] Despite the diversity in form and understanding, these manifestations of Sufism shared the fundamental goal of seeking God through devotion and service which could lead to an intimate and private relationship with the Absolute based on love. One mystic of this period was 'Azīz Nasafī, who was born in Central Asia and gathered a circle of followers in Bukhārā and various locations in Iran. His works are of great interest because they contain descriptions of the different Islamic world views of the age and by a careful analysis of their contents it is possible to piece together Nasafī's own particular mystical perspective which has a striking resemblence to those of Ibn 'Arabī and Najm al-Dīn Kubrā.

There have been many scholarly works on individual Sufis of the medieval era, however, Nasafī has attracted very little attention among contemporary researchers. This is quite surprising since Nasafī was one of the greatest Sufi masters of his time and composed several major works that are distinctive for their clarity and simplicity in explaining the Sufi path. Although Nasafī has been over looked in the modern day and age, he was the subject of academic interest in the West in earlier centuries. In 1665, a Turkish version of Nasafī's *Maqṣad-i aqṣā* along with a Latin translation was published[3] and this was followed in 1821 by F. Tholuck who discussed Nasafī in his handbook entitled "The Pantheistic Theosophy of the Persians."[4] The first English work on Nasafī appeared in 1867 when Palmer paraphrased the *Maqṣad-i aqṣā* under the title *Oriental Mysticism*[5] and this book has been reprinted several times since then. In the middle of the twentieth century there were several excellent studies related to Nasafī. Fritz Meier's German articles were the first to concentrate upon Nasafī's ideas and writings[6] while M. Molé edited two of Nasafī's treatises entitled "The Perfect Man" *(al-Insān al-kāmil)* and "The Waystations of the Travellers" *(Manāzil al-sā'īrīn)*.[7] Molé also included a fifty-seven page introduction in French in which he discussed some of the themes in Nasafī's theosophy as well as continuing Meier's investigation into manuscripts of Nasafī's works.

Since Molé's studies in the early 1960s, western scholars have only made brief references to Nasafī as an interpreter of Ibn 'Arabī[8] and this does not do justice to one of the greatest *shaykhs* of thirteenth century Central Asia and Iran. Recently, several articles about Nasafī's thought and life have been published. Of particular interest is Landolt's study which offers an alternative focus on Nasafī from that presented in this work.[9] During the course of my own research on Nasafī, several articles have been published which have been adapted and included within this work.[10]

One point that will become clear to the reader is that this book includes many translations, some lengthy, from Nasafī's books. The reason for this is that it is best to let the original author speak for himself rather than present watered-down paraphrases which sometimes omit significant details. In addition, the literal approach to translating Nasafī's works has been adopted here in an attempt to avoid the pitfalls of "reader-friendly" interpretations which not only overlook the nuances and technical terminology of the original texts but also becomes lost in a fog of poetic language which may not reflect the intention of the original author.

This book is a result of several years of research undertaken at various universities in England, the United States of America and Japan while I was Ph.D. student. During this period, I was lucky to receive assistance from numerous scholars whose recommendations and comments shaped the course of my studies, and this work would not have been completed without their help. Firstly, I should express my gratitude to Professor A. Matsumoto of Eichi University in Japan, who not only read through Nasafī's *al-Insān al-kāmil* with me while I was studying at the International University of Japan for my M.A., but has continued to take an interest in my research in this field. My study of Nasafī's texts lead me to the State University of New York at Stony Brook from October 1994 to May 1995, where Prof. W. Chittick kindly read through Nasafī's *Kitāb-i tanzīl* with me (in manuscript form). In addition, Prof. Chittick consented to review an early draft of the first section of chapter two, and he unstintingly drew my attention to many of the facets of the *wujūdī* interpretation of Sufism which would otherwise have been omitted.

In England, my understanding of Nasafī's theosophy was nurtured under the guidance of Dr. L. Lewisohn who clarified numerous problems related to Sufi terminology and belief. Always unselfish with his time, Dr. Lewisohn looked at several pieces of this work and suggested various ways to improve it. Another great debt is to Prof. Netton who listened patiently to my ideas and plans for three years. Not only did he provide numerous contacts and give me adequate academic freedom to pursue my studies on Nasafī, but he also was an infinite source of motivation.

I would also like to express my gratitude to all the members of the Imanari family in Muikamachi in Japan where I enjoyed their hospitality for several lengthy periods of time during which I continued my studies on Nasafī in a comfortable and tranquil environment. I would also like to mention my good friend, Vargu Shankar Ajay whose sense of humour, support and insights on a variety of topics contributed to the development of my research.

This piece of research would never have materialised had it not been for the considerable financial assistance that I received from the British Academy and the British Institute of Persian Studies.

Finally I would like to express my thanks to my parents who have encouraged my research from the very start. They have never lacked in understanding or sympathy and their presence has always been the necessary support behind all others.

Notes

1 A. Schimmel, "Sufism and the Islamic Tradition," *Mysticism and Religious Traditions,* edited S. Katz (Oxford: Oxford University Press, 1983), p. 137.

2 For different kinds of Sufism, see H. Landolt, "Two Types of Mystical Thought in Muslim Iran," *Muslim World*, Vol. 68 (1978).

3 A. Mueller, *Excerpta Manuscripti Cujusdam Turcici* (Coloniae Brandenburgicae: 1665).

4 F.A.G. Tholuck, *Ssufismus Sive Theosophia Persarum Pantheistica* (Berlin: 1821).

5 E.H. Palmer, *Oriental Mysticism: a Treatise on Sufiistic and Unitarian Theosophy of the Persians* (London: 1867; second edition, 1938).

6 See "Das Problem der Natur im Esoterischen Monismus des Islams," *Eranos-Jahrbuch* 14 (1946), and "Die Schriften des 'Azīz-i Nasafī," *Wiener Zeitschrift für die Kunde des Morganlandes* 52 (1953). The first of these has been translated into English, see "The Problem of Nature in the Esoteric Monism of Islam," *Spirit and Nature: Papers from the Eranos Yearbook*, ed. J. Campbell (New York: 1954).

7 Nasafī, *Kitāb al-Insān al-kāmil*, ed. M. Molé (Tehran-Paris: Institut Franco-Iranien, 1962). This work also includes Nasafī's *Manāzil al-sā'irīn*. Nasafī's *al-Insān al-kāmil* has subsequently been translated into European languages several times. The first of these was Isabelle de Gastines's French rendition entitled *Le Livre de l'Homme Parfait* (Paris: Fayard, 1984). My own English version was called *The Perfect Man* (Niigata, Japan: The Institute of Middle Eastern Studies, 1992). There also exists an unpublished translation by W. Thackston, which I saw during a research trip to the United States in 1995. Both S.H. Nasr and W. Chittick showed Thackston's work to me.

8 For example, James Morris, "Ibn 'Arabī and his interpreters," *Journal of the American Oriental Society* 106 (1986), pp. 745–51. Also W. Chittick, "Rūmī and waḥdat al-wujūd," *The Heritage of Rūmī*, eds A. Banani and G. Sabagh (Cambridge: Cambridge University Press, 1994). See also S. Murata's passages on Nasafī in her *Tao of Islam: A Sourcebook on Gender Relationships in Islamic Thought* (Albany: SUNY Press, 1992). L. Lewisohn has also focused upon Nasafī, although not merely as an interpreter of Ibn 'Arabī, see *Beyond Faith and Infidelity* (Richmond: Curzon Press, 1995), pp 219–228.

9 H. Landolt, "Le Paradoxe De La "Face De Dieu": 'Azīz-e Nasafī (VIIe/ XIIIe) Et La "Monisme Ésoterique" De L'Islam," *Studia Iranica*, 25, 1996, pp. 163–192.

10 L. Ridgeon, "The Life and Times of 'Azīz Nasafī," *Sufi: A Journal of Sufism*. XXII (1994): 31–35. "'Azīz Nasafī and Visionary Experience," *Sufi: A Journal of Sufism*. XXIV, (1995): 22–28. "The Felicitous Life in Sufism," *Sufi: A Journal of Sufism*., XXVIII, (1996): 30–35. "'Azīz Nasafī's Six Ontological Faces," *Iran*, 1996, pp. 85–99.

1

The Life, Times and Works of 'Azīz Nasafī

I. THE LIFE AND TIMES OF 'AZĪZ NASAFĪ

'Azīz ibn Muḥammad al-Nasafī was born in the beginning of the thirteenth century in Nasaf, a town that was situated some four days travelling distance from Bukhārā.[1] This was the era for seeking knowledge, and the city of Bukhārā was the centre of learning for it had achieved the reputation of being one of the great cities not only of the region, but of the Islamic world. Juwaynī, a contemporary historian, described Bukhārā as ". . . the cupola of Islam and is in those regions like unto the City of Peace. Its environs are adorned with the brightness of the light of doctors and jurists and its surroundings embellished with the rarest of high attainments. Since ancient times it has in every age been the place of assembly of the great savants of every religion. Now the derivation of Bukhārā is from 'bukhar' which in the language of the Magians signifies centre of learning."[2] Whether Nasafī was in Nasaf or Bukhārā or even in Khwarazm among the circle of Najm al-Dīn Kubrā in 1220 when the Mongols appeared is not known, but since his date of birth probably occurred around 1200,[3] he would certainly have been old enough and aware of the events that were to follow.

In 1220, the security and civilised environment of Central Asia and Iran was shattered. One contemporary historian commented: "Who would find it easy to describe the ruin of Islam and the Muslims? If anyone were to say that at no time since the creation of man by the great God had the world experienced anything like it, he would only be telling the truth."[4] In February 1220, the Mongol hordes descended upon Bukhārā, and from the pulpit of the Friday mosque, Chingiz Khān declared: "O people! Know that you have committed great sins and that great ones among you have committed these sins. If you ask me what proof I have for these words, I say it is because I am the punishment of God. If you had not committed great sins God would not have sent a punishment like me upon you."[5] One survivor of the destruction described what had happened: "They came, they sapped, they burned, they slew, they plundered, they departed."[6] Juwaynī believed that Bukhārā had escaped lightly, Chingiz Khān being satisfied with slaughter and looting only once, but not going to the extreme of a general massacre.[7]

Having captured the major cities of Transoxania, Chingiz Khān rested during the summer just outside of Nasafī's birthplace on the plains of Nasaf. His forces then proceeded to conquer all the major cities including Khwarazm which was taken in 1221. Najm al-Dīn Kubrā refused to flee the advancing Mongol armies and was killed in the vain defence of the city. Those cities that surrendered escaped with little damage, but those which resisted suffered a terrible retribution. The case of Nishapur is perhaps the most horrific, for the command was given to destroy the town completely and kill all life including cats and dogs.[8] A daughter of Chingiz Khān had lost her husband during a preliminary skirmish at Nishapur, and once she entered the town with her escort, she had all the survivors slain (save four hundred artisans who were valued for their crafts, and who were carried off to Turkestan). They severed the heads from the slain and proceeded to construct three huge mountains of skulls; one for men, another for women, and one for the children.[9] It was estimated that 1,747,000 people were killed in the massacre at Nishapur,[10] and although this is an exaggeration, at least one can begin to see the proportion of the destruction and terror that the Mongol invasion left in its wake.

Chingiz Khān's hordes were diverted by other issues and departed from the Middle East, however, the Mongols returned to Transoxania in 1254 under Hulegu. Hulegu Khān was the younger brother of Kubilai Khān and he entered Central Asia and Iran to crush the Ismā'īlīs. Having achieved this, he advanced to Baghdād, the capital of the decaying Abbasid Caliphate. The city was sacked and looted and the Caliph was taken prisoner but his ambassadors warned Hulegu that should the deputy of God's messenger be killed, ". . . the whole world will be disorganised, the Sun will hide its face, the rain will cease to fall and the plants will no longer grow." In addition, they predicted that ". . . if Hulegu spills the blood of the Caliph on the ground, he and his infidel Mongols will be swallowed up by the earth." Describing the Mongols' predicament, the Muslims said "the accursed Hulegu feared that if he let the Caliph live, the Muslims would rise up in revolt, and that if he slew him and his blood was spilled on the ground, there would be an earthquake."[11] Hulegu settled the matter by having the Caliph rolled up in a carpet and trampled to death.

The second Mongol invasion in fact turned into an occupation, Hulegu being the first of the Il-Khān dynasty. Of course this had important consequences for Muslims since Chingiz Khān and the Mongols had no special respect for Islam (indeed, during the sacking of Bukhārā, the Mongols had used Koranic stands in the Friday Mosque as mangers for their horses, and worse still for devout Muslims was that leaves of the Koran were trodden underfoot). Yet the Mongols were generally tolerant of all religions, and Chingiz Khān had decreed the freedom of religion: "Kubilai pursued the traditional Mongol policy of toleration for all creeds, whose priests, imams and bonzes continued to be exempt from taxation, and he allowed but two partial exceptions, by suppressing the literature of Taoists and banning the propaganda of the Muslims,"[12] and this policy was generally followed by subsequent rulers. However, the establishment of all religions on a level par with Islam, coupled with the murder of the Caliph, must have thrown Muslims into paroxysms of fear that the end of the world was drawing nigh. It was the first time that Muslims were to suffer the indignity of sharing the same status as Christians and Jews which also meant that non-Muslims were no longer obliged to pay the *jizya* tax. Moreover, Muslims must have felt greater indignation and humiliation since their religion was reduced by the Mongols to the same degree as "idol-worshipping" Buddhism and Shamanism. The Mongol rulers themselves embraced a mixture of Buddhism and Shamanism, for example, at Hulegu's death, several beautiful young women were chosen as "his bed fellows" for the journey to the next world which may have been an old Mongol religious custom.[13] Abaqa (Hulegu's son and second Il-Khān) "followed the path of the Buddhists"[14] and at the same time remained attached to native Mongol beliefs, as he is known to have enjoyed the company of a magician named Baraq.[15] Shaman influence remained under the fourth Il-Khān, Arghun (1284–91), who practised an exorcism of purification by fire which involved walking by two fires while those around him recited incantations and sprinkled water.[16] It was also suggested by some Mongol advisors to the Il-Khān Oljeitu (1304–1316) that he undertake this ceremony (although it is not known if it was performed). In fact Arghun combined Shamanism with his interest in Buddhism, for it is known that he had priests brought from India to conduct Buddhist ceremonies. An interesting account by the famed Kubrāwī Sufi, 'Alā' al-Dawla Simnānī (d. 1336) reveals the nature of religious interaction during Arghun's reign. Simnānī was a member of the Mongol court but had a vision which made him embrace Sufism. After attempting an escape from the court, he was captured and brought back by the Mongols to the city of Sultaniyya. "There, he [Arghun] had assembled Buddhist priests from India, Kashmir, Tibet and Ighur, along with the ascetics and the religious leaders of the idolaters around him, to engage in disputation with me. So I discussed and disputed with them. But God Almighty lent me strength, and I was able to refute all of them, and to disgrace and humiliate them."[17] Arghun was delighted and begged Simnānī to stay with him, permitting him to remain in his dervish clothing. Nevertheless, the true extent of Buddhist influence cannot be evaluated, although as Bausani has commented, "Iran must have been full of Buddhist temples – we hear of them only when they were destroyed in 1295–6."[18]

One interesting point concerning religion under the Mongols is their favourable attitude towards Nestorian Christians. This position may well have been a result of the political dynamics of the time, for Hulegu suffered a defeat at the hands of the Mamluks at 'Ayn Jalut in 1260, and subsequently the Il-Khāns found themselves facing enemies on several fronts; the Mamluks to the west, the Golden Horde in the north and the Chagatai Mongols in the east. Therefore the well-disposed attitude towards Christianity on the half of the Il-Khāns may have been directed at the Byzantine Emperor who was a rival of the Mamluks in the Mediterranean. The extent to which Christianity had penetrated into the Il-Khān court is illustrated by the fact that both Hulegu and his son Aqaba had Christian wives (Aqaba's wife being none less than the daughter of the Byzantine Emperor). Indeed, a Christian named Rabban Sauma[19] was Aqaba's envoy to Rome and at the Vatican he claimed that many Mongols had converted to Christianity. Rabban Sauma's disciple, named Mark, became the supreme head of all Nestorians in Asia (under the protection of Abaqa) and later he was to baptise Arghun's son as Nicholas (in honour of Pope Nicholas IV). It is also during this period that the Gospels were translated in to Persian, but the extent to which the Sufis and Muslims were aware of Christian doctrine is unclear. Although some mystics including Nasafī quoted passages which bear striking resemblance to those in the Gospels,[20] these may have been little more than idioms that were popular at the time.

The displacement of Islam as the official religion of Iran and central Asia lasted until the reign of the Il-Khān Teguder, (1282–1284) who converted to Islam and adopted the name Aḥmad. Although his reign was brief and this changing of religion did little to affect the lot of the Muslim, it is perhaps indicative of the influence that Islam, the belief of the populace, was having upon the Il-Khān court. Islam finally regained its predominant position in the region when the Il-Khān Ghazan (1295–1304) accepted Islam. His conversion is of particular interest because the ceremony was performed by Ṣadr al-Dīn Ibrāhīm Ḥammūya (1246–1322) who was the son of Sa'd al-Dīn Ḥammūya (Nasafī's Sufi master). In addition, it appears that Ghazan was initiated into Sufism in this ceremony.[21]

Ironically, the religious policy of the early Il-Khāns may have contributed to the strengthening of Islam, in particular of Sufism, in the whole region of Central Asia and Iran. Fear of the Mongols and the difficulties of life subsequent to the Mongol invasions may have directed people towards hope in the next world and not in this world. Such a perspective is so pervasive in Nasafī's works:

> Oh dervish! Know for sure that we are travellers and certainly we pass the time hour by hour. If there is wealth it will pass, and if there is affliction it will pass. If you have wealth do not put your trust in it because it is unclear what will happen in the next hour. If you have affliction, do not be excessively sad because it is not clear what will occur in the next hour. You should try not to cause harm to anyone and as far as possible you should try to bring comfort.[22]

Sufism provided a relief for the general Islamic populace, and in all probability, many individuals found solace in meetings at the *khānaqāh*, and in *dhikr* and *samā'* gatherings. Whole communities were affiliated to particular Sufi shaykhs: "At the beginning of the thirties of the thirteenth century, the majority of the population in Balkh were *murids* (followers) of Shaykh Bahā' al-Dīn Walad."[23] This factor, aided by the Mongol tolerance of religion may help explain why Sufism flourished during the Il-Khān period, to which the mystical works of 'Azīz Nasafī, Sa'd al-Dīn Ḥammūya (d. 1252), Najm al-Dīn Rāzī (d. 1256), Sayf al-Dīn Bākharzī (d. 1261), 'Alā' al-Dawla Simnānī and Awḥād al-Dīn Balyānī (d. 1288) all testify. Moreover, the region of Central Asia and Iran under the Il-Khān's was still free and open enough to receive the intellectual and spiritual inheritance of great mystics such as Ibn 'Arabī[24] and Jalāl al-Dīn Rūmī who lived outside of the Mongol regions.

Aside from the religious policies of the Mongols, life in Central Asia and Iran was affected in a whole number of ways. Mongol influence was felt predominantly in the north, for Abaqa had fixed the capital at Tabrīz.[25] Concerning the influence of the Mongols in the north, one scholar commented "under the system set up by Hulegu and his immediate successors, Mongol rule was direct only in Khurāsān and elsewhere in northern Iran, except in Gīlān and in parts of Iraq. Fārs, Kirmān and Shabankara, with Hurmūz and Qais on the Persian Gulf in the south, Luristān in the west and Hirāt in the east, [were] all contained within the Mongol framework under the native ruling families, who suffered little interference and in some cases outlasted the Il-Khāns."[26] By all accounts, the Mongols in the north were rapacious in extorting and appropriating everything and anything from the native peoples who had survived. Finding any source of income must have been difficult enough, and as a result of the destruction of two invasions it was estimated that in 1295, five out of every ten houses in the sacked cities of Iran were uninhabited.[27] Tax collecting was arbitrary and the Mongols imposed new, more severe taxes upon the native population. For example, the "*tamgha*" was a tax of 10% of the value of each commercial transaction which replaced the Muslim *zakat* of 2.5%.[28] The *jizya* tax was abolished for non-Muslims early in the Il-Khān period (to be re-established by Ghazan) and was replaced with a general poll tax. In Transoxania, the highest rate for this tax was fifteen dinars and in 1253 when Arghun was in control of that region, he began to levy seventy dinars from every ten men, turning the maximum into an average.[29] "By extracting taxes greater than the people could pay, and having them reduced to poverty, they began to torment and afflict them. Those who tried to hide were caught and put to death. From those who could not pay they took away their children."[30]

The Iranian economy suffered tremendous losses during the early Il-Khān period. It has been estimated that in their desire for wealth and to finance their campaigns, the Mongols levied taxes twenty to thirty times each year: "the Mongol grandees were the principle culprits; a conquered territory in their opinion existed only to be mulcted, and the terror of their name unlawfully exacted vast sums from the peasants, artisans and merchants."[31] This resulted in the peasants abandoning their land, and nine tenths of cultivable land went to waste.[32] It has been shown that in one region of Fārs, 700,000 ass-loads of grain were yielded annually between 949–983, and in the aftermath of the Mongol invasion and its consequences, this total was reduced to 300,000 ass-loads in 1260.[33]

To say that Nasafī lived during the best of times and the worst of times may not be too much of an exaggeration. The thirteenth century was a century of extremes; on the one hand it developed a tradition of knowledge whose legacy is still regarded as a treasure by millions not only in the Middle East but all around the world, and on the other hand it suffered the devastation and dread of the Mongol invasions and occupation. Nasafī's life spans the whole course of this era, for he was born in Nasaf around the very beginning of the thirteenth century and died towards its end. This is clear because in *Maqṣad-i aqṣā*, Nasafī commented that he was eighty years of age, and this work was compiled some time before 1281.[34]

Of his youth and early adulthood nothing at all is known, indeed, only fragments of information concerning his life emerge from his works. The first of these is his association with an affiliate of the Kubrāwī order, Shaykh Sa'd al-Dīn Ḥammūya, who Nasafī served in Khurāsān.[35] Nasafī also received guidance from an un-named shaykh in Bukhārā[36], and if this shaykh was Ḥammūya, then Nasafī's association with him must have occurred some time during the 1240s and before 1252 when Ḥammūya died. (Prior to this period, Ḥammūya was seeking knowledge further west in the Islamic world).[37] One famous Sufi writer, the great Persian poet and theosopher Jāmī (1414–1492) believed this un-nmaed shaykh was indeed Ḥammūyā.[38] A recent work, however, has suggested that this un-named shaykh (referred to by Nasafī as "Our shaykh") could have been Sayf al-Dīn Bākharzī.[39]

That Nasafī enjoyed companionship with Ḥammūya during the 1240s means that we are still left with a huge gap of perhaps forty years, from Nasafī's birth until his meeting with Ḥammūya. A portion of this may have been taken up with Nasafī's study of medicine, which lasted several years,[40] and although it is not clear when he commenced this study, one can speculate that it was before he encountered Ḥammūya, for Nasafī was probably too old in the 1240s to commence such a difficult field of learning. A knowledge of medicine was one that was, however, fairly typical of the Sufis of the Kubrāwī order for Najm al-Dīn Kubrā and his associates Farīd al-Dīn 'Aṭṭār (d. 1220) and Majd al-Dīn Baghdādī (d. 1219) all spent some time in this occupation.[41]

Aside from enjoying the companionship of Sa'd al-Dīn Ḥammūya, Nasafī may have been spiritually inspired by a son of one of the commanders of Sultan Jalāl al-Dīn of Bukhārā.[42] In a sixteenth century text, Nasafī is called a lover *('āshiq)* and intoxicated *(mast)* with reference to this youth. This was a relatively common phenomena in medieval Persian Sufism, for one finds similar accounts of Jalāl al-Dīn Rūmī who witnessed beauty in the character traits of Shams-i Tabrīzī (d. 1248), Salāḥ al-Dīn Zarkūb (d. 1258) and Ḥusām al-Dīn Chalābī (d. 1284).[43]

By 1260, Nasafī had acquired his own circle of novices who wished to learn from him. His first work appears to be *Kitāb-i tanzīl* which was composed at the request of his followers. The first six chapters were written in Nasaf. By 1261 Nasafī had moved back to Bukhārā[44] where he continued his work on *Kitāb-i tanzīl*. From this period until 1273 nothing is known, perhaps Nasafī continued to teach his theosophy to his circle of dervishes. However his life style was to change dramatically following the events of 22 January 1273:

> In that year the infidel armies came to Transoxania and they destroyed the province, and at that time this helpless one was in the city of Bukhārā with the community of dervishes. At dawn on Friday, at the beginning of the month of Rajab, we left the city – or should I say, that they forced us to make an exit – and we passed the waters of Khurāsān and arrived at the cities of Khurāsān. From that time onwards, each day we were in one location and each night at another, having no security anywhere.[45]

The infidel armies belonged to the Il-Khān Abaqa, whose rivalry and dispute with the Chagatai Mongols was a result of the division of Chingiz Khān's empire. Bukhārā was situated on the border between the Il-Khān and Chagatai areas, and friction between the two sides frequently lead to demonstrations of force. The attack of 1273 was brutal and Nasafī was most likely very lucky to escape with his life. The religious schools and books were burned and as many as 50, 000 people were killed. It was said that no living creature appeared in Bukhārā for seven years after the massacre.[46]

It was impossible for Nasafī to return to Bukhārā so he made his way westwards into northern Iran to visit the tomb of his shaykh, Sa'd al-Dīn Ḥammūya, which was situated in Bahrabād, near Juwayn.[47] Perhaps the Il-Khān control here was strong, because Nasafī moved southwards, and he composed works at Kirmān,[48] Shirāz,[49] Isfahān[50] and Abarqūh.[51] The date of Nasafī's death is not known, but M. Molé has mentioned one of Nasafī's manuscripts which bears the date of 1291. However, his death could have happened anytime between 1281 and 1300. It was on the night of 27 August 1281 that Nasafī was in Abarqūh and had a dream in which the Prophet Muḥammad told him not to reveal the remaining chapters of *Kashf al-ḥaqā'iq* until seven hundred years had elapsed since the hegira (i.e. 1300 A.D.). Nasafī had already composed the first seven of ten chapters for the dervishes, and in all remaining manuscripts of this work, only these seven chapters appear. This suggests that Nasafī passed away before the deadline in the year 1300.

Thus, very little is known about Nasafī's personal life, which perhaps is not so surprising since his works were of a didactic nature. In his treatises, the advice to seek knowledge is predominant, and perhaps Nasafī was speaking of himself when he commented:

> The People of Gnosis . . . have spent many years in the service of Shaykhs in religious effort and spiritual discipline, and they have actualised knowledge of form and knowledge of meaning, and they supposed that they had reached and recognised God. Then after seventy years they understood that they knew nothing, and everything which they had understood was all imagination and fancy; and they saw themselves as ignorant, incapable and helpless.[52]
>
> The People of Gnosis . . . have spent periods among the *'Ulamā'*, periods among the Philosophers, periods among the Transmigrationists, periods among the Sufis and periods among the People of Unity. Each group said, "The truth is with us and falsity is with the others." The People of Gnosis thought to themselves that if each one opposes the others then they cannot all be true because the truth is only one. So they knew for sure that the truth was not with any of them.[53]

One last factor which appears in Nasafī's works is fear and the danger in expressing the esoteric dimension of Islam. This aspect of Nasafī's life is evident in his dream in which the Prophet warned him not to reveal the remaining chapters of *Kashf al-ḥaqā'iq*:

> Know that in 1281 I was in the province of Fārs in the city of Abarqūh. It was midnight on the 27 August and this helpless one had sat down and placed a lamp nearby and was writing something. Then sleep overcame me and I saw my father enter by the door. I stood up and greeted him, and he returned the greeting and said, "The Prophet Muḥammad is sitting with Shaykh Abu 'Abdullah Khafīf and Shaykh Sa'd al-Dīn Ḥammūya in the Friday Mosque of Abarqūh and they are waiting for you." I went with my father to the mosque. I saw the Prophet sitting with them and I greeted them all and they returned the greeting and each one of them embraced me. I sat down and the Prophet said, "Today Shaykh Sa'd al-Dīn Ḥammūya has spoken much about you and he is worried and concerned about your circumstances. He said that all the meanings that he assembled in four hundred books 'Azīz has assembled in ten chapters and although he attempted to write them in

> an obscure and secretive fashion, 'Azīz has attempted to explain clearly and he fears that some bad fortune or harm comes to you."[54]

Another indication of the conditions that prevailed when Nasafī was compiling his works is found in *Maqṣad-i aqṣā*:

> Now I myself do not give my own opinions so that I cannot be accused of infidelity; I report and I say that the People of Unity explain in this way and the Sufis say in that way. O dervish, accept the discourse of this helpless one and recognise yourself so that you can recognise God. Understand all of these discourses which I have set out, and know for sure where the Truth lies.[55]

Nasafī's reluctance to reveal his own views is not surprising given the turbulent times in which he lived. In the generation after Nasafī, the mere possession of Ibn 'Arabī's works was prohibited in Egypt, and such works were confiscated and burnt if found. Moreover, the *'Ulamā'* confirmed that any person advocating the ideas of Ibn 'Arabī would be executed.[56]

II. NASAFĪ'S WORKS[57]

There are many features in Nasafī's treatises which enable scholars to identify his works (although one cannot exclude the possibility of someone else using his name and copying his style and content). The first distinctive aspect in Nasafī's works is the simple but lucid, non-verbose Persian style. His predominant aim is that the reader understands his message and in order to achieve this Nasafī presents each topic from several perspectives, adding at the end of each explanation "I know you have not fully understood so I will explain in another way." This non-condescending style, his direct manner of calling the reader "Dervish" or "Dear Friend," the sections of "advice" at the end of each chapter (in some of his works) in which he offers comfort and encouragement to the Sufi novice and his humility and self rebuking nature endear Nasafī to the reader and one is soon drawn into a warm, intimate relationship with him. The fact that Nasafī used Persian (except for Arabic quotations from the Koran, *ḥadīth* and other sayings) is also of some importance because he can be regarded as among the first of Ibn 'Arabī's commentators who wrote in Persian, thus spreading the message among the non-Arabic speaking populations of Central Asia and Iran.

Secondly, Nasafī's commentaries are both forthright and simple in revealing the non-manifest *(bāṭin)* dimension of Islam. He speaks directly to his readers, advising them to pass over from the formal dimension of Islam to the esoteric, and indicative of this is Nasafī's dream in which Sa'd al-Dīn Ḥammūya states that he had written over four hundred treatises in an obscure and secretive fashion, whereas Nasafī has revealed all of these non-manifest secrets in just ten chapters.

One of the most striking of all of the features in Nasafī's works is the way in which he presents the arguments of each group, that is, he lets each group speak for itself. His chapters frequently begin by "The People of the Holy Law say that . . ." or "The Philosophers say . . ." or "The People of Unity say . . ." If not employing such labels, Nasafī refers to the People of the Holy Law as the "People of Imitation"[58] and the Philosophers are called the "People of definite proof and certain demonstration,"[59] and the People of Unity are the "People of Unveiling."[60] The reason that Nasafī does not reveal his own opinions are firstly that he may have been afraid and so he hid his own beliefs under the shelter of other groups and secondly, he was attempting to describe the beliefs of all the major interpretations of Islam in an impartial manner. While it is true that Nasafī was not the first to undertake such a project, he was most likely the first to record the various beliefs in a non-partisan way. In fact his own dervishes had requested that Nasafī compose his treatises conveying the varying Islamic beliefs "without prejudice and without dissimulation and without making them great and without belittling them."[61] Abū Ḥāmid al-Ghazālī (d. 1111) had studied all the different Islamic beliefs in his attempt to realise the Truth and the results of his intellectual and spiritual investigations are set out in his books in a systematic fashion, describing the beliefs of the *'Ulamā'*, Philosophers and Sufis. However, his preference for the Sufi interpretation of Islam caused him to disparage those beliefs which were at variance with his own, and he describes the Philosophers as "heretics and irreligious men."[62] Nasafī's own portrayal of the different Islamic beliefs did not include such derogatory remarks, and Meier's comment that Nasafī may be considered as a "forerunner of modern comparative religion"[63] captures the essence of Nasafī's spirit. The reality is that while Nasafī was more sympathetic towards the Sufis, he attempted to discover the reality and truth behind other beliefs. This is neatly expressed by Nasafī in his explanation of similar, but different *ḥadīth*.

> In one *ḥadīth* it is stated that "the first thing God created was intelligence," and in another, "the first thing God created was the Pen,"

> and in another, "the first thing God created was the Throne," and there are others like these.[64]
>
> In the Koran and *ḥadīth* there are many references to the First Intelligence. Know that this first intelligence has been referred to through different attributions and viewpoints.
>
> Oh dervish! If one thing has been named in a hundred ways, in truth there is no multiplicity in that one thing, despite its one hundred names.[65]

Yet Nasafī's method of ascribing certain beliefs to particular groups does have the disadvantage in that one is never quite sure when that discourse comes to an end, or whether the beliefs of the same group are carried over into the following discourse (which may not be attributed to any particular group). Moreover, the difficulty in identifying Nasafī's own beliefs has lead to several contemporary scholars[66] seeing Nasafī's own beliefs within those which are attributed to other groups (such as the Transmigrationists). It is more likely that Nasafī believed that the explanations of other groups revealed an aspect of the truth, depending upon which station the wayfarer had reached.

Another distinctive point in Nasafī's works is the similarity in content, and this reaches the extent that there are passages which appear in different books virtually word for word, or else the imagery is exactly the same. One reason for this is that Nasafī's works were all composed during the latter part of his life, and by that time his theosophy had matured to such a degree that he was able to present his teachings in a systematic, coherent manner. There is no development from one work to the next (with the exception of *Kashf-i ṣirāṭ*, which presents several problems that will be highlighted later), only the same message is presented, that is, the unity of being and the perfectibility of man through ascetic discipline and religious effort. So if Nasafī had one fundamental message, the question that must be asked is why did he not write one large book which contained the whole package of his theosophy instead of writing several works which involved a lot of repetition. The reason may be due to Nasafī's teaching in several areas and having different groups of followers. Thus, Nasafī may have composed *Kitāb-i Tanzīl* in Nasaf and Bukhārā at the request of the dervishes, and then he composed *al-Insān al-kāmil* on the Iranian plateau for another group of dervishes, adding new expressions which he thought would be understood easily. This is not to say that his books are completely the same, because this is not the case. For example, *Manāzil al-sā'īrīn* contains discussions which are not found in *Kashf al-ḥaqā'iq* or *Maqṣad-i aqṣā*.

Notes

1 V. Minorsky, art. "Nakhshab," *Encyclopedia of Islam* (Leiden, E.J. Brill), Vol VII, p. 925.
2 'Ala al-Din 'Ata al-Malik Juvaini, *The History of the World Conqueror*, trans, J.A. Boyle (Manchester: Manchester University Press, 1958), Vol. I, p. 97–98.
3 The problems surrounding the dating of Nasafī's birth will be discussed later in this section.
4 Ibn al-Athir, cited by C. Irving, *Cross-roads of Civilisation* (London: Weidenfeld and Nicholson, 1979), p. 123.
5 Juvaini, trans. Boyle, p. 105.
6 Ibid, p. 107.
7 Ibid, p. 96–97.
8 Ibid, p. 177.
9 Ibid, p. 178.
10 Saifi, *Tarikh-nama-yi Harat*, cited I.P. Petroshevsky "The Socio-Economic Conditions of Iran under the Il-Khans," *Cambridge History of Iran*, Vol. V (Cambridge: Cambridge University Press, 1968), p. 485.
11 A. Bausani, "Religion Under the Mongols," *Cambridge History of Iran*, Vol. V. p. 539.
12 J.J. Saunders, *The History of the Mongol Conquests* (London: Routledge & Kegan Paul, 1971), p. 137.
13 See J.A. Boyle, *The Mongol World Empire* (London: Valorium Reprints, 1977), XXII, p. 8.
14 J.J. Sauders, op. cit., p. 130.
15 Bausani, op. cit., p. 540.
16 J.A. Boyle, "Turkish and Mongol Shamanism in the Middle Ages," *The Mongol World Empire*, p. 184.
17 See. L. Lewisohn, *Beyond Faith and Infidelity*, pp. 63–4.
18 A. Bausani, op. cit., p. 541.
19 Rabban Sauma is said to have given communion to King Edward I in Bordeaux, see T. Ware, *The Orthodox Church* (London: Penguin, 1987), p. 12.
20 *Maqṣad-i aqṣā*, in Jāmī's *Ashi"at al-lama'āt*, ed. H. Rabbānī (Tehran: Kitabkhāna-yi 'Ilmīyya-yi Hāmidī, 1973), p. 238, "One cannot enter *(lā yaliju)* the Kingdom of the Heavens and earth unless one is born again," reflects John 3:3, "Truly, truly, I say to you, unless one is born anew, he cannot see the Kingdom of God.
21 See C. Melville, "Padshah-i Islam: The Conversion of Sultan Mahmud Ghazan," in C. Melville (ed). *Pembroke Papers I: Persian and Islamic Studies in Honour of Peter Avery* (Cambridge: Cambridge University Press, 1990).
22 *Maqṣad-i aqṣā*, p. 228–229.
23 Petrushevsky, "The Socio-Economic Conditions of Iran under the Il-Khans," p. 509.
24 This influence can be witnessed in the works of Nasafī and Balyānī in particular. One of Balyānī's works was for many years attributed to Ibn

'Arabi and was published under the title of "*Whoso Knoweth Himself*" (London: Beshara Publications, 1976), although Chodkiewizc has shown this is not a work by Ibn 'Arabī.

25 D. Morgan, *The Mongols* (Oxford: Blackwell, 1986), p. 163.
26 D.E. Philips, *The Mongols* (New York: Frederick A. Praeger, 1969), p. 118.
27 Rashid al-Dīn, *Jāmī' al-tawārīkh*, cited by Boyle, p. 506.
28 Petrushevsky, op. cit., p. 506.
29 W. Barthold, *Turkestan down to the Mongol Invasion* (London: Luzac, 1928), p. 482.
30 Ibid, p. 482, cited from Kirakos.
31 J.J. Saunders, op. cit., p. 133.
32 D. Morgan, op. cit., p. 165.
33 Petrushevsky, op. cit., p. 490–91.
34 *Maqṣad-i aqṣā*, p. 255.
35 *Manāzil al-sā'irīn*, p. 316. Sa'd al-Dīn Ḥammūya came from a very distinguished religious family. His great-grandfather, Muḥammad Ḥammūya, was a tutor of 'Ayn al-Quḍāt Hamadānī, see *Nāmahā-yi 'Ayn al-Quḍāt Hamadānī*, Vol. I, edited 'Afīf 'Ussayrān (Tehran: Intishārāt-i zawār, 1362/1983), pp. 62–63. 'Ayn al-Quḍāt also cites a quatrain composed by his tutor, see *Tamhīdāt*, edited 'Afīf 'Ussayrān (Tehran: Kitābkhāna-yi Manūchihrī, 1373/1994), p. 258. Sa'd al-Dīn's grand-uncle also attained a position of fame since he was appointed the inspector of all the Syrain *khānaqāhs*. See J. S. Trimingham, *The Sufi Orders in Islam* (Oxford University Press, 1971), p. 261.
36 *Kashf al-ḥaqā'iq*, p. 107.
37 Sa'd al-Din Ḥammūya (1198–1252) served under Najm al-Dīn Kubrā in Khwarazm until 1220. At this point he fled the invading Mongols and journeyed to Egypt, Palestine and Syria where he became acquainted with the school surrounding Ibn 'Arabī. During the 1240's he returned to Iran and Central Asia.
38 In his *Nafaḥāt al-uns*, edited M. 'Abidī (Tehran: Mū'assasa-yi iṭilā'āt, 1370/1991), p. 431, Jāmī cites an episode (probably taken from one of Nasafī's treatises) in which he describes Ḥammūya's spirit making an ascent lasting thirteen days. During this period, Ḥammūya's body was like that of dead person. Nasafī offered the very same description about "the shaykh" in *Zubdat al-ḥaqā'iq*, p. 58 and about "our shaykh" in *al-Insān al-kāmil*," p. 108.
39 H. Landolt, "Le Paradoxe De La "Face De Dieu": 'Azīz-e Nasafī (VIIe/XIIIe Siecle) Et Le "Monisme Ésoterique" De L'Islam," *Studia Iranica*, 25, 1996, p. 168.
40 *Kashf al-ḥaqā'iq*, ed. Aḥmad Mahdawī Dāmghānī (Tehran: Bungāh-i tarjuma wa nashr-i kitāb, 1965), p. 125.
41 A.H. Zarrīnkūb, *Justuj, dar taṣawwuf-i Irān* (Tehran: Amir Kabir, 1983), p. 160.
42 See the *Majālis al-'ushshāq* of Kamāl al-Dīn Ḥusayn Kāzargāhī, (Bodleian Library, MS Ouseley, Add. 24, f. 76b).
43 W. Chittick, "Rūmī and the Mawlawiyyah," *Islamic Spirituality II*, edited S. H. Nasr, p. 110–111.

44 *Kitāb-i tanzīl*, John Rylands Library, Manchester University Library, C112, fol. 71b, lines 12–13, and *al-Insān al-kāmil*, p. 80.
45 *Kashf al-ḥaqā'iq*, p. 3.
46 Rashid al-Dīn Faḍl-Allah, *Jāmī' al-tawārīkh*, cited by Haqq-wardī Nāṣirī in his introduction to Nasafī's *Zubdat al-ḥaqā'iq*, p. 7.
47 *Kitāb-i tanzīl*, fol. 82b, line 1, and *al-Insān al-kāmil*, p. 80.
48 *al-Insān al-kāmil*, p. 80.
49 Ibid, p. 80.
50 Ibid, p. 153.
51 *Kashf al-ḥaqā'iq*, p. 4–5.
52 *Manāzil al-sā'īrīn*, p. 436.
53 Ibid, p. 437.
54 *Kashf al-ḥaqā'iq*, p. 4.
55 *Maqṣad-i aqṣā*, p. 277.
56 Lewisohn, op. cit., p. 116.
57 Several western scholars have paid considerable attention to Nasafī's manuscripts without commenting upon their content. However, their efforts have made the task of contemporary researchers that much easier in terms of access to these manuscripts. In particular, the efforts of M. Molé should be mentioned for he gathered microfilms of manuscripts from libraries in Iran and Turkey. These are now stored in Paris in the *Centre National de la Recherche Scientifique: Institut de Recherche et d'Histoire des Textes, Section Arabe.*

On Nasafī's works see Molé, "Die Schriften des 'Azīz Nasafī," *Wiener Zeitschrift für die Kunde des Morgenlandes* 52 (1953), and his introduction to Nasafī's *al-Insān al-kāmil*, pp. 28–57. See also F. Coslovi, "Liste des manuscits Arabe et Persans microfilms (Fond Molé) de L'Insitut de Recherche et d'Histoire des Textes," *Studia Iranica*, 7 (1978), pp. 117–155, and "Second Liste de Microfilms des Manuscrits Arabes et Persans du Fond Molé," *Studia Iranica* 14/2 (1985), pp. 245–254. See also Jürgen Paul, "A Propos de Quelques Microfilms du 'Fond Molé." *Studia Iranica*, 18 (1989), pp. 243–245.

58 *Maqṣad-i aqṣā*, p. 247.
59 Ibid, p. 249.
60 Ibid, p. 250.
61 *Kashf al-ḥaqā'iq*, p. 1.
62 W.M. Watt, *The Faith and Practice of al-Ghazālī*, "al-munqidh min al-ḍalāl," (London: G. Allen and Unwin, 1953), p. 32.
63 F. Meier, "The Problem of Nature in the Esoteric Monism of Islam," p. 150.
64 *al-Insān al-kāmil*, p. 220.
65 Ibid, p. 225.
66 See Meier, "The Problem of Nature in the Esoteric Monism of Islam," p. 182, and J. Morris, "Ibn 'Arabī and His Interpreters part II: Influences and Interpretations," p. 749.

2

Ontology

I. 'AZĪZ NASAFĪ'S SIX ONTOLOGICAL FACES

(Wherever you turn there is the face of God)[1]

Abū Ḥāmid Ghazālī's acceptance of Sufism as a genuine expression of Islamic belief and his composition of treatises in the field of speculative Sufism[2] (*'irfān-i naẓarī*) in the language of the Koran and philosophers may be regarded as something of a watershed in the history of Sufism. After Ghazālī, numerous Sufi texts were composed in a similar style by affiliates of Sufi orders that had established roots in the Muslim world stretching from Andalusia to Central Asia. The movement of explaining Sufism in the lingua franca of the "intelligentsia" of the day perhaps reached a pinnacle in the profound and voluminous theosophy of Ibn 'Arabī, whose writings required and deserved much study and meditation by learned scholars. For the majority of the Islamic populace, his message was delivered in a more simplified and summarised form by interpreters. Some scholars have seen 'Azīz Nasafī's treatises as "popularising the teachings of Ibn 'Arabī"[3] and thus the Greatest Shaykh's message penetrated into areas such as Iran and Central Asia. This section is an attempt to summarise Nasafī's ontological teachings and in so doing, show the similarities between his ideas and Ibn 'Arabī's vast corpus of teachings. Nasafī's audience were Persian speakers and were probably beginners on the Sufi path, so his treatises provided his dervishes with plenty to contemplate and served as a basis from which they could advance to the texts of the Greatest Shaykh (Ibn 'Arabī) himself.

In this section, Nasafī's ontology is discussed by focusing upon one chapter from the treatise *Kitāb-i tanzīl* (the Book of the Descent). It is hoped that this method covers all the main points on the one hand,

and also that the reader will catch something of the flow, directness and simplicity of the original text (which are distinctive characteristics of Nasafī's works).

Incomparability and Similarity

There has been a tendency by scholars to explain Ibn 'Arabī's theosophy in the simple term "unity of existence" *(waḥdat al-wujūd)* and to label the world view of the *wujūdī* school pantheistic or monist.[4] A more suitable way to characterise this theosophy is not unity of existence (a term which Ibn 'Arabī did not use)[5] but He / not He. This axiom neatly encapsulates the Islamic teaching of God's incomparability *(tanzīh)* and similarity *(tashbīh)*. 'Azīz Nasafī's works should also be considered in the same light. The idea of incomparability is expressed in the Koran that "Nothing is like Him,"[6] and in the *ḥadīth* that "none knows God but God,"[7] and "reflect upon all things but reflect not upon God's essence."[8] Similarity is also found in the Islamic tradition, perhaps the best example being the famous *ḥadīth* that "God made Adam in His own form."[9] Adam is of course the archetypal human being, so each person's essence in fact is a mirror of God's essence.

Sufism tended to emphasise the *tashbīh* relationship between God and man, although this should always be considered in the light of *tanzīh*. The first chapter of Nasafī's *Kitāb-i tanzīl* is quite instructive in this respect because the beginning of the work stresses the *tanzīh* position while the remaining sections reflect the *tashbīh* dimension of existence.

From a *tanzīh* perspective, Nasafī comments upon a *ḥadīth* frequently discussed by Sufis that says "He who knows himself knows his Lord."

> O dear friend! The pure essence and Holy Face of the Truth is so great that an individual's intelligence cannot encompass Him; rather, His exalted self is too high for another person to discover Him as He really is. Each one of the Prophets and Friends became aware of God Most High in accordance with their own preparedness and station, and each one of them told the people in accordance with the preparedness and station of the listeners. What they knew compared to what they did not know is a drop in the ocean, and what they said compared to what they understood is also a drop in the ocean. No-one understands his self in the way it is, and he cannot understand. The extremity of man's knowledge is that point where he knows that he cannot know God as God really is. So according to the knowledge one has of one's soul, one also has knowledge of God.[10]

Nasafī then proceeds to say that even the most intelligent of philosophers, and even the Prophets and Friends, cannot understand God, each believing their own knowledge to be the ultimate vision of God. It is impossible to reach God's essence, which is infinite and beyond man's sense perception and intelligence *('aql)*:

> Just as the seekers and the students who are counted among the People of Thought and Reasoning do not like or accept the discourse which their intelligence does not attain to, and just as they judge it correct to deny one another's discourse, because there are ranks *(darajāt)* of intelligence and because the wisdom *(ḥikmat)* in each thing is infinite, so also the wayfarers and spiritual warriors who are accounted as the People of Unveiling and Contemplation do not like or accept the spiritual station *(maqām)* which their view does not reach. They judge it correct to deny one another's station, because there are ranks in unveiling and [God's] self-disclosure *(tajallī)* is infinite. So in whatever station a man is, it is necessary that he makes this prayer his litany: "My Lord! Increase me in knowledge,"[11] because if man could live for a thousand years, and in this thousand years he is [busy] in searching and advancing *(taraqqī)*, he would discover and understand something every day which he had not discovered or understood the day before. . .
>
> O dear friend! If someone fancies that he has understood whatever can be understood and has discovered whatever can be found, this fancy is his idol and this wretched person is an idol worshipper. The reality of an idol is that it keeps a person busy with itself and it becomes an obstacle in his searching and advance.[12]

Yet it is necessary to make an attempt to understand oneself (and in so doing, God's existence) for "He who knows himself knows his Lord." This is a difficult task to undertake and understand as Nasafī himself comments:

> A person may ask, "How can God's essence which is non-delimited and infinite be considered as together with *Jabarūt*, *Malakūt* and *Mulk*?"[13] The Sufis have asked many questions about this and the answer to these questions is extremely difficult and hard. But it is necessary to give an answer. If you want to know that it is difficult, I will give an indication: Understanding the existence of non-delimitation and infinity, and understanding the existence of something else with that such that the non-delimited and infinite possess limits and boundaries, direction, division, separation, breaking apart and coming together is extremely difficult and hard.[14]

The meaning behind such remarks by Nasafī is that man should reach the essence of God as far as it is possible, that is, he should reach the essence of God as seen through *tashbīh*. Thus whenever Nasafī speaks of reaching God's essence, one should read with two eyes (to borrow an analogy from Ibn 'Arabī),[15] that is, with one eye of *tashbīh* and with one eye of *tanzīh*.

Having given a *tanzīh* warning in the opening pages of *Kitāb-i tanzīl*, Nasafī then devotes the rest of the chapter to the *tashbīh* dimension. It is typical that the *tashbīh* section takes up about ninety percent of the whole chapter, for Sufism emphasises the love between God and man, that is, the dimension which can be known. As 'Alī b. Abī Ṭālib is reported to have said, "I only worship a Lord I see."[16] This *tashbīh* position is explained by Nasafī from six different points of view, that is, six ontological perspectives, all of which are the spiritual stations *(maqām)* of the Friends *(awliyā)*, who are those closest to God.

Nasafī's Six Faces

In the Sufi tradition, a spiritual station *(maqām)* describes a relationship between the wayfarer and God. This station is acquired *(kasbī)*, based upon the wayfarer's own spiritual effort, and the knowledge that he actualises in a particular station remains with him even if he progresses on to another station. Spiritual stations are often discussed in the Sufi manuals along with *ḥāl*, or a spiritual state, which is a bestowal by God upon the wayfarer which takes place in a particular station. Nasafī does not employ the term *ḥāl* in *Kitāb-i tanzīl*, but uses *waqt* (present moment) a technical word discussed by Sufis prior to Nasafī, including Hujwīrī[17] and al-Ghazālī.[18] The latter two classified the mystical experience into three stages; the first stage is *waqt*, the second is *ḥāl* and the third is stability *(tamkīn)*. It is not possible to investigate the differences between these three here, suffice to say that the *waqt* is the lowest stage and stability is the highest stage.

Acquisition of the station by the wayfarer and God's bestowal of the *waqt* is referred to by Nasafī at the beginning of each of the stations:

> O dear friend! There is a station for the wayfarer, and in that station there is a *waqt*. When he reaches that station and enters into it, and when that *waqt* reaches him . . .[19]

The *waqt* is based upon the *ḥadīth* which states: "I have a *waqt* with God when no angel brought nigh or Prophet sent embraces me."[20] This *waqt* has been interpreted by some as Muḥammad's ascent, referred to in the Koran: "Glory be to Him, who carried His servant by night from the Holy Mosque to the Farthest Mosque."[21] According to Islamic tradition, Muḥammad rose from his bed and journeyed with Gabriel from Arabia to Jerusalem, and then upwards through all the heavens until he reached the final boundary of the heavens. At this point, Muḥammad had to proceed alone to witness God, for Gabriel said that if he went further towards God he would be burnt.

The *waqt* is not permanent (unlike the station and the knowledge associated with it); it can last less than one hour and may last for longer than ten days.[22] In another work, Nasafī mentions moments experienced by various Sufis:

> Our shaykh stated, "My spirit spent thirteen days in the heavens and then returned to my body. And during those thirteen days my body was like that of a dead man and had no concern for anything. Others who were present said that my body had been in such a way for thirteen days." And another dear one stated, "My spirit remained there for twenty days and then came back to the body." And another good companion said, "My spirit spent forty days and then returned to the body." He remembered everything that he saw in those forty days.[23]

Although the identity of the Friends within these six stations is unclear in the majority of cases, by comparing the contents of these stations with the discourses that appear in other works by Nasafī, one can conclude that the beliefs of the *'Ulamā'*, Philosophers, Transmigrationists and the People of Unity are all mentioned. This shows Nasafī at his best, prepared to endorse the beliefs of groups other than the Sufis if he sees truth in them. Yet, typically, he does not claim that any one group represents his own beliefs. The person with real knowledge witnesses the truth (through experience) in all of the stations:

> At the end of journeying, each wayfarer is in one of these stations, and one of these stations has become his aim and he remains there. There are few wayfarers who are informed of all six stations, and until the wayfarer discovers the information of all six stations and sees the correctness *(ṣalāḥ)* and corruption of each one (not through imitation *(taqlīd)* and supposition *(gumān)* but through unveiling and contemplation) he will neither reach the end point of the journey nor be informed of the extremity of the journey nor discern the truth from the false nor recognise God.[24]

This idea that the wayfarer has to recognise the truth in all expressions of belief is perhaps the fundamental element in Nasafī's theosophy, for it reveals the reality of "no repetition in God's self-disclosure" *(lā takrār fī 'l-tajallī)* which is the basis of the all-embracing nature of Sufism. This idea is discussed in detail within one of the six stations, and so it is not necessary to develop it any further at this point.

The First Station

The first station is the shortest of all the stations, perhaps an indication that Nasafī did not regard it as a profound ontological explanation of the relationship between God and man. God is explained as the essential existent *(mawjūd li-dhātihi)* and He is also termed the *Jabarūt*. This stands in opposition to the world *('ālam)* which is an existent through other than itself *(mawjūd li-ghayrihi)* and comprises *Mulk* and *Malakūt*. *Mulk* is the world of sensory existents *(mawjūdāt-i ḥissī)* and *Malakūt* is the world of intelligible existents *(mawjūdāt-i 'aqlī)*. God, or *Jabarūt*, is real and eternal existence, whereas the world (*Mulk* and *Malakūt*) have metaphorical and created existence. The world is created by God from non-existence through His attributes, that is, through His knowledge, desire and power. These three attributes of knowledge, desire and power were commonly discussed by the theologians in the process of creation; in order to create something, God must have knowledge of it; then He must have the desire to create that thing; thirdly, He must have the power to bring it in to existence. Nasafī then follows the standard explanation of the theologians that there are seven attributes of essence *(ṣifāt-i dhāt)*; the seven are life, knowledge, desire, power, speaking, hearing and seeing. Of course, God's attributes are infinite, but apart from the foregoing seven, they are all attributes of acts.

In this station, creation is seen as a process whereby God makes something existent from non-existence, in other words, it is an interpretation reflecting the idea of *creatio ex nihilo*. This is the meaning behind making something exist *(hast gardānīd)* from non-existence *(nīstī)* and this position is reflected in a small sentence "God was and nothing else was,"[25] which is in fact a *ḥadīth*.[26] Creation from nothing is typically taken by Nasafī as the belief of the People of the Holy Law *(ahl-i sharī'at)*, (who are called the *'Ulamā'* in other works):

> Know that the wise men have had differences of opinion about the possibility of non-existence becoming existence, and existence becoming non-existence. The *'Ulamā'* and *Fuqahā'* believe that it is possible for non-existence to become existence and for existence to become non-existence. This is because the world was non-existent and God Most

> High made the world existent and will make it non-existent when He desires.
>
> The Philosophers and People of Unity believe that it is not possible for existence to become non-existence and it is not possible for non-existence to become existence.[27]

The distinction made between God and the world (that is, between *Jabarūt* on the one hand, and *Mulk* and *Malakūt* on the other) represents a *tanzīh* position. This is counter-balanced by a *tashbīh* explanation that God is with everything, for "it is not possible for a leaf to move on a tree without His knowledge, desire and power."[28]

God's *tanzīh-tashbīh* relationship with the world is described in the following way:

> The God of the world is not inside nor outside of the world, nor contiguous *(muttaṣil)* with or discontiguous *(munfaṣil)* from the world, and not in any direction of the directions of the world or in time or place because these are attributes of bodies, and the God of the world is not a body or bodily.[29]

Although this is the simplest explanation of all the six stations (in terms of an ontological explanation of existence), Nasafī comments that the wayfarer in this station is able to experience the *waqt* with God:

> In this station, when the wayfarer shows perseverance and persistence in the task and does not cease in ascetic discipline and spiritual effort, then *Mulk* and *Malakūt* (which are God's creation) become concealed and forgotten all at once when this *waqt* predominates over him. This is called the station of annihilation *(maqām-ī fanā')*. When the existence of the wayfarer also becomes concealed from and forgotten by the wayfarer and he does not see or know anything else except God, this station is called annihilation of annihilation *(fanā'-i fanā')*.[30]

The Second Station

The first station takes up only twenty-nine lines, whereas the second station comprises a hundred and thirty-four; in fact, it is longer than any other of the stations. Obviously, in this station there are discussions which must have been important to Nasafī.

Whereas in the first station God's essence and attributes are *Jabarūt* and other than God is *Mulk* and *Malakūt,* in the second station God is other than all three worlds. *Mulk* and *Malakūt* are explained in the same way as the preceding station, but *Jabarūt* is an expression for the first substance *(jawhar-i awwal)*, yet God is with all three worlds through His essence and His attributes. The "withness" *(ma'iyyat)* of God with the three worlds is described in terms of the human spirit in the human body. The word *ma'iyyat* is an allusion to the Koranic verse, "God is with you wherever you are."[31] Thus although man is separated from God by the first substance, the *tashbīh* position is maintained through God's "withness."

One of the major discussions in this station is the nature of *Jabarūt* (or first substance), and here the relationship between the first and second stations becomes clear. The first station states a position of *creatio ex nihilo*, whereas the second station suggests a kind of eternity for *Jabarūt*:

> The first substance came from the world of potentiality *('ālam-i quwwat)* to the world of actuality *('ālam-i fi'l)* through one command in the blink of an eye, "And Our command is but one, as the twinkling of an eye."[32,33]

This eternal potentiality is attributed likewise to *Mulk* and *Malakūt*, for the first substance is like a seed and all the substances of *Mulk* and *Malakūt* are existent in the first substance. To use Nasafī's words, everything that "was, is and will be, was potentially existent" in the first substance. However, while these substances are existent in the first substance, they are not distinct *(mumtāz)* from one another; and for this reason, the first substance is also called the undifferentiated world *('ālam-i ijmāl)*. In this state, the potential existents of *Mulk* and *Malakūt* are called non-existent things *(ashyā'-i ma'dūm)* since they have the possibility of existence in contrast to God's real existence.

Both the content and language that Nasafī uses in this discussion reflect an intermingling of Koranic terminology with the kind of philosophical concepts that were discussed by the Ikhwān al-Ṣafā (Brethren of Purity) and Ibn Sīnā (known to the west as Avicenna) among others. Indeed, in this discussion on *Jabarūt*, one finds numerous parallels with Ibn 'Arabī's theosophy, and in other works Nasafī explicitly refers to the similarity of his position with Ibn 'Arabī's, the only difference being one of terminology:

> All potential existents are things, and they are all the objects of God's knowledge *(ma'lūm-i khudā)*. Possible non-existence is one thing and impossible non-existence is another. Possible non-existence is a thing, but impossible non-existence is not a thing. And Ibn 'Arabī calls these things the immutable entities *(a'yān-i thābita)*; Shaykh Sa'd al-Dīn

> Ḥammūya calls these things the immutable things *(ashyā'-i thābitā)*; and this helpless one [i.e. Nasafī] calls them the immutable realities *(ḥaqā'iq-i thābita)*. They are called immutable *(thābit)* because they never change their own state, and they never will.[34]

These possible non-existent things plead with God to have existence bestowed upon them, they say to God "in the tongue of [their] state," *(bā zabān-i ḥāl)* "We have such a preparedness *(isti'dād)* and such a task can be performed through us."[35] The similarity of this passage with chapter sixty-six of Ibn 'Arabī's *al-Futuḥāt al-makkiyya* is unmistakable,[36] and the tongue of their own state is a Persian translation of Ibn 'Arabī's Arabic expression *lisān al-ḥāl.*[37]

If God bestows existence upon these non-existent things by the command "Be!" then they are manifested in the differentiated world *('ālam-ī tafṣīl)* (which is *Mulk* and *Malakūt*) in exactly the way in which they spoke with God. They do whatever they said they would, and this introduces the second major point in the second spiritual station.

God bestows existence upon the non-existent things, but He is not the creator of their actions:

> Everything and everyone has whatever he has from himself and has brought it with himself, nobody has placed it there. This is because only the command to become existent is from God Most High. Everything and everyone became existent in such a way that they were in the world of potentiality. So God Most High is All-Knowing *('ālim)* and All-Aware *(khabīr)*, and his knowledge and awareness follow its object *('ilm tābi' ma'lūm)*.[38]

This last phrase, again, leads back to Ibn 'Arabī,[39] and the significance of God's knowledge following its object is that God does not make the existents act, which "justifies" His rewarding and punishing of creatures. As Nasafī reminds us, "His command, when He desires a thing, is to say Be! and it is," [40] He does not say to the non-existent thing, "Be a wrong doer!" or "Be God-fearing!"

> God Most High commanded the recital of prayers. Recital of prayers is the action of the one who recites the prayer, and the one who recites the prayer brings into existence *(mūjid)* his own actions. If this were not so, why would the performer of good actions deserve reward and praise and the performer of bad actions deserve punishment and blame? Potential existents are the ones who bring into existence their own actions and everything and everyone came to the world of actuality through the command of God and from its own action, just as it was in

> the world of potentiality, and the good ones brought goodness with them and the wretched ones brought wretchedness with them. "A happy man is he who is happy in his mother's womb and a wretched man is he who was wretched in his mother's womb."[41,42]

Although God does not create the acts of the things directly, He knows what they will do once they have existence bestowed upon them. For God not to know this would mean there is a deficiency in Him. Therefore, Nasafī explains God's knowledge as the third main component in the second station. He divides it into two kinds since He is All-Knowing and All-Aware.[43] The All-Knowing refers to God's existentiating command, for He knows the universal condition of each thing:

> When a farmer wants to plant, he takes the seed of the fruit he wants to pick. When he looks at the seed, he "knows" of the existence of the crop before its existence and he recognises the result of the crop. He knows that the barley seed will in fact produce barley and the wheat seed will in fact produce wheat if the earth is wholesome and the air is compatible and there is water on appropriate occasions and no calamity befalls. This knowledge of the farmer is absolute *(muṭlaq)* but it is not complete. Although the farmer knows this, he does not know how many of the wheat seeds that he sowed will rise from the earth and how many will not rise. He does not know how many will reach their full term *(ajal-i musammā)* and how many will become non-existent before the full term through the term of the divine decree *(ajal-i qaḍā')*. He does not know the cause of the non-existence of that which becomes non-existent through the decreed term of life, perhaps because of warmth or cold, too little water or too much water, being eaten by animals or intrusion by people and so on. But when he scatters the seed on the ground, and some rise and others do not, some reach perfection and a calamity befalls others before perfection, then all of this becomes known by the farmer, and this is the farmer's experiential knowledge *('ilm-i dhawq)*.[44]

As Nasafī comments, this is another way of saying that knowledge follows its object. In the first case, the All-Knowing follows the known because the seeds tell the farmer that they have such a preparedness for manifesting what is particular to them. In the second, the All-Aware follows the known, because it is only after the development of the plant that he knows what happens to it. As Nasafī says, this relates to the knowledge of universals and particulars:

> So the farmer is "knowing" and "aware." He is "knowing" of the crop before its existence and he is "aware" of the existence of the crop

after its existence. He is "knowing" of the universals *(kulliyyāt)* before the existence of the universals and he is "aware" of the particulars after the existence of the particulars.

In the same way, God Most High is knowing and aware. He is knowing of the existence of *Mulk*, *Malakūt* and *Jabarūt* before their existence and He is aware of the existence of *Mulk*, *Malakūt* and *Jabarūt* after their existence. He is knowing of the universals before their existence and He is aware of the particulars after their existence.[45]

Nasafī then returns to the statement made in the beginning of the passage that God's essence and attributes are with everything. This begs the question that if God's attribute of awareness is with everything, then why is He aware of a thing only after it has performed the action? If He is aware of it only after the action, then His awareness appears to be defective, which contradicts the idea that his attributes are perfect. Nasafī recognises this problem and he comments that the example of the farmer is only an approximation[46] to help us understand the real situation. Although he does not make the point in this work, in *al-Insān al-kāmil* Nasafī says that time is not a consideration for God but only for humans.[47] There is no dimension of time in God's world, so He is All-Aware of everything all at once, even "before" something takes place.

God's attributes of All-Knowing and All-Awareness are identical to His essence, because there is nothing in true existence except His essence. However, the essence has been called different names by people from various perspectives. Nasafī returns to the seven main attributes which are discussed in the first station:

So God Most High is All-Knowing in essence, a desirer in essence, powerful in essence, a hearer in essence, a seer in essence, speaker in essence and command in essence.[48]

These attributes of essence are then divided into two groups which are the basis of the second station. There are God's existentiating command and His knowledge:

His desire, power and speaking are expressions for His command; and His hearing, sight and life are expressions for His knowledge. So there are not more than two attributes, and there are not more than three things from God's side and there are also three things from the side of potential existents.[49]

From God's side there is the essence (which is infinite and encompasses everything) and two attributes (command and knowledge); from the side of the potential existents there is "thingness" *(shay'iyyat),* acceptance *(qabūl)* and action *(fi'l).*[50] "Thingness" is the essence of the thing, acceptance is the receptivity of the thing of God's command to be, and action is what the thing does when existence is bestowed upon it. Nasafī's portrayal of such a dual triplicity is very reminiscent of that found in Ibn 'Arabī's *Fuṣūṣ al-ḥikām*. Ibn 'Arabī described God's triplicity in terms of Essence, Desire and Speaking (reflecting the main components necessary for creation).[51] The triplicity of the created thing is its own thingness, its hearing of God's command to be and its obedience to the command, Be!

Having described the theory behind this station, Nasafī then explains how the wayfarer perceives the relationship of man and God. This is done with reference to the *ḥadīth qudsī*, "My servant draws near to Me through nothing I love more than that which I have made obligatory for him. My servant never ceases drawing near to Me through supererogatory works until I love him. Then, when I love him, I am his hearing through which he hears, his sight through which he sees, his hand through which he grasps, and his foot through which he walks."[52] From this *ḥadīth*, Muslims distinguish two kinds of acts of worship; the first is the obligatory acts which include praying, fasting and the pilgrimage to Mecca, and the second is the supererogatory which are acts of worship in excess of obligatory worship.

Nasafī's interpretation resembles that of Ibn 'Arabī;[53] Ibn 'Arabī says that the servant is the hearing and seeing of God in obligatory acts of worship and Nasafī expresses this in terms of everything at the level of self of self, hearing of hearing and sight of sight as being God's discourse.[54] It is God's discourse because He looks at the cosmos through man. If He were to look at the cosmos without an intermediary then the cosmos would be "burnt away by the glories of His face." Since the obligatory acts are commanded by God, they are regarded by Ibn 'Arabī as more eminent than supererogatory acts of worship in which the servant has a choice concerning their performance. (Of course, this does not mean that one should not perform the supererogatory acts. The obligatory acts are sufficient for the majority of believers but the supererogatory acts draw each individual even closer to God.) Concerning the supererogatory acts, Ibn 'Arabī states that God is the servant's hearing and seeing and therefore says "I,"[55] and Nasafī comments that everything at the level of self, hearing and sight is the discourse of God's messenger *(rasūl-i khudā).*[56] The distinction between the two sets of acts is very intricate and complex. One way to contemplate the obligatory and supererogatory acts is through the relationship between annihilation *(fanā')* and subsistence *(baqā').* Through the obligatory acts, man annihilates his "self," and therefore it is God performing the acts through man. From this point, the annihilated man subsists in God and so he is able to perform the supererogatory acts. Another way to view the relationship is through *tanzīh* and *tashbīh*. *Tanzīh* stresses God's mastery over His servants through *tanzīh* names, including the majestic *(jalāl)* and the compeller *(jabbār)*, and the obligatory acts establish God's majesty and compulsion over his servant for the latter has no free will in the performance of such acts. *Tashbīh* emphasises the similarity between man and God through *tashbīh* names, including beauty *(jamāl)* and gentleness *(luṭf)*. God and the supererogatory acts draw the servant closer to God since he assimilates God's attributes in the performance of those very acts. Nasafī summarises the obligatory and supererogatory acts of worship in the following way:

> When the wayfarer shows perseverance and persistence in the task in this station and does not cease from ascetic discipline and spiritual effort, then the self of the self, the hearing of hearing, the sight of sight sees, listens and speaks in him. In whomever the self of the self, hearing of hearing, and sight of sight sees, listens and speaks, that person has reached God and the day of resurrection has arrived for him. The dead become living and rise from the graves. Although in form such a person is in the world, in meaning he is in the next world. Outwardly he is with the creatures but inwardly he is with God, since the resurrection of the spirit is different from the resurrection of the body.[57]
>
> So until this point, the wayfarer was alive through himself, heard through himself, saw through himself and spoke through himself. Now he is alive through God, he hears through God, sees through God and speaks through God, "I am his hearing, his sight and his speaking." Moreover, he reaches a point where God hears, God sees, God speaks and God does everything he does. "So you did not slay them, but it was Allah Who slew them, and you did not throw when you threw, but it was Allah who threw."[58] There is much difference between the station where one listens through God, sees through God and speaks through God and the station where God listens, God sees, and God speaks. So everything which the People of Perfection perform is all good. Although some of their actions appear in the form of disobedience *(ma'ṣiyat)*, in the actual situation it is not disobedience, rather it is identical to obedience *(ṭā'at).*[59]

The Third Station

The next station described by Nasafī draws on the Sufi tradition of regarding everything other than God as imagination. The imagination has been the focus of many studies by twentieth-century scholars because it is one of the primary ways in which Ibn 'Arabī explains his theosophy.[60] In the ninth chapter of his *Fuṣūṣ al-ḥikām*, Ibn 'Arabī discusses two kinds of imagination.[61] The first is the cosmos and the second is the individual. It is likely that Nasafī based his third station on Ibn 'Arabī's *Fuṣūṣ* since he follows the same two-fold classification, and not only does he reach the same conclusion that Prophets and Friends are required to interpret the meanings behind imagination, but he also quotes the *Fuṣūṣ*.

The first kind of imagination is the world (which comprises *Mulk*, *Malakūt* and *Jabarūt*). The world has imaginary existence which stands in contrast to God's real existence:

> Real existence *(wujūd-i ḥaqīqī)* which is the existence of God is existence *(hastī)* that appears non-existent *(nīst numā)*. Imaginary existence *(wujūd-i khayālī)* which is the existence of the world, is non-existence that appears existent.[62]

Although the world is imagination and unreal, it can still tell us something about the reality of God because

> . . . there is not one particle of all the particles of the world which God is not with, for imagination cannot exist without reality, and a shadow cannot exist without essence. This discourse will only be clear for you through an example *(mithāl)*.
>
> Know that according to the philosophers *(ḥukamā')*, air is existence that appears non-existent while a mirage is non-existence that appears existent. The existence of the mirage is through the air and the manifestation of the air is through the mirage. Air is the reality of the mirage and the mirage is the form of the air. You should understand God's withness with the world in the same way as the withness of the air with the mirage. Hence, it has been said, "All the world is imagination in imagination and a dream in a dream."[63] This is the meaning of "People are asleep and when they die they wake up."[64,65]

In this station, when man looks at anything, he perceives the forms of the world that are the manifest dimension of meanings[66] (as Ibn 'Arabī so often states, this situation reflects the Koranic verse "We will show them Our signs upon the horizons and in themselves"[67]). These signs within the self introduce the second classification of imagination, which is the faculty of imagination within each person. Although Nasafī does not discuss this faculty in any detail in this chapter, he does refer to it in a later chapter where he explains the imagination and its functions (and his analysis leans heavily upon the teachings of Ibn Sīnā).[68] One of man's sources of intelligence is the five senses which gather in the *sensus communis* and these forms are then stored in the imagination.[69] The store of forms is crucial for man to make sense of God's self-disclosure because the majority of Sufis (including Jalāl al-Dīn Rūmī) held that God's self-disclosure takes a form: "the heart is the antechamber of the eye: For certain everything that reaches the heart will enter into the eye and become a form."[70] Nasafī himself says that God's self-disclosure without a form is impossible (although he makes this comment in the fifth station).[71]

Since everything is imagination, or a form, it is necessary to understand the reality behind the form:

> Everything people see in a dream is all imagination. Everything people see is imagination, so they are all in a dream. Although they see everything in a dream as imagination, that imagination is a denotation *(dalāla)* of reality and [people] will not reach the reality of that imagination as long as they have not "crossed over" *('ubūr)* from it. An interpreter *(mu'abbir)* is called an "interpreter" on the basis of this, and because of this his words are called interpretation *(ta'bīr)*. The Friends *(awlīyā)* and the Prophets are all interpreters and they interpret peoples' dreams so that the people can pass from supposed and imaginary existents *(mawjūdāt-i mutawahham wa mutakhayāl)* and reach real existents *(mawjūdāt-i ḥaqīqī)*.[72]

Even the interpreters of dreams and their interpretations may be considered as imagination. The difference between them and other people is that they have woken up from the dream and they know that everything is imagination (or a dream), while those who are sleeping think that their dreams are reality since they undergo all kinds of "sensory" and "emotional" experience as long as they witness dreams.[73] Those people who are in a dream but think that it is real may not wake up at all. Only at death do they awaken and by then it may be too late. This death is the natural death *(murdan-i ṭabī'ī)* whereas those who have woken up and realised that all is imagination die the voluntary death *(murdan-i irādī)*

> It is necessary to die the voluntary death before natural death in order to awaken from sleep. This is the meaning of "Die before you die."[74,75]

The Fourth Station

The whole tone of the fourth station is very much of a *tashbīh* nature, for God is recognised as the whole world, whether it is imagination or reality:[76]

> In this station, the wayfarer knows and sees the "world," which is an expression for *Mulk*, *Malakūt* and *Jabarūt*, all at once as the existence of God and he sees or knows no existence other than *Mulk*, *Malakūt* and *Jabarūt* which are the levels of the world.[77]

Existence is one. However, it is described by many attributes, since it is manifested in many forms. Therefore the reality of existence is its unity, even though it has been called by many names. As Nasafī says, it may be called God, the world,[78] creature or spirit. In fact, it is best to call this existence by the name which is closer to one's understanding.[79]

Another way to express existence is through the terms substance *(jawhar)* and accident *('araḍ)*. Substance is common for everything, for it is the fundamental reality, however, the distinction between things is through accident:

> . . . there is not more than one substance but there are many accidents for this one substance; growing and not growing, sensory and non-sensory, rational *(nāṭiq)* and non-rational, Philosopher *(ḥakīm)* and other than Philosopher, Prophet and other than Prophet, Friend and other than Friend and others like these have all one substance, and the substance of them all is one. The distinction between them all is through accident.[80]

From this perspective, one can say that everything is God *(kull khudā ast)*,[81] an expression that is very reminiscent of the "everything is He" *(hama ūst)*, which was employed by Sufis including Farīd al-Dīn 'Aṭṭār[82] and Anṣārī (d. 1089).[83] This phrase has also been spoken of in the same breath as the unity of existence *(waḥdat al-wujūd)* which is the doctrine typically attributed to Ibn 'Arabī.[84]

In this fourth station, the unity of God's existence is divided into two forms; the form of essence and attribute *(dhāt wa ṣifāt)* and the form of face and name *(wajh wa ism)*. The form of essence and attribute may also be called the undifferentiated world *('ālam-i 'ijmāl)* and the level of readiness *(martaba-yi ṣalāḥiyyat)*. This is because in origin the substance of everything is in potentiality, as described in the second station, and it is ready to perform its actions. When existence is bestowed upon a thing, substances and accidents may be spoken of as the face and name, because the things are differentiated *(tafṣīl)* and dispersed *(tafraqa)* from one another and also since they are at the actualised level *(martaba-yi ḥāṣiliyyat)*. The two forms which describe this one substance, or God's existence, are summarised in the three levels. Each form is one level and the two combined forms make the third level. So the first level is God's essence, the second level is His face and the combined forms are His breath *(nafas)*.[85]

Level of Essence
(Undifferentiated World/Level of Readiness/Collected Form)

Level of Face
(Differentiated World/Actualised Level/Dispersed Form)

} *Level of Breath*

M. Molé has read this third level as *nafs*, rather than *nafas*. *Nafs* has a variety of meanings ranging from the self, soul, mode and aspect and Molé preferred the word "hecceité,"[86] whereas *nafas* means breath. *Nafas* is etymologically related to *nafs* since both come from the same Arabic root. Thus both of them appear exactly the same way when written because the vowel signs (which would distinguish between *nafs* and *nafas*) are not usually written in Persian. This distinction between the two words is important because the discussion of *n.f.s.* as *nafas* (breath) concerns the Divine breath, which is a major element in the Sufism of Ibn 'Arabī.[87]

The reason for reading *n.f.s.* as *nafas* in this particular passage appears in another of Nasafī's works. In *Bayān-i tanzīl*, Nasafī comments:

> O dervish! If the essence is called the ink-pot, and if the face is called the book, then the breath *(n.f.s)* which is the intermediary *(wāsiṭa)* must be called the pen. If the essence is called the undifferentiated world and if the face is called the differentiated world, the breath is the world of love.
>
> . . .the sigh *(āh)* of the *n.f.s.* comes from the essence and the face comes from the breath *(nafas)*. The face is the self-disclosure of the breath and the breath is the self-disclosure of the essence.[88]

Given that Nasafī uses "sigh," it appears more likely that *n.f.s.* is *nafas* (breath) rather than *nafs* (hecceité). The sound of a sigh is heard when one breathes out or exhales air or blows. (This image calls to mind God's blowing of His spirit into Adam.) The visual image of the breath as an intermediary also makes sense because one cannot see the breath in the undifferentiated world, but when God sighs or exhales, then a "cloud" of breath becomes visible.[89]

In this station there are two questions that may be asked about the nature of this unity of existence. The first concerns the reason for the existence of incompatible *(nā-muwāfiq)* forms and the infinite differences among their attributes, such as one who confesses and one who denies, a powerful person and an incapable person, a just person and a wrongdoer. The answer is that existence

> . . . is described by every attribute which has the possibility to be. Each attribute is perfect in its own level, and this perfection is its greatness. And [existence] is manifested in every form which has the possibility to be and each form is perfect in its own level.[90]

This leads to the next problem, for if all the attributes and forms are manifested perfectly, then is wrongdoing a perfect attribute and is the wrongdoer a perfect form?[91] The reply to this question is linked to God's attributes of power *(qudrat)* and desire *(irādat)* which are perfect attributes. The forms (i.e. the creatures) also have these attributes within them and so they are able to create their own actions, or in other words, they are the cause of their own actions. (This is another way of expressing the point made in the second station that knowledge follows its object *('ilm tābi' ma'lūm)* and God is not responsible for peoples' actions, He only bestows existence upon them.) So if a form employs power at the right time, it is called just *('ādil)* and if it uses power on an inappropriate occasion, it is called wrongdoer *(ẓālim)*. Nasafī repeats that if the situation were not this way, then there would be no point in the call of the Prophets and the instruction of the Friends.[92]

The divine attributes are always manifested in the world, for although the form may differ due to time and place, the substance of the form is always the same. From this perspective

> . . . it is correct if it is said that it is we that existed, it is we that exist and it is we that will exist. And it is also correct if it is said that it is not we that existed and it is not we that exist and it is not we that will exist. You should understand all things in the same way. If, according to you, Moses was the son of 'Imrān and came from Egypt and spoke Hebrew, then Muḥammad was not Moses because Muḥammad was the son of 'Abdullāh and came from Mecca and spoke Arabic. But if Moses was the Perfect Man according to you, then Muḥammad was Moses because Muḥammad was the Perfect Man.[93]

Here an important term is introduced, that is, the Perfect Man.[94] He is God's deputy on earth because he is able to manifest the divine attributes at their appropriate time and place. Such a concept guides each individual towards their own perfection, but whether or not this perfection is actualised depends to a great extent on one's own effort. Since God's attributes always exist, it necessarily follows that the Perfect Man who manifests perfection is always in the world:

> If there was a time when there was Moses and Pharaoh and there was discussion and dispute between them, then there is always Moses and Pharaoh and there is always discussion and dispute between them. The difference is to the extent that one may speak of a time for Adam and Satan, a time for Abraham and Nimrūd, a time for Moses and Pharaoh, a time for Muḥammad and Abu Jahl, a time for Ḥusayn and Yazīd, and a time for Jesus and Dajjāl. If it never was the case that Moses and Pharaoh were, then there would never be Moses and Pharaoh, because nothing comes to the world which was not and everything that was, is and will be; and everything that was not, is not and will not be.[95]

The Fifth Station

There are two interrelated points in the fifth station; God's new creation ("No indeed, but they are in uncertainty as to the new creation")[96] and the non-repetition of this new creation. Many Muslims held that this Koranic verse referred to the resurrection, but Ibn 'Arabī and Nasafī take it as an indication of the renewal of creation at every instant.

God's new creation was accepted by Ash'arī theologians and both Ibn 'Arabī and Nasafī quote the Ash'arī axiom that "the accident does not remain for two moments."[97] However they disagree with the Ash'arī idea that only accidents disappear. Rather, they maintain that both substance and accident are continually destroyed and created again by God. In the quotation below, Nasafī speaks of "accidents" to refer to both substance and accidents. These are both annihilated, while only the real substance, or the One Entity remains:

> This wayfarer in this station says that one Entity *('ayn)* is the Entity of the world and this One Entity *('ayn-i wāḥid)*, that is the Entity of the world, is described with the attribute of unity. In other words, it is one thing that is the reality of the world and this one thing is described with the attribute of unity. All the forms of the world are the forms of the One Entity. This One Entity, which is the Entity of the world, always was and always is and whatever is existent of all the forms and accidents of the world, which are the forms and accidents of the One Entity, becomes non-existent in each moment and a similar *(mithl)* thing becomes existent.[98]

Humans cannot perceive this new creation because of both the extreme speed of the process[99] and also because the thing made non-existent is similar to that which takes its place. One way of explaining how Nasafī perceived this idea is to say that each person is continually changing, whether in his personality, his thoughts, or even his physical appearance. Therefore God's "new creation" is always unique; in other words, His self-disclosure never repeats itself:

> It is one light which has disclosed itself in the whole world. In other words, it is God who has been manifested in all these forms. Whatever is existent becomes non-existent in each moment and something similar to that becomes existent. If He wills, that which becomes existent in the east in a fixed time will become existent in the west, not in the east, and if He wills, that which becomes existent in the west in a fixed time will be manifested in the east, not in the west, since it is God that becomes manifested in the east and west. The sea produces waves in the east, west, south and north and the sea is one, and the waves are the forms of the sea, or rather they are the same as the sea. Just as the sea is constantly billowing, the light of God Most High is continually disclosing itself.[100]

Nasafī offers this self-disclosure which can take place in the east and in the next moment in the west as the explanation for miracles *(mu'jizāt)*, charismatic powers *(karāmāt)* and the manifestation of angels such as Gabriel, and the story of the Queen of Sheba's throne being transported in an instant to Solomon's court,[101] the appearance of Khiḍr and also of the Invisible Shaykh.[102] So miracles and charismatic powers should be regarded as the breaking of enduring habits *(kharq-i 'ādat-i mustamirr)* rather than the changing of reality *(qalb-i ḥaqīqat)*.[103]

God as substance never changes, but the forms or accidents of the One Entity, that is, its self-disclosure is always changing. In this station, Nasafī again refers to the three levels of God to explain existence, that is, the levels of essence, face and breath:

> God's essence, face and breath are not synonymous words *(alfāẓ-i mutarādif)*, for they are distinct words *(alfāẓ-i mubāyin)*. Considering contradictory words is difficult since the light of God cannot be partitioned or divided and cannot alter or change. So one's vision *(naẓar)* must be extremely piercing *(tīzbīn)* and far-sighted *(dūrbīn)* in order to discover these meanings. Know that the wayfarer says that the People of Unveiling and Contemplation have three visions *(naẓar)* in existents: one is towards the existence of that thing, and one is towards the generality *('umūm)* and specificity *(khuṣūṣ)* of that thing; and one is towards the whole *(majmū')* of that thing.[104]

Nasafī offers the example of water: the vision of the existence of water reveals the essence of water; and the existence of water in all plants reveals the generality of water, and the plant is thus the face of God. Water as essence and water as face make up the breath of water. In other words, God's light as essence, and God's light in its forms make up God's breath. So wherever one looks, one sees God; everything is God *(kull khudā ast)*; everything is He *(hama ūst)*:

> The existence of light is an expression for the essence of God because He is independent *(ghanī)* of the world, "God is independent of the worlds."[105] The generality of God's light for all things and the withness of God's light with each one of the world's forms is an expression for God's face and the whole is an expression for God's breath. For each form to which you turn, you have turned to God's face, "wherever you turn there is the face of God,"[106] and each one of the forms of the world is perishing except God's face, "everything is perishing except His face."[107]

Everything man sees is a face of God, thus all beliefs express God's self-disclosure. For this reason Sufis witness truth in all beliefs; however, they stress that one has to recognise the truth in all faces and not become fixed to only one of the faces or forms:

> Whoever reaches God's face *(wajh)* and has not reached the essence has become an associator of others with God *(mushrik)*, and whoever has not passed on from God's face and does not reach the essence is an associator of others with God. Whoever passes on from God's face and reaches the essence is a Unitarian *(muwaḥḥid)*. So whoever worships something worships nothing except God, and whoever turns to something turns to nothing except God, "wherever you turn, there is the face of God."[108] Although all the associators of others with God have turned to God's face and worship God, they were limited *(muqayyad)* to one face and turned their back towards the other faces. Consenting to some and denying others is not acceptable, so the Prophets called them from the limited God to the non-delimited God and they said, "God is one. Whatever you have turned towards, it is all one God that you have worshipped." The associators of others with God were surprised at this and they denied the words of the Prophets, but they marvelled: "What, has he made the gods One God? This is indeed a marvellous thing!"[109,110]

From this point on, Nasafī describes the *waqt* of this station, the explanation of which differs from the other *awqāt* since it contains the ecstatic utterances *(shaṭḥīyyāt)* of several celebrated mystics:

> When he [the wayfarer] becomes completely clean of reproachable descriptions and unpleasant character traits and becomes completely described and characterised with praiseworthy descriptions and pleasant character traits, and when he becomes translucent *(shaffāf)*,

reflective *('aks pazīr)* and glass-like *(zujājī)* through extreme subtleness, then the real light, which is the essence of God, becomes like one thing with the existence of this wayfarer, who is reflective and glass-like. It is like a goblet made of glass which is extremely translucent and reflective, and has wine poured into it, a wine which is extremely pure and fine. One cannot distinguish the goblet from the wine or the wine from the goblet,[111] because the two things are like one. Hence the Prophets said, "Our spirits are our bodies and our bodies are our spirits."[112] Each cry *(awāzī)* which comes from the wayfarer like "There is nothing in my cloak except God,"[113] and "I am the Truth,"[114] is in this station.[115]

In truth, this station requires this, because the body of the wayfarer becomes very glass-like, extremely translucent and reflective through ascetic discipline and spiritual effort. It is in such a way that the wayfarer sees himself as light, and he cannot distinguish the light from the glass or the glass from the light. Whether he desires or not, a cry such as "There is nothing in my cloak except God" and "I am the Truth" comes from him involuntarily That is, at the beginning of this station, the wayfarer is still aware of himself and he sees himself and also sees the light from himself. This cry comes from him, "There is nothing in my cloak except God," and "There is nothing in existence except God." People have called this station the station of incarnation *(maqām-i ḥulūl)*. At the end of this station, the wayfarer is not aware of himself and he does not recognise himself because he sees everything as light and this cry comes from him, "I am the Truth," and "Glory to Me, how great is My majesty!" People have called this station the station of union *(maqām-ittiḥād)*.[116]

The Sixth Station

Whereas the fifth station describes the creatures as the loci of manifestation of God, the sixth station explains the creatures as the loci of manifestation of God's light *(maẓāhir-ī nūr-ī khudā)*. Nasafī is able to use this last station to portray existence in terms of the relationship between God, the macrocosm (big man) *(insān-i kabīr)* and the microcosm (small man) *(insān-i ṣaghīr)*.

The world is again portrayed as a mirror, but not in the sense that it has an imaginary existence. God's world is a mirror in which He can witness His beautiful names.[117] It is like a soulless body or an unpolished mirror, and when God breathes of His spirit into the world it becomes the locus of manifestation of His light. This discussion is based upon the Koranic verse in which God is speaking to the angels concerning his creation of Adam, "When I have fashioned him and breathed of My spirit into him, prostrate yourselves before him." Nasafī's explanation of this Koranic verse seems to be based upon the first chapter of Ibn 'Arabī's *Fuṣūṣ al-ḥikām*, for in another work he mentions that Ibn 'Arabī uses the word *taswiya* in this very sense:

> In Ibn 'Arabī's *Fuṣūṣ al-ḥikām*, in the first bezel, which is the bezel of Adam, he says that fashioning *(taswiya)* is an expression for preparedness and breathing the spirit is an expression for receiving the spirit.[118]

So He is the spirit of the world and the world is His body. The spirit ascends in levels, and in each level it is perfect. When the spirit reaches man, the ascent is complete for man contains all the levels within himself. At this juncture, one can understand the purpose of "creation" which is referred to in the Prophet David's prayer, "O God! Why did you create the creatures?" He said, "I was a hidden treasure and I loved to be known."[119]

In this station, the first thing that God creates is compared to a seed, and the body and spirit of the world are enclosed in this seed and are not distinguishable *(mumtāz)* from one another. In their own time, they are manifested and become differentiated. This portrayal of creation is an alternative to the Neoplatonic hierarchy of creation which some modern scholars have attributed to Sufism.[120] In the first place, Nasafī says that two things come from the seed (that is, body and spirit) whereas the Neoplatonists speak of three things emanating from the first substance (an intelligence, a soul and a heaven). Moreover, in this station, only Koranic imagery is employed in portraying the seed as the first substance which manifests *Mulk* and *Malakūt*: "Do not those who disbelieve see that the heavens and earth were closed up *(ratq)* but We have opened them up *(fatq)*."[121] Nasafī describes this process in another way which again reflects a Koranic rather than Neoplatonic basis:

> As long as the spirit and body were mixed in one another and were not distinguishable from one another, they were like an ink-pot. When they split and become distinguishable from one another, they became like pens. This is the meaning of: "*Nun*, and the pen and what they are writing."[122] "*Nun*" is an oath by the state of closing *(ratq)* and "the pen" is an oath by the state of opening *(fatq)* and "what they are writing" is an oath by the four pens.[123]

This alternative perspective to Neoplatonism is also apparent in Nasafī's other works[124] where he claims that the Philosophers say the first thing that God creates is intelligence *('aql)* and the last thing is the earth *(khāk)*. The People of Unity (who are the elect among the Sufis) maintain that the first thing God creates is earth and the last thing is intelligence, which is manifested only in man. In this way, man is accorded the greatest place in creation. The meaning of man here is the small man (i.e. the microcosm) and not the big man (i.e. the macrocosm), as Nasafī explains:

> Although each individual thing *(fard)* of the world is God's mirror, it is the Perfect Man *(insān-i kāmil)* who is the perfect mirror for "I loved to be known," and some have read it as "I loved to know." Both are correct because the microcosm is both knower and known, both observer *(nāẓir)* and observed *(manẓūr)*, both mirror and the possessor of beauty.[125]

Man is superior to the macrocosm because the macrocosm does what it does through its specific characteristics and properties, so it is impossible for it not to do the task which God commands. However, man does what he does through his specific characteristics and through activity *(fi'l)* which means he also has the choice in some things.[126] He can choose to manifest God's beautiful names in the appropriate situation, and thereby hope for the reward of Paradise. The macrocosm does not possess free will or desire to the same extent that man has. Thus man is closer to God and he can reach a point where God is the seer, hearer and speaker. For this reason, man is both knower and known, observer and observed, mirror and possessor of beauty. Of course, this refers to the *ḥadīth* that Nasafī discusses in the second station.

In this station, human bodies are compared to windows *(darīcha)* and man's spirit, which is God's light, shines out of all these windows. Sometimes the light shines from many windows, and sometimes it shines from fewer windows. When the windows are fewer in number (if there is a plague, or natural disaster) the light is stronger in the remaining windows, and this helps the spirit of one person reach the extremity in knowledge. Such a person becomes the leader of people; he may be a Prophet, Friend, commander or sultan.[127]

Although the light is the same for each person, its manifestation in the world is different and so people are not aware of the knowledge others have had or have. The reason for this difference in manifestation is explained as follows:

> Know that the self-disclosures of God's light are not repeated. Any occasion that He discloses Himself is not identical with the previous self-disclosure; it is similar *(mithl)* to the first. If it were in such a way that the second was identical with the first, then you would be aware of the first form *(qālib)* and would recognise and remember whatever you had seen in that form. But it is not so. If a water jug is dipped into the

sea a thousand times, and a thousand times it is filled from that sea, the water of the first time is not the same as the water of the second time, even though the jug is filled with sea water each time. Hence, it is said that His self-disclosures have no end point.

In addition, know that when the water jug is filled with sea water, in fact the water takes on several attributes from the adjacency *(mujāwarat)* of the jug, and the jug takes on several attributes from the adjacency of the water. When the jug is smashed, the water goes to water and the earth goes to earth. Each one goes to its own state and takes on the attributes of the whole *(ṣifāt-i kull)*.[128]

Nasafī closes the first chapter of *Kitāb-i tanzīl* by relating the famous story of the blind men and the elephant. The story goes that there was a city of blind people who had heard of elephants but could not imagine what they were like. When a caravan (in which there was an elephant) passed their city, some blind men went out to the caravan and each of the blind men touched the elephant. One felt its trunk, another its leg, another its ear, and so each one discovered something about the elephant, about which the others had no knowledge. When they told each other about the "reality" of the elephant, each one said something which did not accord with the experiences of the others.[129] All of them were correct from one perspective but not one of them could grasp the whole picture.

This of course is the reality of the *tashbīh-tanzīh* nature of God. Each one of the six stations reflects an element of truth, and the task of the wayfarer is to realise that his own station is not the only one which reveals God's similarity. However, as Nasafī remarks, even if one person comprehends this fact, the majority (even philosophers and Sufis) do not accept this truth:

This is the state of the People of Thought and Reasoning concerning the objects of intelligence because intelligence has degrees, and the wisdom of things is immeasurable and innumerable. And this is the state of the People of Unveiling and Contemplation concerning the objects of unveiling, because unveiling has degrees and divine self-disclosure is immeasurable and innumerable. Among a hundred thousand people who set out on this road, one reaches the end and is aware of the ultimate goal of the task. The rest remain in way stations *(manāzil)* and they consider the station is their aim.[130]

Each of the six stations represents a way of considering the relationship between God and man, in other words, the *tashbīh-tanzīh* relationship. In the first station, *creatio ex nihilo* expresses man's contingent nature and is on the whole more representative of *tanzīh*. The second station stands in contrast to the first where man is also eternal in potentiality and the *tashbīh* nature is portrayed through the concept of knowledge following the known and also through the *ḥadīth* of supererogatory acts. The third station acts as a kind of isthmus between the previous two, for although the world is imagination and thus *tanzīh*, it does at least reveal something of reality and from this perspective it is *tashbīh*. The fourth station also reflects the *tashbīh-tanzīh* relationship. *Tashbīh* is evident through the idea of "everything is He," and God's existence being a single entity which has three levels; essence, face and breath. *Tanzīh* is clear when Nasafī comments that individuals are responsible for their own acts and thus liable to God's wrath if they are disobedient. In the fifth station, creation at every instant and non-repetition in self-disclosure also manifest the *tanzīh-tashbīh* nature. Although things are annihilated each moment by God *(tanzīh)*, his mercy bestows existence upon something similar to the annihilated thing *(tashbīh)*. The non-repetition of self-disclosure also expresses the *tanzīh-tashbīh* nature, for although everything is a self-disclosure of God *(tashbīh)*, it is only a "face" and not existence as it really is *(tanzīh)*. The non-repetition of God's self-disclosure is a theme continued in the sixth station, but Nasafī also focuses upon the important concept of the Perfect Man. The Perfect Man is crucial for an understanding of Prophecy and Friendship. He is the goal of creation because he acts as a link between God and His creation; he is the mirror by which God sees Himself and he is the form in which the creatures can see God's perfect creation. Thus the Perfect Man fuses *tanzīh* and *tashbīh* together and he realises these two aspects of the God-man relationship in their appropriate places.

All issues considered in the first chapter of *Kitāb-i tanzīl* are among the major points which concerned Ibn 'Arabī and his interpreters. The discussion of these issues combined with Nasafī's style of fusing Koranic imagery and the language of the *kalām* with the use of the Greek-inspired terminology of Philosophers such as al-Farābī and Ibn Sīnā, reflects the *wujūdī* world view of Ibn 'Arabī. Yet the significance of Nasafī's work goes far beyond a shared vision with Ibn 'Arabī. Nasafī's works give a certain simplicity and clarity to Ibn 'Arabī's idea of He/not He, which Sufi novices may have found difficult to find in the Greatest Shaykh's voluminous treatises. In addition, Nasafī's explanation of the six stations which describe the various ontological perspectives of his time, reveals his interpretation of Sufism as all-embracing. The beliefs of the *'Ulamā'*, the philosophers and the different Sufi schools all represent some aspect of truth and are therefore genuine expressions of Islamic belief.

II. NASAFĪ AND IMAGINATION

In the previous section, it was shown that Nasafī described existence through the worlds of *Mulk*, *Malakūt* and *Jabarūt*. Of the six spiritual stations, the most sophisticated is the second where God is other than the worlds of *Mulk*, *Malakūt* and *Jabarūt*. Similar discussions to this second spiritual station occur in most of Nasafī's other works and therefore it is likely that he preferred such a position to any others. This ontological ordering is neatly encapsulated in *Manāzil al-sā'irīn*:

> Know that *Mulk* is the world of testimony and *Malakūt* is the invisible world *('ālam-i ghayb)* and *Jabarūt* is the invisible, invisible world *('ālam-i ghayb-i ghayb)* and God Most High is the invisible, invisible, invisible world *('ālam-i ghayb-i ghayb-i ghayb)*.
>
> O dervish! *Jabarūt*, which is the invisible, invisible world, is the world of potentiality, and the world of potentiality is above *Mulk* and *Malakūt*. This is because existents are actual in *Mulk* and *Malakūt* and they are potential in *Jabarūt* and potential existents are prior to actual existents. First is readiness *(ṣalāḥiyyat)* and then is special quality *(khāṣṣiyyat)*. In addition, potential existents have no beginning and actual existents have a beginning.[131]

Nasafī's interpretation of *Jabarūt* is in fact the same as Ibn 'Arabī's immutable entities. This appellation of the immutable entities as *Jabarūt* is somewhat idiosyncratic, for most Sufis, and not only those of the *wujūdī* school, described *Jabarūt* in an altogether different fashion. To demonstrate the specific nature of Nasafī's *Jabarūt*, it is necessary to see how the term was used by his predecessors and contemporaries.

Imagination and the Divine Presences

Mulk and *Malakūt* are Koranic terms. The term *Jabarūt* does not appear in the Koran although one finds it in a *ḥadīth* which states: "Glory to He of the *Jabarūt* and *Malakūt* and Majesty *(al-kubriyā)* and Greatness *(al-'aẓma)*."[132] Thus, the use of the term *Jabarūt* enters the Islamic vocabulary at an early stage, but its meaning as a technical term in not entirely clear. Some scholars have not been able to see a difference between *Malakūt* and *Jabarūt* in the works of early Islamic philosophers such as al-Farābī and Ibn Sīnā.[133] However, it has suggested that Ibn Sīnā's system differentiates between *Malakūt* and *Jabarūt*, the former being the realm of intellectual realities (or disembodied intellects) and the latter being the realm of symbols that affect the imagination, which is the realm in which Ibn Sīnā locates the celestial souls.[134]

A contemporary of Ibn Sīnā was Abū Ṭālib al-Makkī (d. 998) who also makes a clear distinction between *Mulk*, *Malakūt* and *Jabarūt* in his work entitled *Qūt al-qulūb*. *Mulk* is witnessed by intellectual light; *Malakūt* which is the next world, is witnessed by the light of faith; the Majesty *(al-'izza)* which is the (divine) attributes, is witnessed by the light of certainty; and *Jabarūt*, which is the Unity *(al-wāḥidāniyya)* is witnessed by the light of gnosis.[135]

Abū Ḥāmid Ghazālī was familiar with the works of both Ibn Sīnā and Makkī. Within his works there are many references to *Jabarūt* which is portrayed in two main ways. The first is found in his *Durra* in which the lowest world is *Mulk*, then *Malakūt* and the highest world is *Jabarūt*. *Mulk* pertains to "Adam and his posterity," *Malakūt* pertains to the classes of angels and *jinn*, while *Jabarūt* pertains to the elect among the angels. The elect of the angels are the Cherubs, the bearers of God's Throne and the chamberlains of the godhead.[136]

This ranking appears in treatises of other Sufis, such as the author of *Tabṣirat al-mubtadi'*, who is thought to be Ṣadr al-Dīn Qūnawī.[137] Nasafī copied several passages from this work in his *Maqṣad-i aqṣā*, some of which are discussions related to the existents of *Malakūt (mawjūdāt-i malakūtī)*. Nasafī describes various kinds of existents. The first are those who pay no attention to the world of the creatures, and these are the "Enraptured Angels." Another kind who also are not concerned with the world of bodies and who continually contemplate God are the door-keepers of the Divinity *(ḥijāb bārgāh-i ulūhiyya)* and they are also known as the Folk of *Jabarūt*. A second kind of spiritual existent are those who order, govern and pertain to this world and they are called "spirituals" *(rūḥāniyyān)*. Among these are the Folk of Higher *Malakūt*, who have free disposal in the heavens, and the Folk of Lower *Malakūt* who are the guardians over minerals, plants and animals. The *jinn* and Satan are included among the Folk of Lower *Malakūt*.[138] This particular ordering by Nasafī resembles Ghazālī's hierarchy found in the *Durra*, but this system is not repeated in any of Nasafī's other works. The first chapter of *Kitāb-i tanzīl* is much more representative of his discussions of *Mulk*, *Malakūt* and *Jabarūt*.

Returning to Ghazālī, his second way of portraying *Jabarūt* owes more perhaps to the systems of Ibn Sīnā and Makkī that were described previously. In this second ordering of the three worlds, *Jabarūt* is a unity of *Mulk* and *Malakūt* within man but it is not the origin of *Mulk* and *Malakūt* as in Nasafī's system. Ghazālī's *Jabarūt* in fact prefigures the discussions of the imagination that became one of the predominant features in many of the Sufi works of the *wujūdī* school.[139] For Ghazālī, *Mulk* is the world of sense perception and *Malakūt* is the invisible world. "The realm of the world of *Jabarūt* lies between the two worlds; partly it may become visible in the world of *Mulk*, partly it is related to the eternal Power and belongs to the world of *Malakūt*."[140]

In other words, *Malakūt* is a realm which cannot be witnessed by the physical eye, however, that which pertains to *Malakūt*, such as spirits and angels, takes a form within the imagination. In this way *Malakūt* and *Mulk* combine, resulting in *Jabarūt*. Ghazālī explains: "Now the world of *Jabarūt* [141] between that of *Mulk* and *Malakūt*, resembles a ship which is moving between the beach and the water; it has neither the utter fluxity of the water not the utter stability and fixidness of the beach. Everyone who walks on the earth walks in the world of *Mulk* and of sensual apperception. And when he has sufficient power to sail on a ship, he is as one who walks in the world of *Jabarūt*. And when he has reached such a stage that he can walk on the water without a ship, he walks in the *Malakūt* without sinking."[142]

This is the imaginal world which was described and developed in the course of Sufism. Ghazālī's ranking of *Jabarūt* as the realm where one can understand spiritual realities through a mental form was also explained by 'Ayn al-Quḍāt Hamadānī (d. 1132). For 'Ayn al-Quḍāt, it is intelligence which acts as a broker between the brain and the heart, enabling spiritual realities to become embodied.

> Now know that my brain *(damāgh)* would not understand the discourses of my heart if my intelligence *('aql)* were not between the two. The brain pertains to the realm of *Mulk*, the heart pertains to the realm of *Malakūt* and intelligence pertains to the realm of *Jabarūt*. Know that intelligence is the interpreter that understands both the tongue of the *Malakūtī* heart and also the tongue of the *Mulkī* brain.[143]

Another Sufi who had much to say about this imaginal world was Shaykh Shihāb al-Dīn Yaḥyā Suhrawardī (d. 1191). According to his Oriental Theosophy *(ḥikmat al-ishrāq)*, there are several worlds, the highest of which is the Light of Lights. From this emanates one Victoral Light *(qāhir)* which is referred to under the Mazdean name "Bahman."[144] From Bahman, innumerable lights, independent of material bodies are emanated, and this, according to Corbin, is the world of *Jabarūt*.[145] Then from this world of *Jabarūt*, two groups of substances of light are emanated which may be perceived by man. The first are luminous suspended forms *(al-ṣuwar al-mu'allaqa al-mustanīra)* and is also known as the imaginal world *('ālam al-khayāl)*.[146] The second are dark suspended forms *(al-ṣuwar al-mu'allaqa al-ẓulmāniyya)* which include evil spirits and satans.[147] Corbin calls these last two categories together the world of *Malakūt*.[148]

Nasafī's portrayal of *Jabarūt* is much closer to Suhrawardī's interpretation than those of Ibn Sīnā, Ghazālī or 'Ayn al-Quḍāt, since they understood it as the imaginal world. The reality of the imaginal world was discussed in more detail from the thirteenth century onwards by Sufis of the *wujūdī* school. In many ways Nasafī was influenced by this school as was shown in the previous section, however his works do not discuss the imaginal world in the same manner or detail as Ibn 'Arabī or Ṣadr al-Dīn Qūnawī. Nasafī's most detailed ontological hierarchy posits four levels which are God, *Jabarūt*, *Malakūt* and *Mulk*, omitting the world of imagination from his order. This is not the case with the leading members of the *wujūdī* school who include the imaginal world within their ontological hierarchy which contains five (and sometimes six) levels of existence.[149] These five levels were formulated by members of the *wujūdī* school into the "Five Divine Presences," *(al-ḥaḍarāt al-ilāhiyya al-khams)*. With a lack of a detailed discussion about the imaginal world in Nasafī's theosophy, it is perhaps inevitable that his works are not as sophisticated as those by Sufis such as Ibn 'Arabī, Ṣadr al-Dīn Qūnawī, Sa'īd al-Dīn Farghānī (d.c. 1300), Mu'ayyid al-Dīn al-Jandī (d.c. 1300), Kamāl al-Dīn 'Abd al-Razzāq Kāshānī (d. 1329) and Sharaf al-Dīn Dāwūd al-Qayṣarī (d. 1350).

In order to elucidate Nasafī's position *vis-a-vis* the *wujūdī* school, it is useful to compare his "four seas" from his *Maqṣad-i aqṣā* with the interpretation of the Five Divine Presences by Sa'īd al-Dīn Farghānī. The reason for looking at Farghānī's exegesis rather than any other interpreter is because the former's works probably exercised a more widespread influence on the Islamic world.[150] Before focusing upon Farghānī's Divine Presences, Nasafī's "four seas" will be briefly analysed (it is not necessary to examine them in detail because the four levels of existence have already been discussed).

In the final two chapters of *Maqṣad-i aqṣā*, the topic of discussion is "the four seas," which are "the invisible, invisible, invisible world," *Jabarūt*, *Malakūt* and *Mulk*.[151] The first of these is God's essence which is an infinite, non-delimited light and is a sea without end and without shore.[152] This essence is explained with reference to the *ḥadīth*, "I was a hidden treasure and I desired to be know." Since it desired to be known, the first essence made itself a mirror and this is the second sea (which is the mirror in potentiality).[153] The second sea acts as an intermediary between the *tanzīh* first sea and the third and fourth seas. This second sea is the world of *Jabarūt* and is called by other names including the Attributed Spirit *(rūḥ-i iḍāfī)*,[154] the Muḥammadan Spirit, the Greatest Light and the Muḥammadan Light,[155] and it is also an infinite and non-delimited light and a sea without end and without shore.

> It encompasses the world, and there is not one particle in the world which the Attributed Spirit is not with and which it does not encompass and about which it is not aware. It is the life of the world and of the creatures of the world, and it is the governor of the world and of the creatures, it is the master *(mutaṣarrif)* in its world and it governs the world. Its task is existentiating *(ījād)*, annihilation *(ī'dām)*, reviving *(iḥyā)*, putting to death *(imātat)*, honouring *(i'zāz)* and holding in contempt *(idhlāl)*. [156]

The reason that Nasafī gives the name *Jabarūt* to this particular level may be found in the etymology of the word. *Jabarūt* is not found in the Koran although the derived name *al-Jabbār* (the All-Compeller) appears in 59: 23. So the things in *Jabarūt* are those which are fixed and which cannot change their nature or quality. In other words, they are determined or compelled *(jabr)* in their state from eternity.

Nasafī describes the Attributed Spirit (or *Jabarūt*) as a seed, which contains *Mulk* and *Malakūt* (the third and fourth seas). A seed has the potential to existentiate a plant and it also has a set limit for a plant's life, for a seed contains everything which has the potential to be manifested, from the stalk, to the leaves and petals. The second sea is also described as a pen:

> "The ink-pot *(nūn)*, by the pen and what they are writing."[157] *Nūn* is an expression for the first sea because "I was a hidden treasure and I desired to be known,"[158] and the pen is an expression for the second sea because "the first thing God created was intelligence,"[159] and "what they are writing," is an expression for the third and fourth seas, and they are continually writing and the three kinds of children[160] were and are created from their writing, and the three kinds of children are words and they are not repeated, rather, there is no end as the Most High said "Say: if the sea were ink for the words of my Lord, sooner would the sea be exhausted than would the words of my Lord, even if we added another sea like it for its aid."[161]

The words are existent in the pen in an undifferentiated mode, and when the pen splits them into the third and fourth seas, it is able to compose them in a differentiated mode.

Aside from Nasafī's four seas, there is a discussion in *Maqṣad-i aqṣā* of another level of existence which other Sufis of the *wujūdī* school consider a Divine presence. This is the Perfect Man. Nasafī frequently refers to the aforementioned *ḥadīth* that "I was a hidden treasure and I desired to be known." He explains how *Mulk* and *Malakūt* are combined together in man, for all existents are compounds of light and darkness. Each compound has its nature (its spiritual dimension) and its body (its sensory dimension). These two are mixed together and need to be separated, a process which is started through eating pure food. The process leads from the stomach through the liver and to the brain where the attributes of light can be manifested. According to Nasafī, animals and men are constantly performing this "alchemy," but the Perfect Man takes this alchemy to the limit. The Perfect Man is God's perfect mirror:

> The answer that the Truth Most High gave to David (peace be upon him) that "I was a hidden treasure and I loved to be known," becomes apparent and recognised here. He sees His own glory and He witnesses His own attributes, names, works and wisdom.[162]

So within one chapter of *Maqṣad-i aqṣā*, Nasafī discusses the ontological hierarchy of the four seas and the Perfect Man who comprehends them all.

Turning now to Sa'īd al-Dīn Farghānī's Divine Presences, the first thing to note is that he speaks of six levels rather than five levels. His first level is that of God in His *tanzīh* nature, which is called *aḥadiyya* or Exclusive Unity. This is the level beyond man's conception, and it is Nasafī's "invisible, invisible, invisible world." The second level is that of Inclusive Oneness *(wāḥidiyya)* which is another expression for God as Creator, the source of all things, Who has knowledge of all things and can bestow existence upon them. This is the world of immutable entities, or in Nasafī's terminology, it is *Jabarūt*. Once God bestows existence upon His knowledge, there are three modes or levels in which they are the loci of manifestation. The first is the spiritual world, or the level of intelligible things; the second is the sensory world, or level of sense perception; third is the level of imagination where spirits are corporealised and bodies are spiritualised. The last level is that of the all-encompassing Perfect Man, who comprehends all the prior levels.

Nasafī does not use the terminology of the divine presences although the predominant theme in his theosophy is the hierarchical nature of existence. His four main levels and the Perfect Man accord with Farghānī's *aḥadiyya*, *wāḥidiyya*, spiritual and sensory worlds and Perfect Man. That Nasafī did not include detailed discussions in his works of the central concept of the imaginal world is quite surprising given the fact that he explains the other main aspects of *wujūdī* theosophy (albeit in a summarised manner). The significance of this omission becomes clear when Nasafī's explanation of what happens to the soul after death is compared with the descriptions given by Ibn 'Arabī and other Sufis of the *wujūdī* school.

Imagination and the Return to God *(Ma'ād)*

The unity of God, Muḥammad being God's last prophet and the return of each individual to God to be judged are the three fundamental principles of Islam. As one would expect, each one is discussed in all of Nasafī's works. With respect to the return, the Sufis of the *wujūdī* school discussed three worlds: this world *(dunyā)*, the grave, and the next world *(ākhira)*. Nasafī discusses this world in detail and his references to the next world are many but he hardly mentions the grave. In the whole of *Kitāb-i tanzīl* there is only one paragraph which refers to the grave:

> Know that the Prophets and Friends were informed of the states after death, like the questioning in the grave, the tortures of the graves, becoming alive and rising from the grave, reading the letter of one's works, the reckoning *(ḥisāb)* of each person, the scales *(tarāzū)*, the straight path *(ṣirāṭ al-mustaqīm)*, hell and the various tortures in hell, paradise *(bihisht)* and the numerous comforts in paradise, and all the others are the truth. It is necessary for each person to have faith in each one of them even if he does not know the manner *(kayfiyyat)* of these things. If a person does not have faith in some of them then he is not a believer. There is no damage to faith if a person discusses the manner of these things and makes an explanation *(sharḥī)* even if he is mistaken on some of them, because he is searching. But it is better if he does not say anything and does not become busy in giving explanations.[163]

Yet there can be little doubt that Nasafī was aware of the *wujūdī* discussion of the grave because this topic is included within *Tabṣirat al-mubtadi'*[164] a text with which he was familiar and passages of which he copied in *Maqṣad-i aqṣā*. Nasafī in fact does deal with concepts that are similar to the discussions of the *wujūdī* school but there are fundamental differences. Before reflecting on Nasafī's explanations, it is necessary to summarise the position of the *wujūdī* school on the return to God.

As stated earlier, the *wujūdī* school discusses three worlds: this world, the grave and the next world. The grave is understood as an isthmus *(barzakh)* between this world and the next world and its nature is different for each individual soul. This is because the experiences in the grave are dependent upon the attributes that were predominant in the individual soul while it was in this world.

Since realities in this world are veiled by corporeal bodies, it is difficult to understand the motivations and intentions of people. Their outward dimension or appearance remains relatively fixed while their inward states, moods and thoughts are constantly fluctuating and changing, so most people can only witness the outward appearance and not the inward state. This is not the case in the grave where there are no corporeal bodies to veil realities. Each soul takes an "imaginal" form appropriate to its state which is determined by the attributes or character traits that were predominant over it in this world. This is clarified by the author of *Tabṣirat al-mubtadi'*, who says, "If for example, love of position dominated, the person will appear in the form of a leopard. If the faculty of appetite dominated over the other attributes, he will appear as a dog."[165]

The inner reality of each individual, that is, in terms of attributes, in the grave is fixed. However the manifestations of these attributes at the outward dimension are constantly changing in the forms of their works during this world. The grave then is this world inside out where the intentions and motivations of the soul are apparent in form. If the intentions and motivations are worthy then the form will be pleasant and if they are blameworthy then the form will be hellish. So the grave gives a foretaste of the next world, which may be paradise or hell. Corporeal bodies of this world are dense whereas imaginal bodies are relatively subtle, therefore the experiences of the soul in the grave, be they felicitous or wretched, are more intense than those in this world. The next world is even more real "because it lies closer to the spiritual side of things and is therefore subtle and more luminous."[166]

As stated earlier, Nasafī does not discuss the grave. His explanation of the return to God is connected with the idea of the spirit rising through several levels until it perfects itself. Of his portrayal of the beliefs of the People of the Holy Law, the Philosophers, the Transmigrationists and the People of Unity, it is the discourses of the Transmigrationists that appear similar to those of the *wujūdī* school concerning the grave. However, it will be shown that there are fundamental differences between the two.

(i) Imagination and the Return According to the Transmigrationists

Nasafī's discussions of the return to God are similar to those of the *wujūdī* school in his explanations of the People of Transmigration *(ahl-i tanāsukh)*. These occur in several of his works which indicates that he held them to be quite significant.[167] The identity of this group is somewhat unclear. In *Kashf al-ḥaqā'iq*, Nasafī states that they may be accounted among the Philosophers *(ahl-i ḥikmat)*,[168] while in *Mazāzil al-sā'irīn*, he comments that they have existed for several thousand years and four parts out of six *(chahār dāng-i 'ālam)* in the world follow the beliefs of the Transmigrationists[169] which indicates a pre-Islamic, possibly Indian belief.

According to the People of Transmigration, all souls are existent in the higher world *('ālam-i 'ulwī)* and they come to the lower world *('ālam-i suflī)* to actualise their perfection because this can only be achieved with a body. If this perfection is achieved then the soul returns to the celestial world.[170] The individual soul at first has the form of a plant, then an animal and then a human. Nasafī explains that this ascent is known as "progressive transmigration" *(naskh)*. The lowest plant form is moss *(ṭuḥlub)* and the highest form of plant are trees such as the mandrake *(dirakht-i lūffāh)* and *dhāq dhāq* trees whose fruit are similar to animals. The ascent continues to the lowest form of animal which is the worm, until the non-rational animals *(ḥaywān-i ghayr-i nāṭiq)* appear such as the elephant, ape and *nasnās*.[171] From here, the human form appears, the lowest of which is the negro and it rises in levels until it reaches the Philosopher where it is called the Rational Soul, then it reaches the degree of the Friends where it is named the Holy Soul, and finally it reaches the form of the Prophets where it is called the Soul at rest.[172]

Nasafī also gives the Transmigrationists account of the ascent of the spirit from plant to human form within one lifetime. Some trees bear fruits whose outward appearance is like that of humans. If these trees grow in areas where the air is moderate in regions beneath the equator, such as Sri Lanka, their fruit will gradually become rational and speak. The tradition that Adam came to earth first in Sri Lanka is used to illustrate this belief.[173]

Progressive transmigration is when the individual soul appears in a form higher than the one that it had previously and regressive transmigration works in the opposite direction. Once the spirit has reached the human level it has the ability to reach its ultimate perfection. According to the Transmigrationists, the spirit below the level of Philosopher is in hell. The rank of Philosopher reaches heaven, the rank of the Friend passes on from the heavens and reaches the universal intelligence and the spirit of the Prophet reaches God.[174] If the spirit reaches its perfection in this world, then at the time of death when the spirit separates from the body *(mufāriqat)*, it returns to the world of intelligences and souls. The individual soul connects to the soul of a sphere with which the knowledge and piety that it acquired in this world accords. If it does not reach its perfection in this world then after separation from the body, the soul cannot return to the world of intelligences and souls but remains beneath the firmament of the moon (i.e. this world of creation and corruption, which is hell).[175] In this case, the spirit is resurrected *(ḥashr)* in another body until it reaches its perfection. Some of the Transmigrationists held that it was impossible for the human spirit to be resurrected in anything other than a human body,[176] while others have said that the spirit may regress below the world of animals and become resurrected in the kingdom of plants.[177] In regressive transmigration the spirit suffers in proportion with its sins and then it has the chance to rise again through the various forms until it reaches its perfection. If it does not reach its perfection again, then the process is repeated. The spirit is always resurrected in a form which is suitable to it, in other words, it is raised in the form of the attribute that was dominant over it when it was alive in this world.[178]

This is the point where the beliefs of the Transmigrationists appear similar to those of the *wujūdī* school. It was shown that the Sufis of the *wujūdī* tradition held that in the grave, individuals have "imaginal" bodies which accord with the works of the individual while they were in this world. However, the Transmigrationists believed that if the individual soul did not actualise its perfection, then it was resurrected in this world in the form appropriate to its acts. This superficial similarity was pointed out by Ṣadr al-Dīn Qūnawī:

> In the *barzakh* – or rather, a short time before the Mustering – some people appear in the form of lions, wolves and birds, as the Shariah has mentioned, and as unveiling and divine instruction have given witness.
>
> But this does not happen by means of metempsychosis *(maskh)* or transmigration *(tanāsukh)* that is denied, for people who believe in such things hold that it occurs in this world. But what we are speaking about occurs in the *barzakh* after death.[179]

Generally speaking, Sufis view the ascent of man's spirit as passing through several stages before reaching its perfection, but the form always remains the same in this world, only the non-manifest dimension changes. Rūmī captures the essence of this concept in a well known passage from the *Mathnawī*:

> I died from the mineral kingdom and became a plant; I died to vegetive nature and attained to animality.
> I died to animality and became a man. So why should I fear? When did I ever become less through dying?
> Next time I will die to human nature, so that I may spread my wings and lift up my head among the angels.
> Once again, I will be sacrificed from angelic nature and become that which enters not the imagination.[180]

In the grave the manifest dimension, that is, the imaginal body changes to reflect the attribute of the spirit. This was a theory that was developed prior to Ibn 'Arabī and the *wujūdī* school by Sufis including 'Ayn al-Quḍāt:

> The structures of the existence of the Next World are through imaginalisation, and recognising [the reality] of imaginalisation is not an easy task.[181]
> The first thing that becomes clear for the wayfarer concerning the Next World is the [different] states of the grave. The first imaginalisation that he witnesses, such as snakes, scorpions, dogs, fire, which have all been promised to the people who are to be punished, appears to him in the grave through imaginalisation. All of these things are in man's inner dimension since they are [imaginalised] through him, in fact they are continually with him.[182]

(ii) Imagination in the Return According to the People of Unity

One might expect Nasafī to explain the beliefs of the Sufis or People of Unity regarding the forms of souls in the grave in the same manner as Ibn 'Arabī and Ṣadr al-Dīn Qūnawī. However within the sections of the People of Unity where the discussion is related to the return to God, there is no mention of the imagination in the same sense in which the *wujūdī* school employ the term. For example, in two chapters of *Kashf al-ḥaqā'iq* entitled "Unity" and "the Resurrection of Man," Nasafī presents the discourses of four different groups among the People of Unity. The first two are called the Advocates of Fire *(aṣḥāb-i nār)*. The first of these explains that man's body is the creation of God and his spirit is the God of creation. At death, there is no more existence for the body but the spirit continues to exist because it is eternal. People in this particular station, according to Nasafī, have included Shaykh Shihāb al-Dīn Suhrawardī (attributed by modern scholars to be the Shaykh al-Ishrāq[183]) and Shaykh 'Abdallāh Anṣārī of Herat.[184] The second party among the Advocates of Fire hold that both man's spirit and body are unreal, for they are opposites and there are no contraries in God's world. This is the station of Shaykh Ibn Sab'īn.[185]

The second two groups are called the Advocates of Light *(aṣḥāb-i nūr)*. The first of these says that the spirit and body are with each other and cannot be separated. They rise together in levels and reach their ultimate perfection in man. Then they return to their origin which is earth. Bodies return to the element of earth and spirits return to the nature of earth, and the process of seeking perfection commences again. There is no distinction in the element of earth for each person or in the spirit of each person: the differences among individuals arise due to the movements of the spheres.[186] The second group say that man's body and spirit form a temporary union and after perfection is reached they separate, in other words, the body returns to its world and the spirit returns to its world. However there is no distinction or differences in the body when it returns to its own world and the same applies to the spirit.[187]

These discussions by Nasafī are short and limited and there is no mention of the grave or the resurrection. Therefore it is difficult to make any comments about them. However, if the beliefs of Advocates of Light concerning the return of the spirit and body refer to the resurrection, then there are several issues which need to be raised. This is because there appears to be a lack of individuation after death which runs contrary to the Koranic belief in reward and punishment for each individual based upon his or her works in this world. Moreover, the Koran also states that man will be resurrected in both body and spirit, which the second group of Advocates of Light seems to deny.

The beliefs of the Advocates of Fire also present some interesting problems, especially the group that is representative of Shihāb al-Dīn Suhrawardī (and which also is similar to the theories of Ibn Sīnā). The difficulty lies in the fact that this group sees man's spirit as eternal and that the body is not necessary in the next world, which as already mentioned, contradicts the Koran. Ibn Sīnā regarded the resurrection of the body as an "imaginal" body (and in this respect he is a forerunner of the *wujūdī* school) for the disembodied spirits enjoy pleasure and suffer torture by virtue of the application of their imaginations.[188] According to one contemporary scholar, Ibn Rushd (1126–1198) could not accept this idea of imaginal bodies because the imagination pertains to sense perception.[189] The imagination is a faculty of the soul and the soul cannot exist without a body. When the body dies, so too the soul (and therefore the imagination) ceases to function. Therefore, the resurrection takes place for each individual in both his soul and also in a physical body (created by God) similar to the one that was united with the soul in this world. In this respect Ibn Rushd defends the Koranic doctrine of the resurrection of man's body and spirit and at the same time rejects the idea that man conquers death through the intrinsic nature of his soul. The process is God's second creation.[190]

The *wujūdī* school did not interpret the soul as pertaining to the body in the same way as Ibn Rushd. The soul had a somewhat undetermined position between matter and the spiritual, or between darkness and light. Therefore it shares the qualities of the two. Moreover, it is able to experience things in the grave because God creates *barzakh* bodies for the soul.[191]

Nasafī's explanation of the Return to God for the People of Unity leaves many questions unanswered. There is no detailed discussion of the nature of the grave or of the next world and there is no mention of the imagination, which as demonstrated in this section, is the key to how many Sufis explained several aspects of the Return to God. Given Nasafī's limited explanation of the imagination in his portrayal of the ontological hierarchy, it is not really surprising that there is no discussion of the grave and "imaginal bodies" in his works.

Despite the above shortcomings, one should not under-estimate Nasafī's major contribution to the ontological discussions of the thirteenth century. His portrayal of the hierarchical levels of existence (*Mulk*, *Malakūt* and *Jabarūt*) continued the tradition of providing even more specific and precise explanations of the existential levels. After Nasafī, this trend was developed further by 'Alā' al-Dawla al-Simnānī[192] and the mystics of the *wujūdī* tradition.

III. NASAFĪ AND NEOPLATONIC ONTOLOGY

In the nineteenth and early twentieth centuries, several eminent scholars of Sufism believed that Neoplatonic thought was one of the major influences upon Sufism. For example, R.A. Nicholson commented that "we are drawn irresistibly to the conclusion . . . that Neoplatonism poured in to Islam a large tincture of the same mystical element in which Christianity was already steeped."[193] This train of thought was also adopted by A.J. Arberry (Nicholson's student) who held Neoplatonism on the one hand and the "transcendental theism of the Koran" on the other, as the "twain fountainheads of Sufi theosophy."[194] In more recent years, the Neoplatonic influence has been identified by P. Morewedge in the works of 'Azīz Nasafī, who described ". . . a Neoplatonic system of 'emanation and return' as a mystical depiction of the world."[195] Indeed, one can find many passages in Nasafī's works which one might classify as being of a Neoplatonic persuasion. This is especially the case when he portrays the descent and return which is suggestive of the Neoplatonic idea of emanation through the intelligences until the individual things of the earth are created, and then a return to the One through the compounds.[196]

The influence of Neoplatonism upon Sufism has been questioned by other scholars, such as W. Chittick, who believes the world view of mystics such as Ṣadr al-Dīn Qūnawī was in fact founded upon both spiritual unveiling and the contemplation of Koranic images. However, the extent to which Neoplatonism affected Sufism is still open to debate and much research is required to provide a clearer picture. Nasafī's position in this respect is interesting because scholars have emphasised different elements in his world view; while P. Morewedge seems to witness Neoplatonic tendencies in Nasafī's thought, Chittick has indicated that he was primarily in the *wujūdī* tradition of Ibn 'Arabī and Ṣadr al-Dīn Qūnawī.[197] Before concentrating upon the similarities or differences of Nasafī's theosophy with that of the Neoplatonists, a brief description shall be given of the points where Islam and Neoplatonic thought meet.

Similarities Between Islam and Classical Neoplatonism

By 840 A.D. the so-called "Theology of Aristotle" had been translated into Arabic and was soon utilised by Islamic philosophers such as al-Farābī[198] in their world views. The "Theology of Aristotle" was in fact, a résumé of books IV, V and VI of Plotinus's "*Enneads.*" The fundamental tenets of Plotinus's visionary theosophy are fivefold; God is one: He is eternal: there is a perpetual emanation from the One: the Universal Intellect then acts as a means between the One and the emanations that result from the Universal Intellect: these emanations finally return to the One.[199] These five fundaments of Neoplatonism bear strong similarities to certain verses and meanings which can be found in the Koran. This will be illustrated in the next few paragraphs.

(i) The first tenet, which is that of God's unity is described by Plotinus in the following manner: "Think of the One as Mind or God, you think too meanly; use all the resources of understanding to conceive this Unity and, again it is more authentically one than God, even though you reach for God's unity beyond the unity the most perfect you can conceive. This self sufficiency is the essence of its unity. Something there must be supremely adequate, autonomous, all transcending, most utterly without need."[200]

Unity is of course the backbone of Islam and it is the basis of the testimony of faith, "There is no god but God." The Koran is littered with references to God's unity, for example: "Invoke no other God with Allah. There is no god but Him. All things perish except His face,"[201] "Why, were there gods in earth and heaven other than God they would surely go to ruin,"[202] "Say: He is God, the One."[203]

(ii) The eternity of God, the second tenet of Neoplatonism, was defined by Plotinus in the following manner: "This principle, at rest within the One, is Eternity; possessing this stable quality, being itself at once the absolute self identical and none the less the active manifestation of an unchanging Life set towards the Divine and dwelling within It untrue, therefore neither on the side of being nor on the side of Life – this will be eternity."[204]

The eternity of God is taken for granted in the Islamic tradition for it is the very nature of God that He is eternal. In many verses, the Koran contrasts the eternal God with His temporal, created world. "All that dwells upon the earth is perishing, yet still abides the face of thy Lord, majestic and splendid,"[205] "God, there is no god but He, the Living, the Everlasting *(qayyūm)*."[206] In addition one of the ninety-nine names of God is *baqā'* the meaning of which is permanent, or eternal.

(iii) The third principle of Neoplatonic thought is perpetual emanation. Creation was expressed by Plotinus in terms of generation or emanation, for example: "If the First is perfect, utterly perfect above all, it must be the most powerful of all that is, and all other powers must act in partial imitation of it. Now other things coming to perfection are observed to generate . . . How then could the most perfect remain self set – the First Good, the Power towards all, how could it grudge or be powerless to give of itself? If things other than itself are to exist, things dependent upon it for their reality, it must produce since there is no other source."[207] Plotinus also commented, "... all that is fully achieved engenders: therefore the eternally achieved engenders eternally an eternal being. At the same time, the offspring is always minor: what then are we to think of the All Perfect but that it can produce nothing less than the very greatest that is later than itself? This greatest must be the Divine Mind, and it must be the second of all existence . . . (it) is the loftiest being in the universe, all else following upon it – the Soul for example, being an utterance and act of the Intellectual Principle."[208]

If one replaces the Neoplatonic word of generation or emanation with the Koranic term of "creation," it is possible to find references that can be interpreted in a way which imply eternal creation. For example, "No indeed, but they are in uncertainty as to the new creation,"[209] "Each day He is upon some labour,"[210] "To God belongs the Command before and after."[211]

(iv) The universal intellect of Plotinus acts as an intermediate between the One and many and this preserves the One in transcendence, beyond the limits of rational human understanding and also guards the One from multiplicity which is incompatible with Unity. The One engenders the Intellectual Principle, and the latter's vision of the One's overflowing and exuberance causes the Intellectual Principle to imitate this. In such a way, the Intellectual Principle generates the Soul. These then are Plotinus's three initial hypostases.[212] The One generates the Intellectual Principle which in turn generates the Soul which generates the entire universe and the return to the One follows the same linear route (but in the reverse order).

In the Koran, it is difficult to find such a doctrine of God creating one thing from which the whole universe was created. However, such an idea became one of the linchpins of Sufism, and numerous mystics quoted the *ḥadīth* "the first thing God created was the intellect," to demonstrate this. Sufis including Nasafī frequently quoted the above *ḥadīth*[213] and also one Koranic verse (which attested to the universe appearing from one thing): "Do not those who disbelieve see that the heavens and earth were closed up but we have opened them."[214] Nasafī interpreted this verse in such a way that the heavens and earth were closed up together as if they were in a seed.

(v) Having descended from the One down to the Intellect, the Soul and the universe, the ascent back to the One commences. Plotinus describes the return to the One in this famous passage: "Many times it has happened: lifted out of the body into myself; becoming external to all other things and self encentred; beholding a marvellous beauty; then more than ever, assured of community with the loftiest order; enacting the noblest life, acquiring identity with the divine."[215] "But what must we do? How lies the Path? How come to vision of the inaccessible Beauty, dwelling as if in consecrated precincts, apart from the common ways where all may see, even the profane? He that has strength, let him arise and withdraw into himself, foregoing all that is known by the eyes, turning away from the material beauty that once made his joy."[216]

The return to God is stressed innumerable times in the Koran, for the meeting with God at the end of time is one of the fundamental purposes of life. Those who have lead a good life in conformity with the *Sharī'a* are rewarded with eternity in heaven, and those who have not are sent to Hell: "Are they not in doubt touching the encounter with their Lord?"[217] "He originates creation, then He brings it back again that He may recompense those who believe and do deeds of righteousness, justly. And those who disbelieve – for them awaits a draught of boiling water, and a painful chastisement, for their disbelieving,"[218] "O soul at peace! return unto thy Lord, well pleased, well pleasing! Enter thou among my servants! Enter thou My Paradise."[219]

On the basis of the above five tenets, it is possible to find a degree of compatibility between Neoplatonism and Islam. However, several of the five key Neoplatonic pillars are integral to Islam, and it seems highly unlikely that Muḥammad was influenced by Neoplatonic ideas. It is advisable to bear in mind Nicholson's adage that "the identity of two beliefs does not prove that one is generated by the other."[220] In fact, when both sets of thought are scrutinised more carefully, it becomes apparent that Classical Neoplatonism is very different from the "Neoplatonism" of the Islamic Philosophers and also from the world view of the Sufis.

Yet Neoplatonism did seep in to the Islamic world, indeed, once the "Theology of Aristotle" had been translated into Arabic, Islamic philosophers structured their world views around the emanationist framework, using Arabic equivalents for Neoplatonic terminology (such as *fayḍ* for emanation and *'aql-i kull* for universal intellect). This does not mean that such philosophers embraced everything in the Neoplatonic system, for despite the similarities between the two positions, modern scholars have noted many differences between Classical Neoplatonic thought and that of the Islamic Philosophers such as Ibn Sīnā. Morewedge has commented that it is incorrect to call Ibn Sīnā an advocate of Islamic Neoplatonism, rather, his mystical philosophy "contains development of Neoplatonic themes," and at the same time it is a "development of themes found in Islamic philosophy."[221] He summarises his standpoint by stating that ". . . there is no doubt that Islamic intellectual thought grew through the rich nourishment it received from the Neoplatonic spirit in the same sense that Aristotle's philosophy flourished on a Platonic basis; in both cases, however, the similarity does not warrant a total reductionism."[222] And furthermore, in the same way that there are major distinctions between Classical Neoplatonism and Islamic Neoplatonism, there are also fundamental differences between Islamic Neoplatonism and Sufism.

Differences Between Classical Neoplatonism and Sufism

(i) One of the major differences was that Plotinus had described three hypostases (the One, the Intellect Principle and the Soul) and then followed the universe. Al-Farābī and Ibn Sīnā developed this to the extent that there were ten intelligences before existents appeared on the earth. Nasafī described the beliefs of the Islamic Philosophers in the following manner:

> Know that the Philosophers say that not more than one substance was emanated *(ṣādir shud)* from the essence of God Most High and the name of this substance was the First Intelligence. The First Intelligence is a simple substance and it cannot be divided or separated. Therefore real oneness was emanated from God Most High – Who is Real Oneness – and that is the First Intelligence. From the First Intelligence, the remaining mothers and fathers were emanated, because in this First Intelligence there is real oneness and there is multiplicity from different viewpoints and relations, that is, regarding the essence of intelligence and regarding the cause of intelligence and regarding the relationship between the cause and effect. So from these relations of the First Intelligence, three view points came to be and something was emanated from each relation of the First Intelligence. That is, an intelligence, a soul and a heaven. In such a way, an intelligence, a soul and a heaven emanated from the First Intelligence until nine intelligences, nine souls and nine heavens came to be from the First Intelligence. And then the element and nature of fire were produced under the firmament of the moon. Then the element and nature of air were produced, and then the element and nature of water were produced and then the element and nature of earth were produced and the fathers and mothers were completed and descent was finished. Fourteen levels descended and there will be an

ascent in fourteen levels in the opposite way to the descent; therefore there are fourteen levels of ascent so that the circle can be completed.[223]

The first point to note is that in Plotinus's system, only one thing emanates from the First Intelligence (i.e. the Soul), whereas for Nasafī's Philosophers, three things emanate from each intelligence. Nasafī describes the views of the People of Unity which differ from both the Classical Neoplatonists and also the Philosophers:

> The Prophets posited this First Intelligence as the greatest level and they praised it very much. They called it many names and did not see anything wiser than it, and they said nothing else was nearer to God. Mankind is cherished and is the noblest of existents and exists through intelligence. Sermons are by means of intelligence and punishments are by means of intelligence. The Philosophers also posited this First Intelligence as the greatest level and praised it very much. The Philosophers said that not more than one substance *(jawhar)* emanated *(ṣādir shud)* from the essence of God Most High and Holy, and that substance was the First Intelligence. The rest, including creatures and the objects of intelligence and perception *(ma'qūlāt wa maḥsūsāt)* emanated from the First Intelligence.
>
> O dervish! The Friends say it better. They say that the objects of intelligence were manifested from the First Intelligence and the objects of perception were manifested from the First Sphere *(falak-i awwal)*. The First Intelligence and the First Sphere were manifested from *Jabarūt* and became existent. These two substances arrived at the shore together from the sea of *Jabarūt*.
>
> Since you have understood this introduction, now know that some say that a divine command came to this First Intelligence which is the Pen of God: 'Write upon the First Sphere which is the writing tablet *(law?)* of God.' The Pen said: 'O God! What shall I write?' There came a divine command: 'Write whatever was, is and will be until the day of resurrection.' The Pen wrote all of this and became dry, but according to this helpless one [i.e. Nasafī] a divine command came to the First Intelligence which is the Pen of God: 'Write upon yourself and the First Sphere!' It wrote in the blink of an eye, so that the intelligences, souls and natures appeared *(paydā amadand)* from the first intelligence and the spheres, stars and elements appeared from the First Sphere.[224]

Thus there is a major difference here, for the First Intelligence of the Philosophers corresponds to Nasafī's *Jabarūt*, which contains both the First Intelligence and the First Sphere. These two things which emanate from *Jabarūt*, are explained further in the following manner:

> Know that *Jabarūt* is one world, but this world is called different names. The quiddities of perceivable and intelligible things, and individual and composite things, and substances and accidents are all in *Jabarūt* but they are all concealed and undifferentiated. In addition, they are not separate from one another. It is because of this that *Jabarūt* is called the ink-pot.[225]
>
> Since you have understood this introduction, now know that a divine command came to the ink-pot of the universe to 'Split!' In a wink of an eye it split and there were two parts. One part was the First Intelligence which is the Pen of God and the other part was the First Heaven which is the Throne of God.[226]

The fact that two things emanate from *Jabarūt* reflects imagery from the Koran, for Nasafī frequently quotes the verse "Do not those who disbelieve see that the heavens and earth are closed up."[227] In addition Nasafī uses the image of the Pen for the First Intelligence because of the verse, "By the Ink-pot *(Nun),* the Pen and what they are writing."[228]

(ii) Another difference between Nasafī's vision of creation and that of the Islamic Philosophers is that for Plotinus and the Islamic Philosophers, the First Intelligence is a spiritual intelligence which has no contact with matter, and the universe appears as a result of the chain of emanation which starts at the One and continues through the First Intelligence (down through the nine other intelligences in Ibn Sīnā's case). Nasafī portrays the system of one of the groups of the People of Unity which contrasts considerably with the above.

> According to the People of Unity, the first substance *(jawhar-i awwal)* is the earth *(khāk)* and then the rest of the things appear by means of the earth until intelligence is reached. And according to the Philosophers, the first substance is intelligence and then other things appear until earth is reached.[229]

Thus on the basis of this comment, the People of Unity dispense with the whole chain of Neoplatonic emanation. Again, such a belief reflects the Koran, "His command, when He desires a thing, is to say 'Be!' and it is."[230] Although Sufis including Nasafī did use the terminology of Neoplatonic emanation (e.g. *fayḍ*), it conveyed a totally different meaning to that of the Islamic Neoplatonists. This point has been elaborated upon by Izutsu, discussing the *wujūdī* school, which had a very strong influence upon Nasafī's thought: "It is to be remembered that Ibn 'Arabī uses the Plotinian term 'emanation' *(fayḍ)* as a synonym for *tajallī* (self-disclosure). But 'emanation' does not mean as it does in the world view of Plotinus, one thing overflowing from the Absolute One, then another from that first thing, etc., in the form of a chain. 'Emanation' for Ibn 'Arabī, simply means that the Absolute itself appears in different, more or less concrete forms, with a different self determination in each case. It means that one and the same Reality variously articulates and determines itself and appears immediately in the forms of different things."[231]

Thus the *wujūdī* interpretation of emanation as described by Izutsu is rather far removed from that of Nicholson who commented, "the idea of emanation, or rather the particular form of it exhibited in Sufism proceeded, if we are not mistaken, from the Neoplatonic mint."[232]

In the system of the People of Unity, God exists in His unknowable aspect and secondly there is *Jabarūt* (which is God's knowledge, otherwise known as the immutable entities). When God bestows existence upon His knowledge it comes immediately into the world. Nasafī comments that the first thing is earth; earth is the First Intelligence and the First Sphere closed up together as the Koran states. In other words, the nature of earth is the spiritual or intelligible aspect (or "*amr*" in Koranic terminology) and the element of earth is the material or perceptible aspect (or "*khalq.*")

By placing earth first and intelligence last, the People of Unity have stood the Philosophers on their heads. So far, this interpretation accords completely with the Koranic portrayal of creation. Moreover, it remains faithful to the Koran by placing intelligence last in the scheme, as will become clear in the following point.

(iii) In *Kashf al-ḥaqā'iq*, earth *(khāk)*, according to the People of Unity, is the first thing created from *Jabarūt*. Nasafī proceeds to explain how everything is manifested in the universe from earth until intelligence is finally reached. This manifestation is also the way in which earth attains its perfection. In fact there are two ways in which this is done, that is, there are two ways in which existence becomes completely manifested.

The first way to perfection leads from earth to the sphere of spheres:

> Know that the select *(zubdat)* and quintessence *(khalāṣa)* of a body *(jism)* is earth, and it becomes water, and the select and quintessence of water becomes air, and the select and quintessence of air becomes fire, and the select and quintessence of fire becomes the body of the firmament of the moon.[233]

This order then proceeds in the same manner through Mercury, Venus, the Sun, Jupiter, Saturn, the Fixed Stars and the Great Firmament. Nasafī continues:

> Whatever is the (select and quintessence) of the Sphere of Spheres returns to the body of earth and the children from the horizon by means of the light of the Fixed Stars and Wandering stars.[234]

This idea that in ontological terms, the earth is the first substance and not intelligence, is reconfirmed in another chapter of *Kashf al-ḥaqā'iq*:

> Know that according to the People of Unity, heaven *(samā')* is an expression for a thing which is higher *('ulwī)* and the giver of emanation *(mufīḍ)* to the level which is lower than itself, and the giver of emanation may be from the world of bodies and may be from the world of spirits.
>
> And the earth *(arḍ)* is an expression for a thing which is relatively lower *(suflī)* and is a seeker of emanation *(mustafīḍ)* from the level which is above it, and this seeker of emanation may be from the world of bodies or the world of spirits. So the one thing may be earth and may be heaven and for this reason the heaven and earth are called Adam and Eve.
>
> Know that although the heaven is the giver of emanation and the earth is a seeker of emanation, the level of earth is prior to the level of heaven, so Eve is prior to Adam. Although there never was a time when there was no earth and heaven (because there has always been heaven and earth), the level of earth is prior to the level of heaven and for this reason the nun is mentioned first and then the pen *(qalam),* in such a way as it is said, "*Nun*, by the pen and what they are writing." (68:1).[235]

The second way of perfection from the earth leads to man:

> Know that the levels of children are threefold; mineral, plant and animal. Matter is earth which rises in levels and in each level it has a name. It rises from the elements to plant, and from plant to animal, and one of the types of animal is man, and man is the final type. Whatever is existent in all individual things is existent in man. The body of earth attains its perfection when man is reached. It will return to the earth and rise again in levels until it reaches man. When man is reached it will return again to the earth, once, twice, three times, eternally and this is the meaning of, "Out of the earth We created you; and We shall restore you into it."[236] That is, the perfection of the earth is reached when it reaches the body of man and the perfection of nature is when it reaches intelligence. And everything which attains perfection will return to its origin and this is the meaning of "Everything returns to its origin, once, twice, thrice, maybe indefinitely."[237,238]

This description in *Kashf-al-ḥaqā'iq* of two ways to the perfection of earth becomes clearer with Nasafī's remarks in *al-Insān al-kāmil:*

> Know that Abū Turāb Nasafī,[239] who is one of the People of Unity says that intelligence and knowledge are not included in anything other than mankind. The purpose of Abū Turāb in this discourse is to negate the discourses of the *'Ulamā'* and Philosophers. The *'Ulamā'* and Philosophers say that spheres and stars have intelligence and knowledge, desire and power, that is, each sphere has an intelligence, and there are nine spheres and the nine intelligences. They are constantly acquiring knowledge and extracting lights and their movements are voluntary. The *'Ulamā'* say that the angels have knowledge, but it is not increased. That which each one knows is its inherent knowledge. Abū Turāb does not accept either of these discourses and he says that the spheres and stars and angels do not have intelligence and knowledge, for intelligence and knowledge are particular to mankind. The spheres, stars and angels are continually occupied, each one has an action and they can not refrain from it or perform another one; so that action came in to existence from themselves without their knowledge or desire, and the spheres and stars and angels are compelled in their actions. The spheres, stars and angels are the loci of manifestation for action and mankind is the locus of manifestation for knowledge.[240]

Thus the first route to perfection through to the Sphere of Spheres is inferior to that which leads to intelligence in man. Initially, earth is the first thing to be created and intelligence comes last. Once created however, the heavens and stars have an important role to play upon the states and circumstances and the make up of each thing. For this reason, it sometimes occurs in Nasafī's works that the heavens are placed in a position which is prior to the earth. However, the heavens and stars can only exercise their influences upon that which has already been created (that is, upon something which is prior to them).[241] This creation is constantly occurring because God creates the world anew every moment, thus the whole process of earth being created first commences again and again).

The reason that the philosophers are stood on their heads by placing earth first and intelligence last is because intelligence in found only in man. Man is the centre of the universe. This point was of course stressed by other Sufis prior to Nasafī, for example, Rūmī expressed the superiority of man over the universe by saying: "We have honoured the children of Adam (17:70), God did not say, 'We have honoured the heavens and earth.' So man is able to perform that task which neither the heavens nor the earth nor the mountains can perform. When he performs that task, he will no longer be sinful, very foolish."[242] The honour that Rūmī refers to is the gift of knowledge, the knowledge by which man is able to acquire more knowledge. Not even the angels (who are merely messengers) possess this kind of knowledge. Indeed, in the Koran, the angels are required to bow down before man, a verse which Nasafī quoted: When I have breathed of My spirit into him, you [the angels] should bow down before him all together.[243] Rūmī also quotes the *ḥadīth*, "But for thee I would not have created the heavenly spheres," which also emphasises man's superior position to any other created thing. Such an idea, that the universe was created for man's benefit and to serve him, is commonplace in Nasafī's works:

> O dervish! It is man and whatever he needs that is existent. Nothing else is existent other than this. If man could exist without the spheres, stars, elements, natures, plants and animals, then he would live without them. But he cannot exist without them and he cannot live without them, so the aim of all of them is man, and the existence of all other things is for man's sake.[244]

This relationship is described in another way by Nasafī as man being the fruit of a tree, with all other existents being part of the tree, serving the fruit:

> Know that according to the People of Unity all of the existents are one tree; the first sphere (which is the sphere of spheres and is simple and not illuminated) is the ground *(zamīn)* of this tree. And the ground of the second sphere (which is the fixed sphere) is the root of this tree. The seven heavens *(haft āsmān)* are the trunk of this tree, Saturn in the first heaven and the moon in the seventh heaven. Saturn, which is further from us, is in the first heaven; and you should understand the rest in the same way. Each one which is nearer to us is higher up. And the fourfold elements and natures are the branches of this tree while the minerals, plants and animals are the leaves, flowers and fruit of the tree. Since you have understood the levels of the tree, now know that the fruit is the end of the tree; it is the select and quintessence of the tree and is more noble and subtle than the tree. Whatever is nearer to the fruit in the tree is higher and more subtle and noble.[245]
>
> O dervish! The People of Unity say that the levels of this tree were always complete and are always complete. But some of the levels of this tree exist in such a way that they cannot release the form which they have and they cannot take another form. This is the lower world *('ālam-ī suflī)* which is the spheres and stars that are the roots and trunk of this tree. It must be in this way because the roots and trunk of the tree have a form which they do not release and they do not take another form. But some [of the levels of the tree] exist in such a way that they release the form which they have and take another form, and this is the higher world *('ālam-i 'ulwī)*, which is the

minerals, plants and animals and they are the leaves, flowers and fruit of this tree. And it must be this way because the leaves, flowers and fruit are not always in one state, sometimes the flowers drop off, and the fruit of some falls when it is not ripe and some falls when it is ripe. Moreover, the leaves, flowers and fruit appear; they themselves grow, they themselves are born, they themselves exist and they themselves die. However, this tree rises up in levels and becomes more subtle and more delicate *(nāzuktar)*, and for this reason it may suffer a calamity and move from place to place contrary to the roots, trunk and branches.[246]

Know that the People of Unity say that there is no sense perception, voluntary movement or desire in all the levels of existents except for animals. Sense perception, voluntary movement and desire is particular to animals. And there is no intelligence *('aql)* or knowledge *('ilm)* in existents except in man; intelligence and knowledge is particular for man. The spheres, stars, angels, elements and natures do not have sense perception, voluntary movement, intelligence or knowledge. They are continually working and each one has a task; each one is engaged in performing that task and it can not perform a task other than that [which it is performing]. So that task without knowledge, and without thought and without their desire, comes in to existence through them. That is, sense perception, voluntary movement, desire, intelligence and knowledge is particular for the fruit of this tree, but there is no sense perception, voluntary movement, desire, intelligence and knowledge in the other levels of this tree.[247]

In Rūmī's words, "The outward form of the branch is the origin of the fruit; but inwardly, the branch came into existence for the fruit's sake."

The significance of the microcosm being regarded as superior to the macrocosm can also be seen in the light of the *wujūdī* interpretation of the divine names *Raḥmān* and *Raḥīm*, which Nasafī appears to make. He comments:

One name of the names of the spirit of the sphere of spheres is the Compassionate *(al-Raḥmān)* and the body of the sphere of spheres is the Throne, and the Compassionate is seated upon the Throne: "The Compassionate is firmly established upon the Throne,"[248] and one name of the names of the spirit of the Perfected Man is the Merciful *(al-Raḥīm)*: He is gentle to believers, merciful,[249] and the body of the Perfected Man is the Throne and the Merciful is firmly established upon the Throne. The Compassionate and Merciful (who are the select and quintessence of the macrocosm and microcosm and the last of existents and extremity of levels) are God's Throne and God is firmly established upon the Throne.[250]

Nasafī's interpretation of *Raḥman* and *Raḥīm* was discussed by Meier, who visualised the relationship in the diagram below.

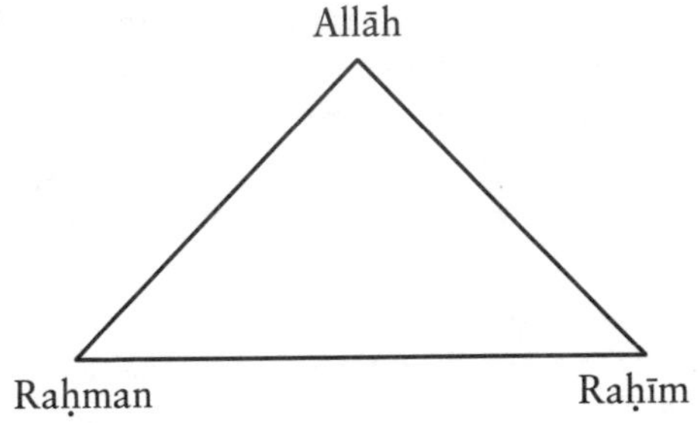

Meier has seen in this a kind of Islamic trinity in which "Nasafī's conception is . . . that man, by mystical growth into the knowledge of the All (i.e. the macrocosm – or Raḥman) ultimately arrives at a kind of coincidence with the All, and with God. All and Man the Perfecter are two all-embracing loci: the All in that it is nature, man in that he reflects this nature. And God is exalted above these two only to the extent that he is symbol and concept of their unity, wherein all antagonisms are resolved."[251] Meier's explanation is illuminating, but we can advance one step further by recognising the fundamental distinctions between *Raḥman* and *Raḥīm* of the *wujūdī* school which emphasises a uniqueness enjoyed by *Raḥīm*.

Ibn 'Arabī regards *Raḥman* as an inclusive mercy which is bestowed upon the macrocosm and the microcosm. *Raḥman* is the existence which is blown upon the immutable entities which then immediately appear in this world as Nasafī states: "*Raḥman* is a name for Him, for that face where existence is distributed to the possible things."[252] *Raḥīm*, however, is particular to man, for it is an obligatory mercy in the sense that God rewards those who are worthy of it, and He is wrathful upon those who are not. So man in fact receives *Raḥman* (i.e. existence) and has the potential to receive *Raḥīm* (God's reward). *Raḥīm* is bestowed on those individuals who employ their knowledge, desire and power in a way that is appropriate in serving God. Since the macrocosm has no knowledge, it cannot be a recipient of *Raḥīm*.

(iv) Aside from this major difference between Nasafī's theosophy and that of the Islamic Philosophers and Classical Neoplatonism, there are several other factors which make Classical Neoplatonism distinct from the beliefs of Nasafī and the Islamic Philosophers.[253] The first of these concerns the concept of being. For Plotinus, the One is completely transcendent, to the extent that in some passages of the "*Enneads*," it appears that the One is not even conscious of itself.[254] Moreover, in some passages, the One is beyond being: "What is this which does not exist? But the existence of That, in the sense which we say it exists, is known from the things that come after it."[255] It appears that there were some Islamic Philosophers who followed this line, for in *Kashf al-ḥaqā'iq*, Nasafī comments:

> . . . and the Philosophers have different opinions regarding the existence of God Most High and Holy. Some have said that God has quiddity and also existence, since existence is impossible without quiddity. Some have said that God has quiddity but not existence, in order that "manyness" *(kathrat)* and plurality *(ijzā')* is not necessary [for God]. Some have said that God's quiddity is the same *('ayn)* as God's existence and is not prior to God's existence in order that "manyness" and plurality is not necessary [for God].[256]

For Nasafī, God's quiddity is His existence; one of Nasafī's favourite phrases, which occurs numerable times in all of his works, is "existence is not more than one and that is the existence of God Most High and Holy."[257]

(v) There is quite a distinction between Nasafī and Neoplatonic thought in the stance taken towards matter. Plotinus regards matter as intrinsically evil, while later Neoplatonists such as Proclus modify this idea and come to regard it in a more positive light.[258] For Nasafī, it is unthinkable that matter can be evil because it is one of the modes in which God manifests Himself. It has already been seen that Nasafī views the world as divided into two parts, that is, the sensual and spiritual. Matter belongs to the sensual world but it co-exists with the spiritual world and is not separate from it. Nasafī repeatedly uses the Koranic concepts of non-manifest *(bāṭin)* and manifest *(ẓāhir)* to describe how these two should be regarded as one:

> Existence is not more than one and that is the existence of God, and other than God nothing else has existence. But there is a *'ẓāhir'* and a *'bāṭin'* for this one existence. Its *'ẓāhir'* is creation *(khalq)* which is an expression for the world of bodies, and its *'bāṭin'* is called 'command' *(amr)* which is an expression for the world of spirits.[259]
>
> Know that the call of the Prophets and the instruction of the Friends are for the sake that people adhere with good words, good actions and character traits so that their *'ẓāhir'* becomes correct. If the *'ẓāhir'* is not correct then the *'bāṭin'* is not correct, because the *'bāṭin'* is like a thing

which is poured into the body. So if the body is erect, the thing that is poured into the body will also be erect, but if it is bent, that thing poured into the body will also be bent.[260]

(vi) The last difference involves the practical manner of Sufism and Neoplatonism, in particular, the role of an intermediary between the individual and the One/God. Modern commentators have seen different mediator figures in the "*Enneads*" ranging from an "ascetic sage" to love, and it has also been speculated that there is no intermediary at all.[261] This stands in contrast to Sufism and Nasafī's theosophy where the role of the intermediary figure plays a crucial role. The identity of this figure is not the same in all cases. One possibility is the Sufi Shaykh or wise man *(dānā)*:

> Without the association of a wise man it is not possible that someone can reach his target. The fruit of the desert which grows by itself is never equal with the fruit of the orchard which the gardener has nurtured. In the same way, each wayfarer who has not found association with a wise man will never be equal to a wayfarer who has found association with a wise man.[262]

Another possible intermediary is the so-called "invisible shaykh" *(shaykh al-ghayb)* who may appear before the wayfarer following the ascetic disciplines and spiritual exercises that are performed under the supervision of the Sufi shaykh. The invisible shaykh is an important element in the theosophy of Najm al-Din Kubrā for the former is no other than the realisation of the perfected self, or the "theophanical ego."[263]

The last possible mediator described by Nasafī is God's love. Nasafī portrays God's love in a discourse on *dhikr* in such a way that it is regarded as a gift from God:

> The glory of the Beloved empties the heart of the lover of everything but Himself, everything is taken out of the heart . . . at that time the lover does not see himself and he sees everything as the Beloved.[264]

The possibility that God draws one of his servants towards him on the basis of His love was a common belief in Sufi circles. Indeed, Nasafī describes how Shaykh Shihāb al-Dīn Suhrawardī portrayed four types of Sufis, one of which he called "*majdhūb*" (or divinely attracted) who are involuntarily drawn by God's divine attraction *(jadhb)* and they arrive at the level of love in the love of God.[265]

Conclusion

Several eminent scholars, in particular P. Morewedge, have highlighted the distinctions between Neoplatonic thought and that of the Islamic Philosophers such as Ibn Sīnā. This has provided a basis to re-investigate the relationship between Sufism and Neoplatonism (and Islamic Neoplatonism/Philosophy). It is not an easy task to research Nasafī's position in regard to Sufism and Neoplatonism because it is not always clear which particular Islamic interpretation he is discussing. However, the system portrayed in *Kashf al-ḥaqā'iq* posits earth as the first thing created by God, and everything else, including the heavens and man reach perfection from earth. This is the belief of one of the groups of the People of Unity, and therefore it would seem likely that Nasafī had more sympathy with this group than with the ideas of the Philosophers. One can speculate that Nasafī's portrayal of the "Philosophers" was based upon his familiarity of works such as the "Theology of Aristotle" and the eclectic mixes of al-Farābī and Ibn Sīnā whereas the explanation of the People of Unity way well have been a result of spiritual unveiling and contemplation of the Koran. Labelling Nasafī's works as "a Neoplatonic system of 'emanation and return' as a mystical depiction of the world,"[266] does not do justice to the many levels of interpretation that are contained within them. It is equally as valid to remark that his works depict the Koranic belief of creation and return.

Notes

1 Koran, 2: 115.
2 For example, *Mishkāt al-anwār*, translated W.H.T. Gairdner (London: Royal Asiatic Society, 1915; repr. Lahore: SH Muḥammad Ashraf, 1952).
3 S. Murata, *The Tao of Islam*, p. 331.
4 A.E. Affifi comments that Ibn 'Arabī is a "thoroughgoing pantheist who tried his best to reconcile his pantheistic doctrine with Islam." See "Ibn 'Arabī," *A History of Muslim Philosophy*, ed. M.M. Sharif (Wiesbaden: Otto Harrassowitz, 1963), Vol I, p. 420. See also I.R. Netton's relevant comments in *Allah Transcendent* (London: Routledge, 1989), pp. 272–274. F. Meier's article on Nasafī , "The nature of monism in Islam," refers to his theosophy as monist countless times.
5 W. Chittick, "Rūmī and waḥdat al-wujūd," p. 72.
6 Koran, 42: 11.
7 *Ḥadīth* frequently quoted by Sufis.
8 *Ḥadīth*, See *al-Suyūṭī, al-Jāmi' al-ṣaghīr (Fayḍ al-qadīr fī sharḥ al-Jāmi' al-ṣaghīr)*, (Beirut: Dār al-Ma'rifa, 1972), Vol. III, pp. 262–63.

9 *Ḥadith*, ed. B. Furūzānfar, *Aḥādīth mathnawī* (Tehran: 1955), no. 346.
10 *Kitāb-i tanzīl*, fol. 38a, lines 9–13.
11 Koran, 20: 114.
12 *Kitāb-i tanzīl*, fol. 39a, lines 5–11.
13 These three terms, *Mulk, Malakūt* and *Jabarūt* are crucial in Nasafī's theosophy. The first two appear in the Koran, (for *Mulk* see for example 2: 101, 3: 186, 5: 20, 21, 44, 120. For *Malakūt* see 23: 90, 36: 83). *Jabarūt* does not appear in the Koran, but it is derived from the divine name *al-Jabbār*, or All-compeller (59: 23). Scholars have translated *Mulk* as "kingdom" and *Malakūt* as "dominion" and *Jabarūt* as "invincibility" (see Chittick, *The Sufi Path of Knowledge*, p. 282). However, I have refrained from translating these terms in this way because such translations do not reflect the meaning that Nasafī generally gives to them. *Mulk* is connected with the world of sense perception and *Malakūt* is connected to the world of spirits, and *Jabarūt* stands higher than both of them in this hierarchy.
14 *Maqṣad-i aqṣā*, p. 231.
15 See Chittick, *The Sufi Path of Knowledge*, chapter 20.
16 A saying frequently quoted by Sufis, for example see Chittick, *Faith and Practice*, p. 14.
17 *Kashf al-maḥjūb*, Hujwīrī, trans. R.A. Nicholson (London: Luzac, 1911), pp. 367–370.
18 See Margaret Smith, *al-Ghazālī the Mystic* (London: Luzac, 1944; repr. Lahore: Hijra International Publications, 1983), pp. 130–131.
19 *Kitāb-i tanzīl*, fol . 39b, lines 3–4.
20 *Ḥadīth*, Furūzānfar, no. 100. See S. Murata, op. cit., p. 265.
21 Koran, 17: 1.
22 *Kitāb-i tanzīl*, fol. 40a, lines 9–10.
23 *al-Insān al-kāmil*, p. 109.
24 *Kitāb-i tanzīl*, fol. 51a, lines 13–17.
25 Ibid, fol. 39b, lines 16–17.
26 This *ḥadīth* is often quoted by Sufis but given various interpretations. For example, see Ibn 'Arabī's usage in Chittick, *The Sufi Path of Knowledge*, p. 88.
27 *Maqṣad-i aqṣā*, p. 254.
28 *Kitāb-i tanzīl*, fol. 39b, line 10. (This alludes to the Koran 6: 59, "Not a leaf falls but He knows it.")
29 *Kitāb-i tanzīl*, fol. 39b, lines 15–16.
30 Ibid, fol. 40a, lines 1–4.
31 Koran, 57: 4.
32 Koran, 54: 50
33 *Kitāb-i tanzīl*, fol. 41a, lines 1–2.
34 *Manāzil al-sā'irīn*, p. 364.
35 *Kitāb-i tanzīl*, fol. 41a, lines 14–15.
36 For an English translation of this chapter, see Chittick, *Imaginal Worlds*, p. 129–136.
37 See Chittick, *The Sufi Path of Knowledge*, p. 387, n. 14.
38 *Kitāb-i tanzīl*, fol. 41a, lines 16–18.
39 See Chittick, *The Sufi Path of Knowledge*, p. 298.

40 *Kitāb-i tanzīl*, fol. 41b, lines 5–6. (Koran, 36: 82).
41 A *ḥadīth* reported by Bukhārī, Muslim and Ibn Ḥanbal, frequently quoted by Sufis; see Najm al-Dīn Rāzī, *Mirṣad al-'ibād min al-mabdā ilā'l-ma'ād*, translated H. Algar, *The Path of God's Bondsmen from Origin to Return* (New York: Caravan Books, 1982), p. 162.
42 *Kitāb-i tanzīl*, fol. 41b, lines 8–13.
43 Ibid, fol. 42a, line 1. This discussion of God being All-Knowing and All-Aware is based on two of God's Ninety-Nine Names. The All-Knowing occurs in the Koran in verses 32: 1, 35: 2, 27: 1, 37: 1, and the All-Aware is found in verses 6: 18 and 34: 1. God's names were the topic of many Sufi works, such as Ghazālī's *Maqṣad al-asnā*, translated R.C. Stade, "The Ninety-Nine Names of God in Islam" (Ibadan, Nigeria: Caystar Press, 1970).
44 *Kitāb-i tanzīl*, fol. 42a, lines 2–12.
45 Ibid, fol. 42a, line 17 – fol. 42b, line 1.
46 Ibid, fol. 42b, line 2.
47 *al-Insān al-kāmil*, p. 242.
48 *Kitāb-i tanzīl*, fol. 42b, lines 18–19.
49 Ibid, fol. 43a, line 2–3.
50 Ibid, fol. 41b, line 6.
51 Ibn 'Arabī comments "For God says, 'Our only word to a thing, when We desire it is to say to it 'Be!' and it is.' (16: 40). Here we have an Essence, a desire and a word," cited by S. Murata, op. cit., p. 151. See also R. Austin, *Ibn al-'Arabī: The Bezels of Wisdom* (New York: Paulist Press, 1980) chapter 11.
52 This *ḥadīth* in this form is found in Bukhārī, *Riqāq*, 38.
53 See Chittick, *The Sufi Path of Knowledge*, pp. 325–31.
54 *Kitāb-i tanzīl*, fol. 43a, line 18.
55 Ibn 'Arabī, translated by Chittick, *The Sufi Path of Knowledge*, p. 329.
56 *Kitāb-i tanzīl*, fol. 43a, line 19.
57 Ibid, fol. 43a, lines 3–7.
58 Koran, 8: 17.
59 *Kitāb-i tanzīl*, fol. 43a, lines 14–16.
60 For example, see Henri Corbin, *Creative Imagination in the Sufism of Ibn 'Arabi* (Princeton: Princeton University Press, 1969) and Chittick *Imaginal Worlds*. Ibn 'Arabī defines three types of imagination. "Non-delimited imagination" is the widest sense of the concept for it includes existents in potentiality and in actuality; "discontiguous imagination" refers to the intermediate world of the macrocosm; "contiguous imagination" is used to describe both the soul and also one of the faculties of the soul called imagination in each individual.
61 Austin, op. cit., pp. 120–127.
62 *Kitāb-i tanzīl*, fol. 43b, lines 18–19.
63 A quotation from Ibn 'Arabī's *Fuṣūṣ al-ḥikām*. ". . .whole earthly life was after this fashion, being a dream within a dream," and several paragraphs later, "all existence is an imagination within an imagination." See Austin, op. cit., p. 121, p. 125.
64 *Ḥadīth*, Furūzānfar, no. 222.
65 *Kitāb-i tanzīl*, fol. 44a, lines 1–6.

66 Ibid, fol. 44a, line 1.
67 Koran 41: 53. For Ibn 'Arabī's use of this verse see Chittick, *The Sufi Path of Knowledge*, p. xv.
68 See F. Rahman's *Avicenna's Psychology* (London: Oxford University Press, 1952), pp. 30–38.
69 *Kitāb-i tanzīl*, fol. 59b, line 4 – fol. 60 a line 2.
70 Rūmī, quoted by Chittick, *The Sufi Path of Love*, p. 279.
71 *Kitāb-i tanzīl*, fol. 48a, lines 16–17.
72 Ibid, fol. 44a, lines 6–10.
73 Ibid, fol. 44a, lines 11–14.
74 *Ḥadīth*, Furūzānfar, no. 352.
75 *Kitāb-i tanzīl*, fol. 44a, lines 15–16.
76 Ibid, fol. 44b, line 11.
77 Ibid, fol. 44b, lines 9–10.
78 Ibid, fol. 44b, lines 15–16.
79 Ibid, fol. 45a, line 9.
80 Ibid, fol. 45a, lines 4–6.
81 Ibid, fol. 45a, line 7.
82 See A. Schimmel, *As Through a Veil* (New York: Columbia University Press, 1982), p. 61.
83 See W.M. Thackston's translation of Ansārī's *Munājāt, Intimate Conversations* (New York: Paulist Press, 1978), p. 215.
84 A. Schimmel, *As Through a Veil*, p. 61.
85 *Kitāb-i tanzīl*, fol. 45a, line 14.
86 See M. Molé's introduction to *al-Insān al-kāmil*, p. 13. Heccéité is the French form of haecceity, an obsolete English word meaning a quality or mode of being in virtue of which a thing is or becomes a definite individual.
87 See H. Corbin's *Creative Imagination in the Sufism of Ibn 'Arabī*, and Chittick, *The Sufi Path of Knowledge*, pp. 127–30.
88 *Bayān-i tanzīl*, fol. 9, lines 9–13.
89 See Chittick, *The Sufi Path of Knowledge* concerning the Divine Breath and the Cloud, p. 126.
90 *Kitāb-i tanzīl*, fol. 45b, lines 8–10.
91 Ibid, fol. 45b, lines 13–14.
92 Ibid, fol. 46a, line 3.
93 Ibid, fol. 46a, lines 14–18.
94 The Perfect Man is a major element in Ibn 'Arabī's theosophy and his commentators discussed this issue at length. Indeed, Nasafī himself composed a book entitled the Perfect Man.
95 *Kitāb-i tanzīl*, fol. 46a, line 18 – fol. 46b, line 3.
96 Koran, 50: 15, quoted by Nasafī, *Kitāb-i tanzīl*, fol. 46b, line 19.
97 *Kitāb-i tanzīl*, fol. .46b, line 6. For Ibn 'Arabī see Chittick, *The Sufi Path of Knowledge*, p. 97.
98 *Kitāb-i tanzīl*, fol. 46b, lines 11–16.
99 Ibid, fol. 47a, line 9.
100 Ibid, fol. 47a, line 6 – fol. 47b, line 3.
101 See the Koran, 27: 40 and also Austin, op. cit., pp. 188–189.
102 *Kitāb-i tanzīl*, fol. 47a, lines 14–16.

103 Ibid, fol. 47b, lines 10–11.
104 Ibid, fol. 47b, lines 16–19.
105 Koran, 3: 97. *Kitāb-i tanzīl*, fol. 48a, line 4.
106 Koran, 2: 115. *Kitāb-i tanzīl*, fol. 48a, line 7.
107 Koran, 28: 88. *Kitāb-i tanzīl*, fol. 48a, line 8.
108 Koran, 2: 115.
109 Koran, 38: 5.
110 *Kitāb-i tanzīl*, fol. 48a, lines 8–15.
111 Such a description is found in Ghazālī's *Mishkāt al-anwār*, translated Gairdner, p. 108.
112 I have not been able to trace the origin of this statement.
113 The *shaṭḥ* of Abū Sa'id b. Abi'l Khayr.
114 The *shaṭḥ* of Hallāj Ibn Mansūr.
115 *Kitāb-i tanzīl*, fol. 48b, lines 4–10.
116 Ibid, fol. 48b, lines 10–17.
117 A reference to the Koran, (7: 180), "To God belong the most beautiful names."
118 *Maqṣad-i aqṣā*, p. 264.
119 *Kitāb-i tanzīl*, fol. 49a, line 13. This is a *Ḥadīth qudsī*, Furūzānfar, no. 70.
120 See below, Section III, Nasafī and Neoplatonic Ontology.
121 *Kitāb-i tanzīl*, fol. 50a, line 7. Koran 21: 30.
122 Koran, 68: 1.
123 *Kitāb-i tanzīl*, fol. 50a, lines 5–8. The four pens are the four primal elements (earth, water, air and fire) of the world. They mix together to form the composite things, which are the three kingdoms of mineral, plant and animal.
124 See *Kashf al-ḥaqā'iq*, pp. 57–58.
125 *Kitāb-i tanzīl*, fol. 49b, lines 13–17.
126 Ibid, fol. 51a, line 10.
127 Ibid, fol. 51a, lines 12–16. Compare with Ibn 'Arabī's ideas on this point in Austin, op. cit., p. 251–252.
128 *Kitāb-i tanzīl*, fol. 50b, lines 5–11. The imagery of the jug in this passage resembles Junayd's axiom that the water takes the colour of the cup.
129 *Kitāb-i tanzīl*, The story of the elephant extends from fol. 51a, line 17 to fol. 51b, line 17. F. Meier has commented on the origin of this story, suggesting a Buddhist origin before it was picked up by Sufis such as Sanā'ī, Ghazālī, Rūmī and Nasafī. See F. Meier, "The Nature of Monism in Islam."
130 *Kitāb-tanzīl*, fol. 52a, lines 7–11.
131 *Manāzil al-sā'īrīn*, p. 364.
132 Nasā'ī, Taṭbīq, bāb 12, 25, 73, 86; Aḥmad b. Ḥanbal, vi. 24. Cited by A. J. Wensinck, "On the Relation Between Ghazālī's Cosmology and His Mysticism," *Mededeelingen der Koninklijke Akademie wan Wetenschappen* (Amsterdam: Noord-Hollandsche Uitgevers-Maatschappij, 1933).
133 A. J. Wensinck, op. cit., p. 188–190.
134 L.E. Goodman, *Avicenna* (London: Routledge, 1992), p. 89–90.
135 A. J. Wensinck, op. cit., pp. 191–92.

136 Ibid, p. 193.
137 See Chittick, *Faith and Practice*, p. 263.
138 *Maqṣad-i aqṣā*, pp. 238–240.
139 See Chittick, *The Sufi Path of Knowledge*, p. 408, n.8.
140 Translated by Wensinck, op. cit., p. 195.
141 Wensinck's translation reads *Malakūt,* but this must be an error. To make sense of the passage, one should read *Jabarūt.*
142 A. J. Wensinck, op. cit., p. 194–195. For another account of Ghazālī's interpretation of *Jabarūt,* see K. Nakamura, "Imam Ghazali's Cosmology Reconsidered with Special Reference to the Concept of Jabarut," *Muslim World*, 1994, pp. 29–46.
143 'Ayn al-Quḍāt, *Nāmahā-yi 'Ayn al-Quḍāt*, ed. 'Afīf 'Ussayrān, Vol. 1 (Tehran: Intisharāt-i Zawār, 1362), p. 277.
144 Shaykh Shihāb al-Dīn Yaḥyā Suhrawardī, *Ḥikmat al-Ishrāq*, translated into Persian by Sayyid Ja'far Sajjādī (Tehran: Tehran University, 1978), p. 230.
145 H. Corbin, *Spiritual Body and Celestial Earth*, translated from the French by N. Pearson (Princeton University Press, 1977), p. 55.
146 H. Ziai, "The Source and Nature of Authority: A Study of al-Suhrawardī's Illuminationist Political Doctrine," in *The Political Aspects of Islamic Philosophy*, ed. C. Butterworth (Harvard Middle Eastern Monographs, Harvard University Press, 1992), p. 319, n.40.
147 H. Ziai, ibid.
148 H. Corbin, *Spiritual Body and Celestial Earth*, p. 55.
149 For an account of the *wujūdī* school's interpretation of the different levels of existence see Chittick's article, "The Five Divine Presences," *Muslim World*, pp.107–28.
150 Ibid, p. 119.
151 *Maqṣad-i aqṣā*, pp. 275–285.
152 Ibid, p. 279.
153 Ibid, p. 281.
154 So called because the spirit is attributed to both God and man. The Koran says that God blew of His spirit into Adam.
155 *Maqṣad-i aqṣā*, p. 275.
156 Ibid, p. 280.
157 Koran, 68: 1.
158 *Ḥadīth*, in Furūzānfar, no.70.
159 *Ḥadīth*, in Furūzānfar, no. 342.
160 The children are the kingdoms of mineral, plant and animal.
161 Koran, 18: 109. *Maqṣad-i aqṣā*, p. 258.
162 *Maqṣad-i aqṣā*, p. 274.
163 *Kitāb-i tanzīl*, fol. 67b lines 8–14.
164 *Tabṣirsat al-mubtadi'*, trans. Chittick, *Faith and Practice*, pp. 99–100.
165 *Tabṣirsat al-mubtadi'*, trans. Chittick, *Faith and Practice*., p. 99.
166 Chittick, *Imaginal Worlds*, p. 103.
167 See *Manāzil al-sā'īrīn*, p. 408–420, also *Kashf al-ḥaqā'iq*, p. 17–19. In *Kitāb-i tanzīl*, the Transmigrationists are not named although the discussions are the same as those attributed to the Transmigrationists in other works, see fol. 68 a, line 2 – fol. 71 b line 13.

168 *Kashf al-ḥaqā'iq*, p. 17.
169 *Manāzil al-sā'irīn*, p. 408
170 Ibid, p. 410.
171 For an explanation of the *nasnās,* see Algar, *The Path of God's Bondsmen from Origin to Return*, p. 82, n. 18.
172 *Kitāb-i tanzīl*, fol. 68 b line 1 – 68 b line 17.
173 Ibid, fol. 69 aline 13.
174 Ibid, fol. 68 b line 15–68 b line 17.
175 *Manāzil al-sā'irīn*, p. 410.
176 *Kashf al-ḥaqā'iq,* p. 188.
177 Ibid, p. 189.
178 Ibid, p. 188.
179 See Chittick, *Faith and Practice*, p. 227–228.
180 Translated Chittick, *The Sufi Path of Love*, p. 79.
181 'Ayn al-Quḍāt, *Tamhīdāt*, ed. 'Afīf 'Ussayrān (Tehran: Intishātāt Manuchihr, 1373/1994), para. 385.
182 'Ayn al-Quḍāt, *Tamhīdāt*, para. 376.
183 See Sajjādī's introduction to his Persian edition of *Ḥikmat al-ishrāq* (Tehran University Press, 1978), pp. 16–18.
184 *Kashf al-ḥaqā'iq*, p. 156.
185 Ibid, p. 158.
186 Ibid, p. 192.
187 Ibid, p. 192.
188 O. Leaman, *An Introduction to Medieval Islamic Philosophy* (Cambridge: Cambridge University Press, 1985), p. 94.
189 Mohammed, O.N. *Averroes Doctrine of Immortality* (Ontario: Wilfrid Laurier University Press, 1984). See Chapter III, pp 84–114.
190 Ibid, p. 112–113.
191 Chittick, *Imaginal Worlds*, p. 99.
192 For Simnānī's discussion of the ontological levels see J.J. Elias, *The Throne Carrier of God* (Albany: SUNY Press, 1995), pp. 154–157.
193 R.A. Nicholson, *The Mystics of Islam* (London: G. Bell & Sons, 1914), p. 13.
194 A.J. Arberry, *Fifty Poems of Hāfiz* (London: Cambridge University Press, 1947), p. 31.
195 P. Morewedge, "Sufism, Neoplatonism, and Zaehner's Theistic Theory of Mysticism," in P. Morewedge (ed). *Islamic Philosophy and Mysticism* (Albany: SUNY Press, 1981), p. 225.
196 See for example, *al-Insān al-kāmil*, p. 190.
197 Chittick, *Imaginal Worlds*, p. 179, n. 1.
198 Concerning the influence of Neoplatonism upon al-Farabi, see I.R. Netton's *Al-Farabi and His School* (London: Routledge, 1992).
199 D. Martin, "The Return to the One in the Philosophy of Najm al-Din Kubra," in P. Morewedge (ed), *Islamic Philosophy and Mysticism*, p. 212.
200 Plotinus, *Enneads*, trans. Stephen MacKenna, VI.9.6 (London: Penguin, 1991), p. 542.
201 Koran, 28: 88.
202 Koran, 21: 22.

203 Koran, 112: 1.
204 Plotinus, *Enneads*, III.7.6, p. 219.
205 Koran, 55: 26.
206 Koran, 2: 255.
207 Plotinus, *Enneads*, V.4.1, p. 388.
208 Ibid, V.1.6, p. 354.
209 Koran, 50: 15.
210 Koran, 55: 29.
211 Koran, 30: 4.
212 Plotinus, *Enneads*, V.2.1, p. 361.
213 Nasafī also quoted variations of this *ḥadīth*, for example, "the first thing God created was intelligence," "the first thing God created was spirit," "the first thing God created was the Pen." *Kashf al-ḥaqā'iq*, p. 47.
214 Koran, 21: 30.
215 Plotinus, *Enneads*, IV.8.1, p. 334.
216 Plotinus, *Enneads*, I.6.8. p. 53.
217 Koran, 41: 54.
218 Koran, 10: 4.
219 Koran, 89: 27.
220 R.A. Nicholson, Introduction to *Selected Poems from the Diwan-i Shams Tabrizi* (Cambridge, Cambridge University Press, 1898; repr. Richmond: Curzon Press, 1994), p. xxx.
221 P. Morewedge, Introduction to *Neoplatonism and Islamic Thought*, (Albany, SUNY Press, 1992), p. 4.
222 P. Morewedge, "Sufism, Neoplatonism, and Zaehner's Theistic Theory of Mysticism," p. 231.
223 *al-Insān al-kāmil*, p. 71.
224 Ibid, p. 189.
225 Ibid, p.186.
226 Ibid, p. 186–187.
227 See for example, *Kitāb-i tanzīl*, fol. 50a, line.3.
228 Koran, 68: 1.
229 *Kashf al-ḥaqā'iq*, p. 57. See also, *Kitāb-i tanzīl*, fol. 52a, lines 5–16.
230 Koran, 36: 82.
231 T. Izutsu, *Sufism and Taoism* (Berkeley and Los Angeles: University of California Press, 1984) p. 154. Corbin was perhaps the first to remark on the distinctions between the emanationist position compared with that of the *wujūdī* school. He remarked, "This cosmogony is neither an emanation in the Neoplatonic sense of the word nor, still less, a creatio ex nihilo. It is rather a succession of manifestations of being, brought about by an increasing light, within the originally undifferentiated God; it is a succession of tajalliyat of theophanies." *Creative Imagination in the Sufism of Ibn 'Arabī*, translated R. Manheim (Princeton: Princeton University Press, 1969), p. 114.
232 R.A. Nicholson, *Selected Poems from the Diwan-i Shams Tabrizi*, p. xxx–xxxi.
233 *Kashf al-ḥaqā'iq*, p. 57.
234 Ibid, p. 57.
235 Ibid, p. 225.

236 Koran, 20: 57.
237 *Ḥadīth*, (source not given).
238 *Kashf al-ḥaqā'iq*, p. 58.
239 Abū Turāb Nasafī was a Sufi from Transoxania who emphasised trust in God *(tawakkul)*. He met an unfortunate end in 859 A.D for he was eaten by lions in the desert.
240 *al-Insān al-kāmil*, p. 263.
241 In this system, emanation still has an important role to play, because the emanations from the spheres determine the fortune of each child's life, and there are four times when these emanations take place:

"... there are two kinds of preparedness *(isti'dād)*; one is actualised at the origin without the free will and acquisition of the child, and this is the preparedness of the effects of the qualities of time and place; and the other is actualised after the origin through free will and acquisition and this preparedness is through effort and endeavour."

"O dear friend! There are strong effects and complete qualities on the preparedness and states *(aḥwāl)* of the child for when the sperm falls in to the womb, the time when the form of the child appears, the time when the spirit appears in the form and the time when the child leaves the mother's womb." (*Kitāb-i tanzīl*, fol. 60b lines 11–17).

The states of each person are different because the emanations each day (and thus the four times of each person) are different:

"The spheres and stars are the managers of the lower world and they have no free will and their function is to continually spread torment and comfort in this world and spread felicity and wretchedness in a universal way, not in a particular way." (*al-Insān al-kāmil*, p. 197).

242 Quoted from Chittick, *The Sufi Path of Love*, p. 63.
243 *Kashf al-ḥaqā'iq*, p. 85, Koran 15: 29.
244 *Maqṣad-i aqṣā*, p. 266
245 *Manāzil al-sā'īrīn*, p. 430–1.
246 Ibid, p. 431–432.
247 Ibid, p. 433.
248 Koran, 20: 5.
249 Koran, 9: 129.
250 *Kitāb-i tanzīl*, fol. 66a, lines 5–15.
251 F. Meier, "The Problem of Nature in the Monism of Islam," p. 187.
252 Nasafī, *Maqṣad- Aqṣā*, p. 237.
253 See P. Morewedge, "Sufism, Neoplatonism, and Zaehner's Theistic Theory of Mysticism," p. 228–229.
254 Plotinus, *Enneads,* VI.9.9.
255 Ibid.
256 *Kashf al-ḥaqā'iq*, p. 39.
257 It is interesting that Ibn 'Arabi also uses the expression "There is no existent but God," and "there is no existent other than He." See Chittick, "Rumi and waḥdat al-wujūd," p. 108, n. 52.
258 See I.R. Netton, *Muslim Neoplatonists* (London: Allen and Unwin, 1982), p. 34.
259 *Kashf al-ḥaqā'iq*, p. 190.
260 *al-Insān al-kāmil*, p. 88.

261 For this discussion see P. Morewedge, *Neoplatonism and Islamic Thought*, p. 70.
262 *al-Insān al-kāmil*, p. 109.
263 T. Izutsu, "The Theophanical Ego in Sufism," *Sophia Perennis*, Bulletin of the Imperial Iranian Academy of Philosophy, Vol. IV, No. 1 (Tehran, 1978).
264 *al-Insān al-kāmil*, p. 139.
265 *Maqṣad-i aqṣā*, p. 226.
266 P. Morewedge, "Sufism, Neoplatonism and Zaehner's Theistic Theory of Mysticism," p. 225.

3

Epistemology

I. ATTAINING KNOWLEDGE

'Ayn al-Quḍāt Hamadānī (d. 1131) claimed the idea of the equidistance of all things from their ultimate ontological Source in terms of knowledge (or *ma'iyyat*, "withness") to be his own.[1] This understanding of God's proximity reflects the Koranic verse which states that God is with man wherever he is[2], but the practical reality is that man is negligent and he forgets this "withness," so he must strive to acquire such knowledge and once attained, keep it in mind constantly. By Nasafī's era, the idea of "withness" expressed in terms of knowledge had become common in Sufi circles, and is explained in Nasafī's own works:

> O Dervish! God is very close, just as the Most High said: "We are nearer to him than the jugular vein,"[3] and there are many examples like this in the Koran and *ḥadīth*, but what is the use if the people have fallen far, far behind and remain without any share or portion in the gnosis of God and God's proximity. Every day they boast and say that we are searching for God, but they do not know that God is present and there is no need to search. O dervish! God is neither far from some nor close to others. He is with everyone. All the existents are equal in proximity with Him. The highest of the high and the lowest of the low are the same in proximity with Him. We have spoken of proximity in terms of knowledge *('ilm)* and ignorance, that is, whoever is more knowledgeable is nearer.[4]

The knowledge of the various groups that Nasafī portrayed agreed upon the general principles of Islam, such as the unity of God and how He could be described. For example:

Know that the Sufis say that all the Prophets and Friends have said that there is a creator for the world. After the Prophets and Friends, all the *'Ulamā'* and Philosophers have also said that there is a creator for the world and in order to prove this they have given many reasons and they have written and continue to write books, so it is not necessary for me to give any proof for the [existence of a] creator of the world.

> Since you have understood that there is a creator for the world, now know that the Sufis say that there is one creator and He is eternal, and has no beginning or end, no like or partner, and He cannot change or alter, and He cannot be non-existent or annihilated, and He has no place *(makān)*, time or direction. He is endowed with the appropriate attributes and He is free from inappropriate attributes. The *'Ulamā'* and Philosophers agree on this point with the Sufis.
>
> The Sufis say in addition to this that the essence of God is unlimited and infinite. O dervish! The *'Ulamā'* and Philosophers also say that the essence of God Most High is infinite, and they say that this infinity of God has no beginning or end, above or under, before or after, that is, it has no direction. It is a light, unlimited and infinite. It is an ocean without shore or end. The totality of the universe is a drop in the ocean considered in relation to the greatness of God's essence, perhaps less than a drop. There is not one existent particle which God is not with, or which God does not encompass and of which He is not aware.[5]

Thus the beliefs of both the *'Ulamā'* and Philosophers are regarded as Islamic and worthy in their own right, however, their knowledge of things does not match that of the Sufis or People of Unity. In fact, Nasafī makes a distinction between the groups which reflects the well-known *ḥadīth* of Gabriel, in which Muḥammad divides Islam in to three stages. The first stage is submission *(islām)*, the second is faith *(īmān)*, and the third is excellence *(iḥsān)*. According to this *ḥadīth*, submission is performing the five pillars of Islam: bearing witness that there is no god but God and Muḥammad is His messenger, reciting the ritual prayer *(ṣalāt)*, paying the alms tax, fasting during Ramadan and making the pilgrimage to Mecca. Faith is having faith in God, His angels, His books, His messengers, the Last Day and the measuring out *(qadar)*. Excellence means worshipping God as if you see Him, for even if you do not see Him, He sees you.[6] Submission pertains merely to practice, and is the lowest in the hierarchy because people may practice Islam even if they do not want to. There are many reasons for performing actions, ranging from the economic to social, so even a hypocrite *(munāfiq)* can submit to God and the five pillars of Islam. Faith is a stage above practice because the person with faith undertakes submission through sincerity. The relationship between practice and faith can be described in Koranic terms as the manifest *(ẓāhir)* and the non-manifest *(bāṭin)*. Above faith is excellence, and this is the highest degree in the *ḥadīth* of Gabriel because excellence involves a degree of insight or gnosis which faith does not encompass. For Nasafī, the *'Ulamā'* have submission,[7] the Philosophers have faith,[8] and the People of Unity have excellence *(iḥsān)*.[9]

The differences between submission, faith and excellence may also be clarified through another *ḥadīth* which Nasafī quotes on numerous occasions: "The Holy Law *(sharī'at)* is my words, the Path *(ṭarīqat)* is my works and the Reality *(ḥaqīqat)* is my states."[10] Nasafī reworks this *ḥadīth* and states that the Perfect Man has four things: good words, good works, noble character traits *(akhlāq)* and gnosis *(ma'rifat)*.[11] Good words and works pertain to the Holy Law, the character traits pertain to the Path, and gnosis pertains to the Reality. Gnosis is the ability to see things as they are, to see the essences (as far as it is possible) of oneself and God, whereas having the appropriate character traits or being sincere does not necessarily mean that one can see things as they are.

(i) The Knowledge of the *'Ulamā'*

Tradition plays a very important role in the Islamic community and this tradition is based upon memorising the Koran and *ḥadīth* and also by following the *Sunna* of Muḥammad. The importance of this tradition is demonstrated by the fact that Najm al-Dīn Kubrā (the founder of the Sufi order to which Nasafī was probably affiliated) had spent long periods in the study of *ḥadīth* and he also commenced a commentary on the Koran (which was eventually completed by 'Alā' al-Dawla Simnānī)[12]. This kind of knowledge is fundamental for all Muslims, and Nasafī recognises that the *'Ulamā'* provide a crucial role in society by acting as guardians of this knowledge. They act as propagators of the exoteric message of the Koran, *ḥadīth* and *Sunna*, and education (reading and writing) is entrusted to them. Nasafī expresses the importance of the *'Ulamā'* in society:

> O dervish! Whoever puts himself up as a director of creatures, calls himself a shaykh or an ascetic. Know for sure that [such an indiviual] has found no trace of God's fragrance. It was necessary for the Prophets to be the directors of creatures whether they wanted to be or not. It is also necessary for the *'Ulamā'*.[13]
>
> O dervish! Whoever possesses one field of knowledge has a narrow range of thought and his enemy is the *'Ulamā'* who possess [several] fields of knowledge. Whoever possesses [several] fields of knowledge has a wide range of thought and he is a friend of the *'Ulamā'*.[14]

However, the knowledge of tradition is founded upon memory and represents only the first step towards the realisation of things. It is not sufficient to be able to recite the Koran and *ḥadīth* and act in the way of Muḥammad, for one also has to understand the message of the Koran and *ḥadīth* and realise why Muḥammad behaved in any given manner:

> "God Most High sent down the Koran in ten meanings."[15] The grammarians, philologists, jurists, commentators of the *ḥadīth* and expounders *(mufassirūn)* are all at the first stage and are not aware of the second stage.[16]

Nasafī calls the *'Ulamā'* the "People of Imitation" *(ahl-ī taqlīd)* and their belief is based upon the sense of hearing:

> They have heard and accepted, that is, their acceptance is not by reason and demonstration, and not by unveiling and spiritual contemplation. This belief is worthy although it is through the sense of hearing, and this group is included among the People of Submission *(ahl-ī islām)*. At this level, effort and endeavour are dominant over the wayfarer and satisfaction and submission are subdued. There is much difficult asceticism and spiritual discipline and much obedience and worship in this level. They perform very much of everything which pertains to the manifest dimension, and they perform little of anything that pertains to the non-manifest dimension. This is because this group (in this level) believe in existence and oneness, and although they believe that God is Knowing, Desiring and Powerful, they have not seen that His knowledge, desire and power are through the light of reason and demonstration and through the light of spiritual unveiling and contemplation for all secondary causes *(asbāb)* and caused things *(musababāt)*. They have not witnessed that all the secondary causes are incapable and over-powered, like all the caused things. So effort and endeavour is valid according to them and everything is increased by secondary causes, effort and endeavour. This group see by means of secondary causes, effort and endeavour, because such people are still in the level of sense perception and they cannot advance forth.[17]

This belief is merely a preliminary stage, but it provides the foundation upon which to build other forms of knowledge. Nasafī contrasts the results obtained through the religious institution of the *'Ulamā'* (the *madrasa*) with those of the house of Sufis *(khānaqāh)*:

> There is one way which leads to perfection of the path. At the beginning is education and repetition and at the end it is religious effort and remembrance of God *(dhikr)*. One must first go to the *madrasa* and then one must go to the *khānaqāh* from the *madrasa*.

> Whoever does not go to the *madrasa* but goes to the *khānaqāh* may profit and have some reward and may reach God through the journey to God, but will not profit or have any reward through the journey in God.[18]

Nasafī is referring to the Sufi concept of annihilation *(fanā')*, a state when all human attributes which form a veil between man and God are removed. According to Nasafī, it is possible to reach this stage even if one does not learn the knowledge offered through the *madrasa*, that is, belief through sense perception. However, the higher stage of *baqā'*, or subsistence in God, can only be reached by first attending the *madrasa* and then going onto the *khānaqāh*.

(ii) The Knowledge of the Philosophers

Some of the discussions in Nasafī's treatises concerning the Philosophers and their methods of acquiring knowledge are explained with great clarity. However, there are also passages which are quite confusing. To begin with, let us examine those points which are set out in a manifest manner, and on the basis of this we can then investigate those issues which are problematic.

When considering the knowledge of the Philosophers, it is important to remember that their knowledge is a stage above that of the *'Ulamā'*:

> This group [the Philosophers] are among the People of Faith. Satisfaction and submission are dominant in this level and effort and endeavour are subdued. This is because this group has recognised God through definite proofs and certain demonstration, and they have seen His knowledge, desire and power encompassing all existents. They have witnessed secondary causes as incapable and overpowered in the same way as caused things. That is, in the same way that until now they saw a thing as incapable and overpowered, they also see secondary causes as incapable and overpowered. In other words, they reached the Causer of secondary causes and saw the Causer of secondary causes as encompassing everything and powerful over everything and they became satisfied and submitted. They do not place their faith upon anything, neither effort nor endeavour, and neither material wealth nor reputation, neither obedience nor worship.[19]

However, above the knowledge acquired by the Philosophers stands that of two other groups, namely the Prophets and the Friends. Nasafī comments that a Philosopher knows the nature of things; a Prophet understands the nature of things and the qualities of things; but the

Friend recognises the nature of things, the qualities of things and the reality of things.[20] The reason that the Philosophers are limited in knowledge is that their knowledge is dependent upon definite proof *(dalā'il qaṭ'ī)* and certain demonstration, that is to say, upon reason and intellectual argument. The knowledge of the Prophets is through revelation from God and that of the Friends is through gnosis and inspiration from God. This knowledge of the Philosophers is acquired by intelligence *('aql)*, the tool of rational demonstration, but this method is considered deficient by the Sufis because it cannot yield gnosis. Moreover, having a rational mind does not necessarily mean that one acts on the basis of reason. A Philosopher may understand that the Sufi path of ascetic discipline and religious effort may purify the body and prepare the heart for any unveiling that may reach it from the spiritual world, but that same Philosopher may not act on the basis of this knowledge because of the difficulties and hardships of undertaking the Sufi practices. Another limitation in the Philosophers' path is found in the etymology of the word *'aql* itself. The root meaning of *'aql* is tying, binding and constricting. In other words, *'aql* likes to order things into individual units which means that it cannot accommodate God's *tanzīh* nature on the one hand, and His *tashbīh* nature on the other hand. *'Aql* can only work with one or the other but not with opposites. The inadequacy of the Philosopher's methods compared to those used by Sufis (ascetic discipline and religious effort) is described with reference to the story made famous by Niẓāmī and Rūmī about the Greek and Chinese painters:

> O dervish! Some wayfarers say, "We learn the skills of painting so that we can illustrate the tablet of our hearts with all knowledge by the pencil of education and the pen of repetition, so all knowledge will be written in our hearts, and everything which is written in our hearts will become the well preserved tablet *(lawḥ-ī maḥfūẓ)*."
>
> Other wayfarers say, "We learn the skills of polishing so that we make the mirror of our heart clean and pure by the tool of polishing which is asceticism and by the oil of *dhikr*. In this way our heart becomes capable of transparency and reflecting, thus the reflection of every knowledge which exists in the invisible world can be manifested in our hearts."
>
> Reflection is more reliable and correct than a book because mistakes and error are possible in writing, but not in reflection. The story of the Chinese painters and the Emperor is famous.[21] In addition, much knowledge exists for man and there are many different kinds of knowledge. But life is short and it is not possible to fulfil life by making the heart the well preserved tablet by education and repetition, but it is possible to fulfil life by making the heart the cosmos reflecting mirror by the path of asceticism and *dhikr*.[22]

Several other weaknesses which the Sufis saw in the epistemology of the Philosophers have already been noted (see chapter two, section iii), so here we shall remind ourselves of just two fundamental faults. The first, the Neoplatonic idea of emanation, as advocated by Nasafī's Philosophers, does not explain the complete picture of God in His *tanzīh/tashbīh* nature. With the hierarchy of ten intelligences, God remains too remote from His creation. Secondly, the Philosophers (according to Nasafī) believe that the celestial intelligences acquire knowledge, desire and power, and they are the origin of the intelligences and souls of man.[23] This idea, as we have seen, is denied by the People of Unity, since intelligence is found only in man.

Up to this point, Nasafī's discourses concerning the Philosophers present the reader with no problems. Difficulties arise however, when one reads passages relating to the Philosophers in which *'aql* is praised very highly. The trouble is that Nasafī sometimes speaks of more than one kind of *'aql*, and it is not always clear which *'aql* is associated with the Philosophers. The quotation below from *Maqṣad-i aqṣā* discusses two kinds of *'aql*:

> . . . man is a partner with other animals, that is, in having three spirits: the plant spirit, the animal spirit and the soul spirit. This is because all men and all animals have three spirits and man also has other things which animals do not have.
>
> The first is speech *(nuṭq)*, and through this man is superior to other animals. At first he is superior through this spirit of speech which is also called intelligence *('aql)*. Yet this intelligence has no share or part in the gnosis of God. [However], it is the king on earth, makes the waters flow on the earth, prepares the fields, creates gardens, makes boats move on the water, carries merchandise *(rakht)* from east to west and carries merchandise from west to east, and there are many examples like this. I have discussed this intelligence for livelihood *('aql-ī mu'āsh)* in the seventh station of *Manāzil al-sā'irīn*, and [the wayfarer] can study it there.
>
> That intelligence about which the Prophet Muḥammad said "Intelligence is a light in the heart distinguishing between the truth and the false"[24] is different. This light rules the heart and soul whereas the intelligence for livelihood rules water and clay. As long as man has not yielded the human spirit *(rūḥ-ī insānī)*, he has not reached the intelligence about which the Prophet spoke. The human spirit is called the Attributed Spirit *(rūḥ-ī iḍāfī)* because God Most High attributed the human spirit to Himself and said: "And when I have fashioned him and breathed of My spirit into him."[25] Several times it has been said that the Attributed Spirit has many names: the First Intelligence, the Greatest Pen, the Supreme Spirit, the Muḥammadan Spirit and others like these.[26]

Is the *'aql* of the Philosophers the intelligence for livelihood or the Attributed Spirit? The answer is not clear. However, the *'aql* of the Philosophers is able to offer highly esoteric interpretations of the Koran. The following example comes from the fifth chapter of *Kashf al-ḥaqā'iq* in a section explaining the resurrection of man according to the Philosophers:

> The following example makes it clear that the heaven which is promised after death for the pious ones is commanded by God Most High: "This is the similitude of Paradise which the god-fearing have been promised; therein are rivers of water unstalling, rivers of milk unchanging in flavour and rivers of wine – a delight to the drinkers, rivers, too, of honey purified; and therein for them is every fruit, and forgiveness from their Lord – Are they as he who dwells forever in the Fire, such as are given to drink boiling water, that tears their bowels asunder?" [27] Know that water causes life and its benefit is common for everything in all times, and the reality of these rivers of water in heaven is that they are the waters of life for all the People of Heaven who enjoy all of them.
>
> The cause which nurtures children is milk which is more particular than water, since the benefit of milk is common for all but only at a certain time. The reality of these rivers of milk in heaven is that they are rivers of common sense which is the basis and exoteric aspect of wisdom, and the common pleasure in heaven is derived from these rivers.
>
> The cause of healing sickness and suffering is honey which is more particular than milk since the benefit of honey is particular for some people. The reality of these rivers of honey in heaven is that they are the rivers of wisdom for the special ones and the pleasure of the special ones in heaven is derived from these rivers.
>
> The cause which removes grief and sadness is wine which is more particular than honey since wine is unlawful and impure for all the People of the World but it is lawful and pure for the People of Heaven. The purification and reality of these rivers of wine in heaven is that they are the wisdom and pleasure of the special ones among the special ones in heaven and their pleasure is derived from these rivers.
>
> In addition, know that in Hell there are four rivers for the inhabitants of Hell, which correspond to the rivers in Heaven: these are hot water, stagnant water, stagnant water mixed with matter flowing from the bodies of the damned, tar and pus: "And these similitudes – We strike them for the people, but none understands them save those who know."[28,29]

Does rational demonstration, the epistemological tool of the Philosophers, permit such an esoteric interpretation of the levels of Heaven? The answer must be affirmative although it is important to remember that this interpretation of the Philosophers' is based upon reason and not on gnosis, which may provide a completely different vision of the levels of Heaven. Another problem encountered in determining Nasafī's attitude towards *'aql* is that the term is used not only in the discourses of the Philosophers but also in those of the People of Unity. This is highlighted in Nasafī's discussion of the covenant between God and man before existence was bestowed upon man. The Koran states that God assembled mankind and asked all of them, "Am I not your Lord?" and they answered "Yes."[30] Nasafī describes the result of this event:

> That trust *(amānat)* which was presented to all existents, and was denied and not accepted by any of them, was accepted by man, and he reached his perfection through it. That trust was *'aql.*[31]

Two chapters later, continuing the discourses of the People of Unity, Nasafī explains the same covenant and replaces *'aql* with passionate love *('ishq)*.[32] With regard to his explanation of the Sufis, Nasafī is explicitly clear that when he uses the word *'aql*, it refers to something which has been remembered under a variety of names including the Attributed Spirit, the Muḥammadan Light, the First Intelligence, the Greatest Pen and the Supreme Spirit. Despite the problems of determining the true nature of *'aql* as used by the Philosophers, it is apparent that Nasafī sees the Sufi method, founded upon love and worship, of ascetic discipline and religious effort as superior to reasoning and intellectual demonstration. The methods of the Philosophers are better than the blind imitation of the *'Ulamā'*, for reasoning enables man to intellectually comprehend some aspect of God's nature.

(iii) The Knowledge of the People of Unity

Nasafī explains that the knowledge of the People of Unity (also referred to as the People of Unveiling) is superior to that of the *'Ulamā'* and the Philosophers:

> O dear friend! What is heard *(masmū')*, the object of knowledge *(ma'lūm)* and spiritual station *(maqām)* are all different from each other. It is a long way from what is heard to what is known and there are uncountable difficult passes from what is known to the spiritual station. So whoever has read or heard these chapters should not suppose that he has understood *(ma'lūm kard)* the intention and purpose of the author. Whoever has understood the intent and purpose of the author does not suppose that this has become his spiritual

> station. This is because whoever hears that there is a thing in the world called sugar is never equal with the person who knows there is a plant called sugar cane which is extremely sweet, and that when that plant is cut and beaten and the water is taken from it and made thick, sugar and cane-products are made. Whoever knows how sugar is made is never equal to the person who sees how it is made and places sugar in his mouth. First is the level of hearing *(sam')* concerning the experiential knowledge *(ma'rifa)* of sugar, second is the level of knowledge *('ilm)*, and third is the station of tasting *(dhawq)*. When knowledge is completed, it becomes complete through tasting and reaches its perfection through tasting. First in the experiential knowledge of sugar is general knowledge *('ilm-i ijmālī)*, and second is the differentiated knowledge *('ilm-ī tafṣīlī)* and third is knowledge of tasting *('ilm-ī dhawqī)*. First, sugar is heard of, second it is known and third it is seen and tasted. You should understand all things in this way.[33]

This experiential knowledge transcends sense perception and *'aql* because it is based upon unveiling bestowed upon wayfarers by God. Although the wayfarer cannot guarantee that God will ever rip away the veils that conceal Him, the wayfarers among the People of Unity believe that unveiling is more likely if they love God intensely and engage in ascetic discipline and spiritual effort.

> Know that the People of Unveiling confirm with their tongue and testify with their hearts the existence and unity of God and this confirmation and testimony of theirs is by way of unveiling and contemplation. O dervish, these are groups that see and know everything as God since they have passed all the veils and have come close to God's face and have seen and known the knowledge of certainty *('ilm al-yaqīn)* and the eye of certainty *('ayn al-yaqīn)* and they have understood that existence is for God alone, and for this reason they are called the People of Unity, for they do not see or understand anything other than God.
>
> Know that at this level, nothing is predominant for the Unitarian, neither effort nor endeavour, neither satisfaction nor submission, because the Unitarian says that everything in the beginning is good, and everything that exists must be as it is, and if it were not so then it would not be itself. But everything must exist in such a way that it is in the right place and in the right amount, since everything is called bad which is not in the right place, or else is in its right place but not in the right amount. So effort and endeavour are good in the right place and amount, and satisfaction and submission are good in the right place and in the right amount, and the words of the doctors are good in the right place and the right amount, and everything which exists is good in the right amount.[34]

It was mentioned in the first chapter that Nasafī was requested to compose his treatises without prejudice and without belittlement, and in to a remarkable extent, he is consistent in maintaining this, however, there can be no doubt that he preferred his path of ascetic discipline and religious effort to *'aql* and sense perception. He slips in a slight criticism of the other groups:

> The People of Unveiling *(ahl-ī kashf)* attained to the truth of things and they saw and understood things as they are. The rest are in a sleep and are dreaming and they tell stories to one another in their dreams.[35]

II. THE CONVERGENCE OF HELLENISTIC AND ISLAMIC EPISTEMOLOGICAL THOUGHT

The integration of Greek knowledge into the Islamic world resulted in Muslim philosophers discussing ontological and epistemological issues. As some Muslim philosophers were also attracted to Sufi explanations of existence and knowledge, the mystical and the rational philosophical traditions converged, to which some of Ibn Sīnā's works testify. By Nasafī's era and in the tradition of which he was a part, many Sufi works included discussions that on the one hand preserved the basic Koranic doctrines and also employed Islamic terminology and on the other hand borrowed certain rational philosophical structures and occasionally used the language that would have been familiar to students of Classical Greek thought.

This confluence of the Islamic and Hellenistic is apparent in many sections of Nasafī's works. For example, the ontological levels of the soul *(nafs)* reflect the Greek classification of the three kingdoms (mineral, plant and animal) and also the Koranic terminology of the soul commanding to evil *(al-nafs al-ammāra bi'l sū')*, the blaming soul *(al-nafs al-lawwāma)* and the soul at peace *(al-nafs al-muṭma'inna)*. In a discussion of the Transmigrationists in *Manāzil al-sā'irīn*, there is a description of the ascent of the soul which reflects the Greek-Islamic heritage. At the lowest level, the soul is called nature *(ṭabī'at)*, then it develops into the plant soul *(nafs-i nabātī)* which progresses into the animal soul *(nafs-i ḥaywānī)* and then comes the human soul *(nafs-i insānī)* which is also called the rational soul *(nafs-i nāṭiqa)* and the commanding soul. The ascent continues and the soul of the Philosopher is called the blaming soul, the soul of the Friend is the holy soul *(nafs-i qudsī)* and the soul of the Prophet is the soul at peace.[36] In other works, Nasafī also says there is one spirit which is described by praiseworthy and blameworthy attributes, such as the predatory spirit, satanic spirit, the commanding soul, the blaming soul and the soul at peace.[37] He then compares the levels of the spirit to the Light verse of the Koran:[38]

> The body *(qālib)* is like a niche, the plant spirit is like a glass lamp, the animal spirit is like a wick, the soul spirit is like oil, the human spirit is like light, the prophetic spirit is like light upon light and the holy spirit is like light upon light upon light.[39]

A similar ontological hierarchy is utilised in other works in Nasafī's discussions of the other Islamic beliefs to portray how man can know God. The basic epistemological structures are grounded in both the frameworks provided by Ibn Sīnā, who adopted them from Galen[40] and also in the doctrines found in the Koran. Yet there is a crucial distinction between Nasafī's beliefs and those of philosophers such as al-Farābī concerning the knowledge that man can actualise. In order to show this difference it is necessary to portray Nasafī's epistemological order.

The Outer and Inner Faculties of Perception

The faculties of perception *(idrāk)* are of two kinds, outer and inner; and there are five outer senses and five inner senses. The outer senses are seeing, hearing, smelling, tasting and touching. The inner senses are the *sensus communis (ḥiss-i mushtarak)*, imagination *(khayāl)*, sensory intuition *(wahm)*, the memory and the cognitive faculty *(mutaṣarrafa)*. The *sensus communis* is the perceiver of the objects of sense perception *(maḥsūsāt)* and these are stored as forms in the imagination. Thus the *sensus communis* discovers those things which pertain to the world of testimony such as the colour, flavour, scent, sound and coldness of water. Sensory intuition is the perceiver of the meaning *(ma'nā)* of the objects of sense perception and these are stored in the memory. So sensory intuition pertains to the invisible, such as the meaning of friendship in friend.[41] These faculties are governed by the cognitive faculty for it orders *(taṣarruf)* the perceptions which are stored in the imagination through composition *(tarkīb)* and distinguishing *(tafṣīl)*, for example it composes a man with no head. It is also implied in Nasafī's works that the cognitive faculty also needs to order and control sensory intuition.

Nasafī observes that the physicians say that there are no more than three inner senses; the imaginative *(takhayyul)*, sensory intuition *(tawahhum)* and recollection *(tadhakkur)* because the *sensus communis* and imagination are one and are located at the front of the brain, sensory intuition and the cognitive are one and are located at the middle of the brain and memory and recollection are one and are located at the back of the brain.[42] Such discussions are also found in Ibn Sīnā's works[43] and also those of Ibn Rushd.[44]

Although at first it may appear that all knowledge that man can obtain is sensory, this is not the case. This is because the cognitive should also be considered as man's *'aql* which the Philosophers employ in their quest for truth, and which enables the Sufis to make sense of any unveilings which occur in their hearts. According to Nasafī, God's self-disclosure (or unveiling in the heart) is impossible without a form,[45] so the unveiling takes an imaginal form, of which *'aql* can make sense. Thus, only the form of knowledge (which originates in the heart) is sensory, for the form is based upon sensory images that are understood by *'aql*.

Nasafī outlines several problems related to the operations of the faculties of imagination and sensory intuition which pertain to sense perception. These include the manifestation of images when they are not sought which may occur during sleep or during wakefulness (in the latter case Nasafī comments that one says such a thing or such a person just came in to the mind)[46], and the slowness in presenting images that are sought which is called forgetfulness.[47] Imagination and sensory intuition can have such a strong effect upon individuals that they can present images that effect the state of that individual. Nasafī describes imagination's power in an example of a person asleep who witnesses a cup of water. He drinks the water and something of the pleasure in satisfying that thirst remains when that person wakes up. Likewise, sensory intuition has similar power, and people may even become sick and die through its effects. For this reason, *'aql* has to become the master over imagination and sensory intuition.[48]

The superiority of *'aql* to the other faculties is portrayed by Nasafī with reference to man as the microcosm:

> Know that just as Adam, Eve and the Devil *(Iblīs)* are in the macrocosm, so too are they in the microcosm, and just as predatory animals, beasts, satans and angels are in the macrocosm, so too are they in the microcosm.
>
> O dervish! Man is the microcosm and Adam is the *'aql*, and Eve is the body, sensory intuition is the Devil, appetite is the peacock, anger is the snake of this world and good character traits is heaven and bad character traits is hell, and the faculties of *'aql* and the faculties of spirit and body are angels.[49]

Nasafī proceeds to describe how it is the task of man (otherwise known as Adam, Solomon or Jesus) to make his satan (who has the attribute of disobedience), his Devil (who has the attributes of pride, self satisfaction, envy and disobedience) and his angel (who has the attributes of obedience and heeding commands) subservient to him:

> The task of God's deputy is to make all these attributes subjected and subservient to himself and put each one of them in its correct place. Without his command, not one of them can do anything and God's deputy is Solomon and all of them work for Solomon.
>
> O dervish! The angel and the Devil are a single faculty and as long as this faculty is not obedient to Solomon, it is called the Devil and Solomon puts it in chains. When it obeys Solomon it is called an angel and then he puts it to work. Some build, some dive.[50]
>
> So Solomon's task is to change attributes, not to make them non-existent, since this is impossible. He makes the disobedient obedient. He teaches courtesy *(adab)* to the discourteous and he makes the blind see and he makes the deaf hear and he brings the dead to life. So *'aql*, which is God's deputy is Adam, Solomon and Jesus.[51]

When the *'aql* is employed in the appropriate manner, man is then open to understand the reality behind any unveilings that appear in his heart. The store of sensory images in the faculty of imagination provides him with the ability to imaginalise the disembodied realities of the spiritual world. Since each person's store of sensory images are based upon their own unique experiences, it follows that the imagination is particular to each person. This means that God's self-disclosure is different for each person. The manner in which this imaginalisation occurs, that is, the embodiment of disembodied objects is a mystery that is not explained by the Sufis. Such a secret could be not be discovered even by Ibn 'Arabī:

> . . . the gnostic knows who is disclosing Himself and Why He is disclosing Himself. But only the Real knows how *(kayf)* He discloses Himself. No one in the cosmos, no one other than God, knows that, neither angel nor prophet. For that is one of the specific characteristics of the Real, since the Essence is unknown at root. Hence the knowledge of how He discloses Himself in the loci of manifestation cannot be acquired or perceived by any of God's creatures.[52]

Although this is a mystery, the Sufis explained the self-disclosure in man's heart in purely Koranic imagery, for the Greek heritage was unable to provide any assistance. The Koran and *ḥadīth* literature hold man's heart as the locus of greatest proximity between man and God: "My heavens and earth embrace Me not, but the heart of My believing servant does embrace Me;"[53] "The hearts of the children of Adam are like a single heart between the two fingers of the All-merciful."[54] Nasafī also provides many similar examples, such as, "Intelligence is a light in the heart distinguishing between the truth and the false."[55] The actual process of how the heart can "perceive" God remains a mystery as Ibn 'Arabī comments, however, the Koran hints that the heart can be considered in the same way as a mirror: "No indeed, but what they were earning has rusted upon their hearts."[56] Mirrors were made of polished metal in Arabia during the seventh century and they rusted if they were not cleaned. In addition, the verse: "We lay coverings upon their hearts"[57] occurs several times in the Koran and one cannot see a reflection in a veiled mirror. Moreover the *ḥadīth* Nasafī cites that "Knowledge is a light in the heart," suggests a mirror imagery because there can be no reflection in a mirror without light.

The polished heart (also called the non-manifest) has to master the body (the manifest) because if the body predominates over the heart then knowledge from the world of spirits cannot be actualised:

> That side which is the invisible world is always clean and pure and there is no vexation *(zaḥmat)* or darkness *(zulmat)* or turbidity *(kadūrat)* in the non-manifest dimension. As for that side which is the body, it is a slave to greed and anger and it is gloomy and dark, and the non-manifest becomes gloomy and dark as long as one is tied to one's appetites. For this reason, the non-manifest is not able to acquire knowledge and lights from the invisible world – which is the world of angels and pure spirits. When the body becomes clean and pure, the non-manifest is made clean between two worlds. Whatever is in the invisible world – which is the world of angels and pure spirits – is also manifested in the non-manifest dimension of the wayfarer just as two clean mirrors when they are placed opposite one another; whatever is found in one mirror will also be found in the other mirror and vice versa.[58]

When man's heart is polished and dominates his senses, he can become informed of past, present and future events[59] because there is no dimension of time in the spiritual world. This knowledge passes into a form in most cases while man is asleep (when his sensory faculties are dulled and thus do not present any images which would obstruct the creation of forms for the knowledge from the disembodied world). This is known as veridical dreaming *(khwāb-i rāst)*. However, some people are also able to actualise this knowledge even while they are awake. Such cases are rare and Nasafī says that the isolation, ascetic discipline and spiritual effort of the wayfarer are so that his body has the same state in wakefulness that it has while he is asleep.

Yet isolation, ascetic discipline and spiritual effort are not the only ways that contribute to actualising a polished heart. Some people have a constitution *(mizāj)* which is innately perfect and such individuals include Prophets, Friends and the élite among the *'Ulamā'*. They have praiseworthy attributes, pleasant character traits and good qualities and they can acquire lights and knowledge from the spiritual world without much ascetic discipline or spiritual effort.[60] Other people do not have such a constitution and they have nothing but blameworthy attributes and bad character traits which cannot be improved through ascetic discipline and spiritual effort. Between these two are those people whose attributes and character traits are not determined in essence but can be improved through the Sufi practices or may deteriorate if the body dominates over the spirit. Each person's fate is decided by the "four times," in other words, by the movements of the stars and planets during the period of the child's conception and its birth into this world.[61] According to Nasafī, these three kinds of humans are referred to in the Koran: "People of the right hand, o how fortunate shall be the people of the right hand! And the people of the left hand, o how unfortunate shall be the people of the left hand! And the foremost shall still be the foremost,"[62] and: "Now someone among them is being unjust to his own self, and someone is following a middle course and someone is excelling in good deeds by God's leave."[63]

Since the actualisation of a polished heart is in some cases determined by the "four times" it is not surprising that Nasafī states that such a quality does not pertain solely to Islam. Acquiring knowledge from the spiritual world upon the heart may be found in non-believers. This significance of this point will be discussed in more detail chapter five.

The important point to note concerning Nasafī's portrayal of how man actualises knowledge is that it is not intellectual or rational. The Sufi makes an effort to polish his heart, but having done this, it is God that places a certain knowledge in the heart. For the Philosophers, knowledge is acquired through finding the "middle term" rationally which does not involve God. God's action of bestowing knowledge upon the wayfarer is described by Nasafī as love:

> O dervish! Love is a fire which falls into the wayfarer's heart. It annihilates the external secondary causes and inner thoughts of the wayfarer – which are all idols of the soul and veils in the path of the wayfarer – in order that he becomes *qibla*-less and idol-less and he becomes clean, pure and disengaged *(mujarrad)*.

O dervish! Love is the staff of Moses and this world is the magician which plays tricks every day. In other words, everyday it makes illusions *(khayālbāzī)* and the people are deceived by these worldly illusions. Love opens its mouth and swallows this world and everything in this world in one go and it makes the wayfarer clean, pure and disengaged in one go. Now the wayfarer is called "*ṣāfī,*" (pure) for up to this point he was not a Sufi because he was not *ṣāfī*. He becomes a Sufi when he becomes *ṣāfī*.[64]

O dervish! *'Aql* is the staff of the wayfarer as long as he has not reached the level of love and it prepares his worldly structures and tasks because it is engaged with the edifice of this world which has no soul *(jān)*: "He replied, 'It is my staff: Upon it I lean and with it I beat down the leaves for my flock. It has other uses besides.'"[65] The soul of *'aql* is love. *'Aql* without love is "soul-less" and dead. Hence that dear one said:

If there is no heart, where does love build its home?
And if there is no love what would the heart do?

O dervish! A command came to the wayfarer, "Cast aside *'aql* for *'aql* has turned towards this world and there is a danger that it will lead you to destruction *(halāk)*. Turn it around so that it faces Me." The wayfarer cannot cast aside *'aql* at first because it is love that casts it aside. When the wayfarer reaches the level of love, he casts aside *'aql* and regards it as a serpent, and he is afraid that it may even kill him.[66]

The knowledge of the Philosophers such as al-Farābī and Ibn Rushd is purely scientific, however gradually philosophers of the Greek tradition combined Islamic doctrines of revelation or unveiling. For example, Ibn Sīnā "recognises the possibility of man's attaining instantaneous scientific knowledge without following scientific procedures."[67] Nasafī's epistemology bears many resemblences to that of Ibn Sīnā, including the explanation of man's inner senses and also the possibility of actualising intelligible thoughts and foreknowledge of the future from the world of spirits in dreams and in wakefulness.[68] Moreover, Nasafī and Ibn Sīnā appear to be saying similar things concerning the knowledge actualised by the Prophets:

> . . . there might be a man whose soul has such an intense purity and is so firmly linked to rational principles that he blazes with intuition, i.e. with the receptivity of inspiration coming from the Active Intelligence concerning everything. So the forms of all things contained in the Active Intelligence are imprinted on his soul either all at once or nearly so, not that he accepts them merely on authority but on account of their logical order which encompasses all the middle terms . . . This is a kind of prophetic inspiration, indeed its highest form and the one most fitted to be called a Divine Power; and it is the highest human faculty.[69]

Yet Ibn Sīnā's hierarchy of ten intellects between God and man with the Active Intellect acting as the link between man and the higher intellects seems to emphasise God's *tanzīh* nature. Sufis such as Nasafī stress God's immediate self-disclosure, reflecting the *tanzīh/tashbīh* balance of witnessing God through His signs and through gnosis of *Malakūt* and *Jabarūt*.

III. MYSTICAL KNOWLEDGE

Although reason and logical argument are insufficient to grasp the true reality of Ultimate Existence, Nasafī portrays a systematic hierarchy of mystical perception which leads the wayfarer from the very start of the path where multiplicity is witnessed in all things to the termination of the journey where the unity of existence, or unity in multiplicity is apprehended. There are four levels in this hierarchy; the first is "remembrance" *(dhikr)*, the second is "reflection" *(fikr)*, the third is "inspiration" *(ilhām)* and the fourth is "contemplation" *('iyān)*. Nasafī himself comments that no one can comprehend the wayfarer's experiences of the fourth level unless they have also reached this station[70] and this is just as valid for the other three levels too. Nevertheless, Nasafī's didactic works provided a guide of these levels for the wayfarers, perhaps as a foretaste of what one could expect should the path be followed. Even if one did not have the preparedness to reach any one of the four levels of mystical knowledge at least one would be able to comprehend the theoretical explanation that Nasafī provides.

(i) *Dhikr* (Remembrance)[71]

It has been stated that one of the distinguishing features of Sufism around Nasafī's era was the practice of *dhikr*.[72] The verbal form of this term appears in the Koran several times where Muslims are commanded to remember God: "O you who believe! Remember God with much remembrance,"[73] "And remember your Lord within yourself humbly and with awe and under your breath by morning and evening."[74] One of the most common forms of *dhikr* was the repetition of the Islamic testament, "There is no god but God." By uttering this simple phrase in "mantra-style," whether verbally or silently, the Muslim was able to focus his concentration upon God alone and the distractions of this world ceased to be a veil between him and God. Nasafī describes the *dhikr* as the first step towards reaching God:

> Know that for the wayfarer, the *dhikr* is just like milk for a child. . .[75] Just as it is impossible for the body to grow strong and reach its perfection without milk, so too is it impossible for the heart to be nurtured and reach its perfection without the *dhikr*.[76]

Nasafī describes four levels of *dhikr*. The first of these is that of the novice, whose *dhikr* is verbal but whose heart is negligent. This *dhikr* reciter says the *dhikr* but only in form for his thoughts are elsewhere, perhaps buying and selling goods in the bazaar. The effects of this *dhikr* are weak but still beneficial, for at least the journey has commenced. The second level of *dhikr* is when the reciter performs the *dhikr* with his tongue and heart, and although the heart is present *(ḥāḍir)* in a formal manner *(bi-takalluf)* the pure ones are aware of their own disobedience to God. The third level of *dhikr* is when it is performed in such a way that it is both verbal and at the heart. Here the *dhikr* is dominant over the heart which becomes calm and stable. Even though the *dhikr* prevails over the heart, the reciter is able to perform other tasks which pertain to this world in a formal manner. The inner sign of this third level is that one is always aware of one's own obedience *(ṭā'at)* to God. The final level of *dhikr* is when the "object of remembrance" *(madhkūr)*, or God, becomes dominant over the heart. In fact this final level of *dhikr* is also referred to by Nasafī as the beginning of *fikr* or reflection. At this point the novice reaches the start of the Sufi path.[77]

(ii) *Fikr* (Reflection)

Several major Sufis of Nasafī's era, including Jalāl al-Dīn Rūmī and Ibn 'Arabī,[78] considered reflection as pertaining to human intellectual and rational faculties. For this reason they held reflection as an inferior method of obtaining knowledge when compared with *dhikr* (which was a means of obtaining knowledge of a higher dimension). However, there was no real consensus among the Sufis. One of the greatest of mystics of Nasafī's era was Shabastarī (d. 1320) and he portrayed "thinking" *(tafakkur)* in the sense of unveiling *(kashf)*, in other words, as an intuitive grasp of Reality: "It is to see the absolute All in every individual thing."[79] Abū Ḥāmid al-Ghazālī believed *fikr* to be superior to *dhikr* and he defined five stages in obtaining non-rational knowledge:

> What we have said thus far will show you how excellent a thing is meditation *(tafakkur)* and how it surpasses invocation *(dhikr)* and

> remembrance *(tadhakkur)* . . . First: remembrance or invocation *(tadhakkur)*, which consists in bringing to mind two cognitions. Second: meditation or reflection *(tafakkur)*, which is the search for the cognition which one seeks to obtain from the two concepts already in the mind. Third: obtaining the desired cognition, and the heart's illumination by it. Fourth: a change in the heart from its former state, by virtue of the illumination attained. Fifth: service performed for the heart by the bodily members in conformity with the new state prevailing within it.[80]

Like Ghazālī, Nasafī posits *fikr* as more eminent than *dhikr*:

> Just as you have understood the effects and qualities of the *dhikr* for the illumination of the wayfarer's heart, know that the effects and qualities of *fikr* are a hundred times greater, maybe more.[81]
>
> The journey is searching and searching is an attribute of the heart. There is a time when this searching is strong and dominates the heart in such a way that the search is transmitted to the outside which then becomes engaged in the same task as the inside. The inner and outer searching turn to the object of desire and they both engage in that task. The inner task is the resolution of purity and great effort: the outer task is bodily asceticism and constraint of the soul. The inner task is *fikr* and the outer task is *dhikr.*[82]

Nasafī's understanding of *fikr* becomes clearer when he explains how it has been known under different names by various individuals:

> Every person gives *fikr* a name; some call it "reflection" *(fikr)*, some call it "state" *(ḥāl)*, some call it "I have a time with God," and some call it "absence" *(ghaybat)*.[83]

Thus in *Kashf al-ḥaqā'iq*, Nasafī's explanation of *fikr* is a non-rational and non-intellectual process.[84]

> The meaning of all of them [that is *fikr, ḥāl,* etc.] is that there is a time for a person when his inside *(andarūn)* becomes so absorbed and engaged in something that his external senses cease from their activity and in that state his inside pays complete attention to that thing. Such a state lasts for one hour for some people, and for one day for other people, or two or three days for still others, and it is possible for it to last for up to ten days.[85]

Nasafī gives examples of how *fikr* or *ḥāl* can befall a person when he or she is in the middle of any task:

> It is related that one day, a dear one was climbing up a ladder [to reach a place where] he could perform his ritual ablutions. A servant

> had taken a water jug and was following him when that dear one experienced this [mystical] state while still on the ladder. That state remained with him for forty days while he was on the ladder and the servant stood in assistance, still holding the water jug. When the Shaykh came out of the state and climbed to the top of the ladder, the servant followed him to the top and the Shaykh took the water jug and made his ablutions.
>
> The servant said, "It has been forty days since we have prayed."
>
> The Shaykh replied, "You must go and pray the equivalent of forty days prayers since you have been aware of this for forty days."[86]

Other examples of *fikr* befalling people while engaged in day to day activities are given, such as during prayer or even while eating food, and this mystical state may last for one or two days.[87] Despite this, Nasafī's portrayal of *fikr* is somewhat vague and many questions are left unanswered. We may assume quite safely, however, that when Nasafī speaks of the wayfarer's inside being engaged in something, he is referring to the wayfarer meditating on God. Once the external senses are blocked from their functions, the wayfarer's heart is then prepared to receive, or rather "perceive" anything that God bestows upon it. In the Sufi tradition the *ḥāl* (or *fikr* to use Nasafī's term) is "something that descends from God into man's heart." [88] Nasafī does not explicitly say this, since his definition of *fikr* refers only to the external senses being blocked, however, there is an implicit understanding in this that the heart is ready to receive something from God. According to Sufis, the *ḥāl* (or *fikr*) that descend upon the heart are not all the same, as Schimmel states: "The states that come over [the wayfarer] will vary according to the station in which he is presently living; thus the *qabḍ*, 'contraction,' of someone in the station of poverty is different from the *qabḍ* of someone in the station of longing."[89]

(iii) Inspiration *(ilhām)*

The third level of mystical perception which is called "inspiration" is different in nature from *fikr*. The *fikr* is when the wayfarer abides in a particular spiritual station and pays complete attention to God and he experiences a mystical state which reflects the knowledge of that station. The scope of inspiration differs because it is a time when the heart is illuminated with knowledge concerning a past or future event without prior meditation or hearing it from some other person. Again Nasafī comments that inspiration has been known by different names including "heralding" *(adhina)* and "a passing thought" *(khāṭir)*. Inspiration is very similar to the concept of revelation *(waḥī)*, however revelation is limited to prophets which came to an end with the sealing of Prophecy.

Nasafī also describes how the experiences of *fikr-ḥāl* and inspiration may be manifested externally in the wayfarer. He does this by listing the various degrees of insight. The first is called "finding" *(wajd)* of a thing in the heart which has come from the invisible world. When the "finding" becomes more manifest, it is called "unveiling" *(kashf)*, and when this becomes more manifest it is called "gnostic knowledge" *(ma'rifat)* which is then called "witnessing" *(mushāhada)* when it becomes more manifest. When all the veils have been cast aside, the wayfarer reaches the station of contemplation *(mu'āyana)*. Having given this introduction, Nasafī compares the heart to a hearth and gnostic knowledge is like a coal in the hearth, love *(maḥabbat)* is like fire in the coal, and passionate love *('ishq)* is like the flames of the fire. The states and mystical occurrences *(wārid)* and inspiration and mystical audition *(samā')* are like a breeze which blows on the fire.

Thus the wayfarer must first have the preparedness, love and passionate love for God and then God may release a breeze of *fikr-ḥāl* or inspiration upon him. There is nothing rational or intellectual in this process.

> When the fire of love – which is in the heart – flares up in flames as a result of the breeze of mystical audition, the wayfarer cries in tears if it expresses itself through his eyes. He shouts out loud if it expresses itself through his mouth. He waves his hands if it expresses itself through his hands and he rises up and dances if it expresses itself through his legs. States like these are called "finding" because if the fire of love was in the heart but could not be manifested, it resembles a thing that has been lost. When the breeze of mystical audition or mystical occurrences cause this fire to burst forth in flames, it resembles a lost thing which has been found. So these states are called "finding."[90]

(iv) Contemplation *('iyān)*

In the previous section it was shown that Nasafī lists a hierarchy of spiritual experience. This starts with "finding" and progresses to the final level of "contemplation." Unfortunately, in Nasafī's works there is no precise definition of these technical terms so it is difficult to understand how he distinguishes between them (this problem is not solved by referring to the works of other Sufis because there is no consensus among them regarding these technical terms).[91] One clue to Nasafī's understanding of "contemplation" is contained in the following portrayal of God as light:

> The Shaykh of this helpless one said, "I reached and saw this light. It was an infinite and limitless light, it was an ocean, endless and shoreless that had no above, under, left, right, before or after. I remained bewildered in that light. Concerns for sleep, eating and problems of livelihood departed from me and I could not engage in any of them. I said to a dear friend that my condition *(ḥāl)* was in this way and he said that I should go and take a handful of straw from someone's harvest store without God's permission. I went and I took [the handful of straw] and I no longer saw the light."
>
> This helpless one said to the Shaykh, "O Shaykh, in my opinion, one cannot see this light with the eyes of the head, but one can see it with the eyes of the inner heart *(sirr)* because this light is not the object of sense perception *(maḥsūs)*."
>
> The Shaykh said, "O 'Azīz, in my opinion, one can see this light with both the eyes of the head and also with the eyes of the inner heart."
>
> I said, "O Shaykh, the indication of whoever has reached this sea of light is that he drowns in it and he will never see himself afterwards. He sees everything as this sea of light."
>
> The Shaykh said, "One should not witness *(mushāhada)* continually."
>
> I said, "O Shaykh, witnessing is one thing and contemplation *(mu'āyana)* is another."
>
> He said, "One should not witness continually but one should contemplate continually."[92]

The above is an account of Nasafī's Shaykh's experience of "witnessing" which occurs within the heart. This "inner witnessing" of God has been described by one of the foremost scholars of Sufism as "the realisation of one's own nothingness"[93] through witnessing God in the heart, which encapsulates Nasafī's Shaykh's loss of self in the sea of light. "Witnessing" is contrasted with the experience of "contemplation" which is when the mystic sees God with the eyes of the head. This would seem to be heretical, but the Sufis meant the seeing of God through His signs in this world. One realises that although everything, including oneself, has no real existence, the things of this world reveal some aspect of God's existence.

For Nasafī, "contemplation" is a superior level of mystical experience compared to "witnessing" because the mystic has already passed through the stage of "witnessing" and has returned to this world and can now contemplate God in a sober manner and see and understand the things as they are. Moreover, from this elevated stand-point, one can do anything one pleases, such as engage in the *dhikr*, *fikr* or inspiration.

As long as the wayfarer is engaged in *dhikr* and it is dominant over him, he is in the world of body and physical sensation. When he ceases the *dhikr* and *fikr* presents itself and it becomes dominant over him, he passes from the world of body and reaches the world of spirit. When he ceases *fikr* and inspiration presents itself and it becomes dominant over him, he passes from the world of intelligence and reaches the world of love. When he ceases from inspiration, contemplation presents itself and he passes from the world of love and reaches the station of stability *(tamkīn)*, and in [the station of] stability he may choose whatever attribute he desires and he will be attributed with it.

So at first the *dhikr* is dominant for the wayfarer, then *fikr* is dominant, then inspiration and then contemplation. And then he reaches the station of stability and he becomes free from any variegation. In other words, at first the attributes of the wayfarer are dominant over his existence and each day, perhaps each hour, an attribute is dominant over him. But when he passes the station of variegation *(talwīn)* and reaches the station of stability, his existence becomes dominant over his attributes. The indication of the station of stability is that the wayfarer can obtain whatever station or attribute he desires, that is to say, he can choose and all the attributes are his property. If he desires he can recite the *dhikr*, and if he wants he can engage in *fikr*, and if he does not desire then he will not recite the *dhikr* or engage in *fikr*. He has made himself prepared for inspiration so that he can become informed of past and future events. In other words, the mirror of his heart has been cleaned from the tarnishing of both worlds, so that the reflection of whatever occurs or will occur in this world will become apparent upon his heart. If he desires, he can renounce the past and future and enjoy his present time.[94]

The Two Varieties of Mystical Wayfarer[95]

The superiority that Nasafī sees in *fikr* over *dhikr* is highlighted in his comparison of the terrestrial and celestial wayfarer. The terrestrial wayfarer journeys on land and his means of transport is a mount *(markab)* which is in fact, the *dhikr*. The celestial wayfarer journeys through the heavens and his mount which is called Burāq (the name of the horse of the Prophet Muḥammad, by which, according to Sufi tradition, he rode on his night ascent through the heavens) is in reality, *fikr*.

There are four conditions *(sharṭ)* for the terrestrial wayfarer without which the spiritual journey is impossible. These four are association with a wise man, complying with the orders of this wise man, continual *dhikr* and lastly being God-fearing *(taqwā)* and abstinent *(parhizgar)*.

There are also four "wings" *(par)* for the Burāq of the celestial wayfarer, without which it cannot fly in to the heavens of mystical experience. These four wings are firstly spiritual hearing, or hearing and understanding the reality and meaning behind things; second is spiritual seeing which is the ability to see things as they are. These two wings are called manifest revelation *(waḥy-i jahr)*. The third wing is *fikr* and the fourth is inspiration, and these two wings are called revelation of the spiritual heart *(waḥy-i sirr)*.

According to a recent work, this classification of terrestrial and celestial wayfarers is unique and found in no other author preceding or following Nasafī.[96] With the practice of *dhikr*, the terrestrial wayfarer can also become a celestial wayfarer:

> Know that it is necessary for the terrestrial wayfarer to travel on the mount of religious effort and to be engaged in continual *dhikr* until he acquires the Burāq of contemplation. And when he acquires the Burāq of contemplation, he ceases from the *dhikr*, the sign is that the wayfarer has passed from the earth and heavens, and the earth and heavens are one.[97]

Conclusion

For those who have not had any kind of mystical experience, it may be difficult to comprehend Nasafī's epistemological discussion of mystical experience because it transcends the logical and rational processes of acquiring knowledge which are based on sense perception and the intellect. It is perhaps obvious to state that "a full understanding of mystical phenomena requires more than a study of mystical literature."[98] In other words, one has to have had a mystical experience oneself in order to appreciate what is really happening when mystics such as Nasafī are discussing the inner senses and losing themselves in the sea of light.

This ineffability of the mystical experience and the transcendence of logic and reason is the essence of what distinguishes the epistemology of the Sufis from that of the Philosophers. The Sufis of Nasafī's era held that mystical experience occurred through the "inner senses" and by this term they were not referring to the intellectual faculties. Nasafī does not elaborate on these "inner senses" but his contemporaries, such as 'Alā' al-Dawla al-Simnānī constructed a hierarchical framework of inner senses which he called "Subtle Substances" *(laṭā'if)*. These are the essential reality of the human being. Of course reason and intelligence have a role to play in how man acquires knowledge for it is through the imagination that knowledge from *Malakūt* and *Jabarūt* takes a form. It is also vital to note that the pinnacle of Nasafī's epistemology, namely "contemplation" is when one "returns" to this world and is able to understand and see everything as it is and in its right place. Thus Nasafī's Sufism should not be regarded as "otherworldly," or as a form of mystical escapism. Rather, Nasafī provides a path to perfection which leads one away from oneself to God. Thereafter, one remains with God but enjoys a felicitous life in this world. Just how one can achieve this life is the subject of the next chapter.

Notes

1 See T. Izutsu, *Creation and the Timeless Order of Things* (Oregon: White Cloud Press, 1994), p. 112.
2 Koran, 57: 4, "He is with you wherever you are."
3 Koran, 50: 16.
4 *Maqṣad-i aqṣā*, p. 235.
5 Ibid, p. 229.
6 For a discussion of the implications of this *ḥadīth*, see Murata and Chittick, *The Vision of Islam* (New York: Paragon House, 1994).
7 *Maqṣad-i aqṣā*, p. 248.
8 Ibid, p. 249.
9 Ibid, p. 212.
10 For example, *Maqṣad-i aqṣā*, p. 213.
11 *Maqṣad-i aqṣā*, p. 217.
12 This commentary was called *Bahr al-ḥaqā'iq*, see J.J. Elias, *The Throne Carrier of God* (Albamy: SUNY Press, 1995), pp. 204–205.
13 *al-Insān al-kāmil*, p. 291.
14 Ibid, p. 81.
15 *Ḥadīth*, I have not been able to trace this.
16 *al-Insān al-kāmil*, p. 175.
17 *Maqṣad-i aqṣā*, p. 247–8.
18 *al-Insān al-kāmil*, p. 54–55.
19 *Maqṣad-i aqṣā*, p. 249.
20 *Kashf al-ḥaqā'iq*, p. 58. This issue will be explained in more detail in chapter six.
21 See Jalāl al-Dīn Rūmī, *Mathnawī*, I, 3467. Also Niẓāmī, *Sikandar-nāma*, Vol II, pp. 197–200 (Dehli, 1316). For a translation of this story in Niẓāmī, see Sir Thomas W. Arnold, *Painting in Islam* (New York: Dover Publications, 1965), pp. 67–68.
22 *al-Insān al-kāmil*, p. 93.
23 *al-Insān al-kāmil*, p. 74–75.
24 *Ḥadīth*. This is a *ḥadīth* which was quoted by Sufis prior to Nasafī. For example see al-Sarrāj (d. 989) *Kitāb al-luma' fi'l-taṣawwuf*, ed. R. A. Nicholson (Leiden and London, E.J. Brill, 1914), 548.
25 Koran, 15: 29.
26 *Maqṣad-i aqṣā*, p. 263.

27 Koran, 47: 15.
28 Koran, 29: 43.
29 *Kashf al-ḥaqā'iq*, p. 179–80.
30 Koran, 7: 172, 33: 72.
31 *al-Insān al-kāmil*, p. 203.
32 Ibid, p. 299.
33 *Kitāb-i tanzīl*, fol. 68b, l.15 – fol. 69a, l.6.
34 *Maqṣad-i aqṣā*, p. 250.
35 *al-Insān al-kāmil*, p. 270.
36 *Manāzil al-sā'irīn*, p. 412.
37 *Kitāb-i tanzīl*, fol. 58b, lines 9–11.
38 Koran 24: 35, "God is the light of the heavens and earth. The parable of His light is as if there were a niche and within it a lamp enclosed in a glass, the glass as it were a shining star, kindled from a blessed tree, an olive tree neither of the east nor the west. Its oil would almost shine even if no fire touched it. Light upon light. God guides to His light whom He will."
39 *Kitāb-i tanzīl*, fol. 58b lines 16–18.
40 See S.H. Nasr, *Three Muslim Sages* (New York: Caravan Books, 1964), p. 39.
41 As S. Murata has commented, there is no scholarly consensus on how to translate the word *wahm*. See *The Tao of Islam*, p. 351, n. 77.
42 *Kashf al-ḥaqā'iq*, p. 88–89.
43 S.H. Nasr, *Three Muslim Sages*, p. 39.
44 See O.N. Mohammed, *Averroes Doctrine of Immortality* (Ontario: Wilfrid Laurier University Press, 1984), p. 102.
45 *Kitāb-i tanzīl*, fol. 48a, lines 16–17.
46 *al-Insān al-kāmil*, p. 244.
47 Ibid, p. 243.
48 Ibid, p. 240–241.
49 Ibid, p. 149.
50 An allusion to Solomon's power over the satans mentioned in the Koran, 38: 37: "And the satans, every builder and diver, and others also, coupled in fetters."
51 Ibid, p. 150.
52 Ibn 'Arabī, *al-Futūḥāt al-makkiyya* (II 597.4, 35) translated Chittick, *The Sufi Path of Knowledge*, p. 342.
53 *Ḥadīth*, Muslim, *Qadar*, 17.
54 According to Chittick, this *ḥadīth* is frequently quoted in Sufi texts as well as by Ghazālī in *Iḥyā' 'ulūm al-dīn*, but it is not acknowledged as authentic by most of the exoteric scholars. See *The Sufi Path of Knowledge*, p. 396, n. 20.
55 *Maqṣad-i aqṣā*, p. 263. See note 19.
56 Koran, 83: 14.
57 Koran, 6: 25, 17: 46, 18: 57.
58 *al-Insān al-kāmil*, p. 89.
59 Ibid, p. 242.
60 *Kashf al-ḥaqā'iq*, p. 117–18.
61 *al-Insān al-kāmil*, p. 90.
62 Koran, 61: 7–12.

63 Koran, 35: 31.
64 *al-Insān al-kāmil*, p. 297.
65 Koran, 20: 19.
66 *al-Insān al-kāmil*, pp. 297–298.
67 H. Davidson, *Alfarabi, Avicenna and Averroes on Intellect* (Oxford: Oxford University Press, 1992), p. 123.
68 Ibid, p. 119.
69 Avicenna, *Avicenna's Psychology*, translated F. Rahman, p. 37.
70 *Kashf al-ḥaqā'iq*, p. 207.
71 For an alternative discussion on *dhikr*, see J.J. Elias, *The Throne Carrier of God*, p. 119–146.
72 M. Hodgson, *The Venture of Islam* (Chicago: University of Chicago, 1974–77), p. 211.
73 Koran, 33: 41.
74 Koran, 7: 205. See also 76: 25, 73: 8, 3: 41, 4: 103, 18: 24.
75 *Kashf al-ḥaqā'iq*, p. 135.
76 Ibid, p. 164.
77 For these four levels of *dhikr*, see *Kashf al-ḥaqā'iq*, pp. 165–166. Nasafī's discussion of the different levels of the *dhikr* are very similar to those of earlier Sufis such as Maybudī (d. 1126). See M.I. Waley, "Contemplative Disciplines in Early Persian Sufism," in *Classical Persian Sufism: from its Origins to Rumi*, edited L. Lewisohn (London: Khaniqahi Nimatullahi Publications, 1993), p. 531–32.
78 For Ibn 'Arabī on *fikr*, see Chittick, *The Sufi Path of Knowledge*, p. 159. For Rūmī on *fikr*, see Lewisohn, *Beyond Faith and Infidelity*, p. 222–225.
79 Shabastarī, *Gulshān-i Rāz*, v. 72, reproduced in Lāhījī's *Mafātīh al-i'jāz fī sharḥ-i gulshān-i rāz*, edited Kayvān Samī'ī (Tehran, 1965). Cited by T. Izutsu in *Creation and the Timeless Order of Things*, op.cit, p. 59.
80 Abū Ḥāmid al-Ghazālī, *Iḥyā', Bāb al-tafakkur* (vol 4, pp. 412), translated M.I. Waley, cited in Lewisohn, *Beyond Faith and Infidelity*, p. 219.
81 *Kashf al-ḥaqā'iq*, p. 164.
82 Ibid, p. 165.
83 Ibid, p. 149.
84 In *Kitāb-i tanzīl*, Nasafī explains *fikr* in a way which may be interpreted as a rational and intellectual process. He describes the appearance of light within the wayfarer, which at the beginning may have the strength of a star in [the wayfarer's inside]. According to the times of the day, [the light] has the strength of the moon, and with the passing of time that moon becomes just like the sun through ascetic discipline and *dhikr*, until a point when reflection *(fikr)* and thought *(andīsha)* are no longer required for [the wayfarer]. Everything becomes the object of contemplation *(mu'āyana)* for him. (*Kitāb-i tanzīl*, fol. 74b, lines 12–14).
85 *Kashf al-ḥaqā'iq*, p. 139.
86 Ibid, p. 166.
87 Ibid, p. 139–140.
88 Hujwīrī, *Kashf al-maḥjūb*, p. 181.
89 "The states that come over [the wayfarer] will vary according to the station in which he is presently living; thus the *qabḍ*, 'contraction,' of someone in the station of poverty is different from the *qabḍ* of someone in

the station of longing." See A. Schimmel, *Mystical Dimensions of Islam* (Chapel Hill: University of North Carolina Press, 1975), p. 99.

90 *Kashf al-ḥaqā'iq*, p. 136–137.

91 For example, see Hujwīrī: "Therefore the life of contemplatives is the time during which they enjoy *mushāhadat*: the time spent in seeing occurlarly *(mu'āyanat)* they do not reckon as life, for that to them is really death." *Kashf al-maḥjūb*, op. cit., p. 331. Nasafī spiritualises the meaning of *mu'āyanat*, as is shown in this section.

92 *al-Insān al-kāmil*, p. 286–287.

93 C.W. Ernst, *Words of Ecstacy in Sufism* (Albany: SUNY Press, 1985), p. 35.

94 *Kashf al-ḥaqā'iq*, p. 141–2.

95 See Lewisohn's discussion on Nasafī and the celestial wayfarer, *Beyond Faith and Infidelity*, p. 220–222.

96 Ibid, p. 220. However, one can point to similar classifications such as a work by Najm al-Dīn Kubrā, *Risāla ādāb al-sulūk*, edited and translated into Persian by Husayn Muḥyī al-Dīn Qumsha'ī, in *Kīmiyā*, ed. Aḥmad Bihishtī Shīrāzī (Tehran, 1366), pp. 4–13. In this work, Najm al-Dīn Kubrā divides the journey *(safar)* into one of spiritual meaning *(ma'nā)* and the other is a bodily *(jismānī)* journey.

97 *Kashf al-ḥaqā'iq*, p. 141.

98 N. Pike, *Mystic Union* (London: Cornell University Press, 1992), p. xii.

4

The Sufi Journey

Surely God's friends – no fear shall be on them, neither shall they sorrow. Those who believe and are god fearing – for them is good tidings in the present life and in the world to come.[1]

I. FELICITY, THE GOAL OF SUFISM

The origin of the word "Sufism" has been studied in depth by both Muslim and non-Muslim scholars but as yet, there is no consensus concerning its etymology.[2] However, the reality of Sufism is clear, for its paramount aim is felicity *(sa'āda)* which is determined by the knowledge or proximity one has to God. For Sufis, knowledge about God is both "theoretical" and "experiential", the former being worthless unless it is used to bring man close to God. Having discussed many of the issues relating to theoretical knowledge of God in the preceding two chapters, it is now necessary to examine the practical side of Sufism, that is, the methods and disciplines particular to Sufism that distinguishes it from other forms of Islamic worship.

Nasafī's version of felicity is attractive because it reveals the simple and complex nature of the "*shahāda*" or testimony of Islam. The public and voluntary utterance of the *shahāda*, "There is no god but God,"[3] is the foundation of Islam and by this statement, consenting adults become Muslims. At the manifest level, the *shahāda* is an affirmation of the unity of God and negates any multiplicity of deities. The non-manifest dimension of the *shahāda* is more intricate and Nasafī's explanation of this is the means by which the wayfarer can enjoy the felicitous life in Sufism. To understand the non-manifest dimension of the *shahāda*, it is necessary to know the Sufi meaning of felicity.

Felicity and Heaven

Finding real existence, which is the existence of God, is the cause of felicity. This search is the Sufi path in which there are many stages and the closer one comes to real existence, the more one's felicity increases. Nasafī portrays three basic degrees of felicity by revealing the esoteric meaning of the word "*ajr,*" or reward. In Persian, this word is spelt with three letters; *alif*, *jim* and *ra*:

> *Alif* is an expression for return to God *(i'ādat)*, and *jim* is an expression for paradise *(janna)* and *ra* is an expression for vision of God *(rū'yat)*. In other words, those who have faith and have performed good works will return to God and their return is to God's essence. There is no doubt that they reach God's essence when they ascend, and they are in paradise and encounter God.[4]

The distinction in felicity between Paradise and witnessing God is a typical Sufi theme and dates back to the time of Rābi'a (d. 801),[5] a female mystic from Basra who stressed the importance of avoiding any ulterior motive in worshipping God. 'Aṭṭār (d. 1221) cites one of Rābi'a's prayers:

> O my Lord, if I worship Thee from fear of Hell, burn me in Hell, and if I worship Thee from hope of Paradise, exclude me thence, but if I worship Thee for Thine own sake then withhold not from me Thine Eternal Beauty.[6]

The vision of God as the ultimate degree of felicity is not confined to the next world. Through following the Sufi path of ascetic discipline and spiritual effort under the guidance of a shaykh or master, many mystics claim that it is possible to witness God through his signs in this world. Nasafī gives an indication of such Sufis and the subsequent felicity that they experience:

> Know that some of the élite of the élite among the People of the Holy Law say that it is possible that through ascetic discipline and spiritual effort, the wayfarer's body can reach a point that in terms of attributes and subtlety it becomes extremely translucent, reflective, and luminous. The light and the place of manifestation become like one thing just like a glass goblet which is extremely translucent and reflective in which there is an extremely pure and fine *(laṭīf)* wine. One cannot distinguish the goblet from the wine or the wine from the goblet since the two are like one thing.[7] Hence the Prophets said: "Our spirits are our bodies and our bodies are our spirits." Each cry that comes from the wayfarers, like "Glory be to Me, how great is My majesty,"[8] and "I am the Truth,"[9] is in this station. In fact this station requires this

> because when the wayfarer's body becomes glass-like *(zujājī)*, extremely translucent and reflective through ascetic discipline and spiritual effort, he sees things that others cannot see, he hears things that others do not hear, he knows things that others do not know and he does things that others do not do. When it occurs in this way, the wayfarer sees the whole of his self as light and he cannot distinguish the light from the glass or the glass from the light. Even if he does not wish, a cry such as "Glory be to Me how great is My majesty," comes from him involuntarily.
>
> O dervish! At the beginning of this station a cry comes from the wayfarers, like "There is nothing in my cloak except God,"[10] and "There is nothing in the two worlds except Me."[11] In the middle of this station, in fact the cry "I am the Truth," and "Glory be to Me how great is My majesty," comes from the wayfarers. At the end of this station, such a silence and quietness prevail over the wayfarer that he does not speak with anyone at any time unless it is necessary, and such an incapacity *('ajz)* and ignorance *(nā-dānā'ī)* prevail over him that he knows for sure that nobody knows or will know God's essence and attributes just as God's essence and attributes are, and such a tranquillity *(farāghat)* and peace of mind *(jam'iyat)* prevail over him that he renounces everything all at once, and such an entrustment *(tafwīẓ)* and surrender *(taslīm)* prevail over him that nothing remains as a sorrow for him and he recognises God as knowing and powerful over the servants.[12]

Although the ultimate goal is the contemplation of God, in Nasafī's works there are frequent references to the wayfarer being in either heaven *(bihisht)* or hell *(dūzakh)*. In Sufi terms, being in hell is a state of remoteness from God where it is not possible to witness Him. However, heaven is a place where the wayfarer is able to contemplate Him.[13] As Nasafī indicates, some Sufis claim that it is possible to behold God in this world, therefore there is a heaven and hell in this world as well as a heaven and hell in the next world. In this world,

> Hell is love of fortune and fame, greed and avarice, associating others with God *(shirk)* and not recognising God. Heaven is the hatred of fortune and fame, renunciation of seeking them, contentment, satisfaction, unity and recognition of God.[14]

This worldly heaven and hell appear in Nasafī's discourses of both the Sufis and the Philosophers. For example, according to the Philosophers

> the real Heaven is harmony and the real Hell is antagonism, and the truth of felicity is obtaining [one's] desire and the truth of non-felicity is

not obtaining [one's] desire . . . Since you have understood the truth of Heaven and Hell, now know that Heaven and Hell have many gates. All pleasant words and actions and praiseworthy character traits are the gates of Heaven. All unpleasant words and actions and reproachable character traits are the gates of Hell. This is because each torment and unhappiness that befalls man is through unpleasant words and actions and reproachable character traits. Each comfort and felicity that befalls man is through pleasant words and actions and praiseworthy character traits.

Know that some people say that Hell has seven gates and Heaven has eight gates. This is correct because man has eight senses, that is, man has eight perceptions; five external senses, imagination *(khayāl)*, sensory intuition *(wahm)* and intelligence *('aql)*. Everything that man perceives and discovers is through these eight gates. Each time that intelligence does not accompany the other seven, or when they operate without the order of intelligence but operate through the order of nature, these seven are the gates of Hell. And when intelligence is manifested and becomes the master of these seven and when they operate on the command of intelligence, the eight become the gates of Heaven. Therefore all of mankind will pass through Hell and then arrive at Heaven. Some remain in Hell and cannot proceed from there, and others pass Hell and arrive at Heaven.[15]

Nasafī's statement that everyone passes the gates of Hell is based upon a verse in the Koran which states "Not one of you there is, but he shall go down to it [Hell]."[16] In fact, the whole of Nasafī's works reflect a deep knowledge of the Koran and in outlining his thought and that of others, he draws many allusions from it. The following example (which again comes from a discourse of the Philosophers) stresses the immediacy of Heaven and Hell in the present world and portrays the tree in Heaven and the tree in Hell.[17]

Know that the *Tubba'* tree is a tree which has a branch in each pavilion and in all the levels of Heaven. Each comfort and repose for each individual of the People of Heaven comes from a branch of the *Tubba'* tree, since it is in their pavilion. That tree is wisdom, since there is wisdom in every branch. Each person thinks about the final cause of each action he performs and he does not regret any action.

And the *Zaqqūm* tree is a tree which has a branch in each house and in each of the Hells of Hell. Every torment and vexation that afflicts the People of Hell comes from the *Zaqqūm* tree. That tree is nature since there is nature in each branch of this tree. Each person does not think about the final cause of each action that he performs, and this lack of reflection and thought is created by him and he regrets his own action. The sign of the ignorant is that they regret [their] words and actions.

> Know that reward and punishment are the fruits of the *Tubba'* and the *Zaqqūm* trees. The fruit of their branches will be produced for you since there is a branch of both in your house.
>
> Since you have understood that reward and punishment are the fruits of your tree, now know that the nurturing of these trees is through your own planting and rearing. This is because each action which you perform is through the management and thought of intelligence and the prevention of the soul's caprice is in that action.[18]

Although the two previous quotations are from the discourses of the Philosophers, they also reflect the esoteric dimension of Nasafī's brand of Sufism. The only difference that Nasafī has with the Philosophers is that there is another stage beyond intelligence which enables the wayfarer to contemplate God from Heaven. This stage is the love for God where one actualises gnosis *(ma'rifa)*.

> O dervish! Ignorance is a Hell before [attaining] gnosis. Ignorance after gnosis is Heaven. Before attaining gnosis, ignorance is the cause of greed and avarice, and after gnosis it is the cause of satisfaction and surrender.[19]

The Path of Felicity

Sufism is more than a theoretical interpretation of the esoteric dimension of Islam for there is no benefit to the wayfarer in comprehending the theory of felicity without performing those tasks which draw him towards the felicitous life:

> Whoever hears there is a thing in this world called sugar is never equal with the person who knows there is a plant called sugar cane which is extremely sweet and when that plant is cut and beaten and the water is taken from it and made thick, sugar and cane by products are made. Whoever knows how sugar is made is never equal to the person who sees how it is made and places sugar in his mouth. First is the level of hearing *(sam')* concerning the experiential knowledge of sugar, second is the level of knowledge *('ilm)* and third is the level of tasting *(dhawq)*.[20]

In other words, the first level pertains to those members of the *'Ulamā'* or religious scholars who stress the exoteric dimension of Islam, and the second level is that of the Philosophers who emphasise the use of rational knowledge in explaining the world. The third level belongs to the Sufis whose practices enable them to understand the reality of things as they really are. In *Maqṣad-i aqṣā*, Nasafī classifies these practices into two sections, which if perfected together, can lead to the felicitous life. The first factor is renunciation *(tark)* and the second is gnosis of God.

(i) Renunciation

Nasafī lived through the two Mongol invasions of Central Asia and Iran between 1220 and 1258. The subsequent occupation of that area by the Mongols clarified to the local inhabitants the insecurity and impermanence of their lives and circumstances. The horrors perpetrated by the Mongols are infamous and need not be repeated here.[21] It may well be a result of his experiences under Mongol domination that Nasafī was so adamant that "there is no happiness *(khūshī)* in this world *(dunyā)*."[22] The instability of this world and its circumstances *(aḥwāl)* are compared by Nasafī to a wave of the sea:

> O dervish! You must not put your trust in this world or this world's comforts, and you should not put your trust in the life or veracity of fortune and fame. Everything under the sphere of the moon and the stars does not keep its original state. It will certainly change, in other words, the state of this world does not stay in one condition, but is always changing. Each moment it takes a new form and each hour a plan is created, but the first form has still not been completed or found stability when another form comes and annuls the first form. It resembles a wave of the sea, and the wise man never builds his house upon a wave of the sea and he never intends to live there.[23]

As a result of this impermanence, people are always seeking more.

> Nobody is satisfied with his own station. If there is an ignorant person, he seeks something and if there is a wise person, he also seeks something, perhaps more; and if there is a poor person, he seeks something and if there is a wealthy person, he seeks something, perhaps more; and if there is a subject and if there is a king, they are both desirers. This conflict and discord are due to desire and seeking; so there are conflict and discord wherever one desires and seeks. There is no difference between the wise and the ignorant person, the wealthy and the poor person, the subject and the king. But the wise person, the wealthy person and the king have more suffering because their desires and seeking are greater.[24]

The only cure for conflict is the renunciation of whatever one is seeking.

> Know that renunciation is the severing of connections; the severing of connections in its non-manifest dimension is when love of this world is

> expelled from one's heart, and in its manifest dimension it is when a worldly person renounces everything he has and gives it to the poor people.[25]

Desire is not limited to worldly matters, for according to Nasafī, attachment to religion and the next world is undesirable in certain respects. This is particularly the case if the exoteric dimension of a religion predominates in the believer.

> O dervish, everything which becomes a veil in the path of the wayfarer obstructs his path. He must renounce it, whether it belongs to this world or to the next world. That is, just as fortune and fame obstruct the path of the wayfarer, there is also a time when too much prayer and fasting obstruct the path. One is a murky veil and the other is a luminous veil.[26]

Nasafī relates an enlightening story which highlights the extent of renunciation when attachment to religion (even Sufism) can become a veil. The story involves two famous Sufis, Ibrāhīm Adham (d. 790) and Shaqīq al-Balkhī (d. 809).

> It is said that Shaqīq came to Ibrāhīm and Ibrāhīm asked Shaqīq –
>
> "O Shaqīq! How do the dervishes of your city behave?"
>
> "In the best spiritual state," Shaqīq replied.
>
> "How is that spiritual state?" Ibrāhīm asked.
>
> "If they find something they give thanks, and if they do not find anything, they wait," Shaqīq replied.
>
> "The dogs of our city act in the same way; if they find something they eat it, and if they don't find anything, they wait," Ibrāhīm said
>
> "So how should the dervishes live?" asked Shaqīq.
>
> "If they don't find anything, they give thanks, and if they find something, they give it up *(īthār kunand)*," he replied.[27]

The "murky" and "luminous veils" are also called idols *(but)* which come in all forms:

> Old clothes may be an idol for one person and new clothes may be an idol of another. The free person is he who sees both in the same way. The purpose of clothing is the repelling of cold and obtaining warmth, and one should desire whichever serves this purpose. If neither do, then one should desire whichever serves the purpose in an easier way. O dervish, the person who says, "I want new clothes and I do not want old clothes," is in chains. And the person who says "I want old clothes and I do not want new clothes," is also in chains. As long as they are in chains, there is no difference between them. Whether gold or iron, both are chains. The free person is one who has no chains of any type in any way, because chains are idols.[28]

Generally, Nasafī describes the root of all idols in the following way:

> O dervish, there is one big idol and the rest of the idols are small. These small idols derive from the big idol. For some people the big idol is fortune and for others it is fame while for still others it is being accepted by other people. Being accepted by other people is the biggest of all idols, and fame is bigger than fortune.[29]

Nasafī does not advocate the complete renunciation of everything; rather the renunciation of idols means becoming non-attached to everything to such an extent that makes life possible. One has to be practical in renunciation:

> Renunciation is the renunciation of trifling matters, not the renunciation of what is required. This is because too much fortune is unpleasant and obstructs the path. The renunciation of what is necessary is also unpleasant and also obstructs the path because man needs nourishment, clothing and a place to live to a degree that is necessary. If man renounces everything, he needs others and he becomes hungry and hunger is the mother of meanness. In the same way that too much fortune causes much corruption, so too does the renunciation of whatever is necessary. Whatever is necessary is a great blessing and whatever is not necessary is a great affliction. The amount of whatever is necessary is a blessing, but it becomes an affliction when that amount is exceeded.[30]

Renunciation is not an easy task, since one has to determine what is the necessary amount. This is one reason why Nasafī holds it advisable to practice renunciation with the help of someone who is spiritually more mature and advanced, that is, the Sufi shaykh.

> . . . renunciation must have the permission of the shaykh. You must renounce whatever he says, whether it pertains to this world or the next world, for nobody recognises his own idol and nobody sees himself as an idol worshipper. Everyone believes himself to be released and free and recognises himself as a Unitarian and idol-smasher. [31]

Renunciation and idol-smashing have results in two ways: that one may enter Heaven after the Day of Judgement and that one may enjoy a felicitous life in this world in close proximity to God.

(ii) Gnosis of God

Renunciation is a concept that is common in the esoteric dimension of all major religions, but the gnosis of God is perhaps a more particularised aspect in each belief. For Sufis, gnosis of God means seeing God in everything, for His creation reveals something about Him – if one has the ability to see correctly. His creation is all good, for it is impossible that God should create something evil. Nasafī explains:

> No attribute is bad, but some of these are used on an improper occasion, and it is said that the attribute is bad. There is nothing bad in the world. Everything in its right place is good, but the name of some things becomes bad when they are not in the right place. Therefore God Most High does not create anything bad, He has created everything as good.[32]

To take a specific example, force may be a good attribute if one needs to exercise physical strength to break a piece of wood, however, the same force of physical strength should be regarded in a negative light when it is used in robbery. The individual who manifests the right character trait at the right time has the gnosis of God, but the problem of course, is how one knows which character trait to reveal at any given moment.

(a) The simplest way to obtain gnosis of God is to realise that Heaven and Hell exist within the self and to act appropriately, for God is witnessed in Heaven.

> Know that someone asked a wise man, "Each person has a way and that way is called the way of salvation, and each person denies the way of the others. I am confused and I do not know where my salvation lies or what way will make me sorrowful." The wise man said, "Go and be a man of good conduct, since no evil befalls a man of good conduct in this world or the next world and the man of good conduct never regrets his actions." He asked the wise man, "What is good conduct?" The wise man said, "Don't do anything evil against anyone and do good with everyone, and do not wish evil against anyone but wish well for everyone, since the quality of a well-wisher and a good soul is that at first his own state and affairs prosper and the quality of a bad soul and an evil-wisher is that at first his own state and affairs deteriorate. So whoever does evil and wishes evil upon people, in truth does it against his own soul."
>
> O dervish! The bad-souled, evil wishing person has a state right now in Hell and burns in Hell and his heart is tormented. His fire and torture become more severe on the basis of other peoples' states and to the extent that other peoples' states improve.[33]

Thus the person who steals for no good reason, steals from himself, and the person who torments other people or even animals without purpose, in fact torments himself: "whatever evil visits you is from yourself."[34] The manifestation of such character traits at the improper time leads straight to Hell: "For them is chastisement in the present life; and the chastisement of the world to come is yet more grievous."[35]

(b) The second way is by following the laws that God has sent down to His community. The laws of Islam (the *Sharī'a*) are quite specific, ranging from issues on inheritance to those on marriage. However, Nasafī is aware that in some cases, the *Sharī'a* needs to be understood in an esoteric manner:

> The Unitarian says that recognising good and bad, and obedience *(ṭā'at)* and disobedience *(ma'ṣiyat)* is a great task and nobody understands them except the wise man and perfect ones.
>
> O dervish! All the religions and Islamic schools have agreed that telling lies is a great disobedience, and they have seen and spoken the truth, but there is a time when speaking the truth is a great disobedience and there is a time when lying is a great act of worship, so it is clear that understanding good and bad is a difficult task.
>
> O dervish! Actions according to intent may be good and they may be bad, so recognising the intent is a great task.[36]

So it is incumbent upon each individual to make an attempt to recognise the intent behind each person's action, but this does not mean that everyone can ignore the laws of the *Sharī'a* on the basis of their own esoteric interpretations of the Koran (however much the intent may be in the spirit of the *Sharī'a*). Indeed, having composed treatises on the esoteric nature of Islam, Nasafī concludes both *Maqṣad-i aqṣā* and *Manāzil al-sā'irīn* with warnings that the ultimate recourse of the Muslim must be to the *Sharī'a*:

> O dervish! In whatever station you are in, do not trust in your own intelligence and knowledge, and do not see or name yourself "Verifier of the Truth." Neither make a special way *(ṭarīqī)* for yourself nor establish a religious school *(madhhab)* through your own thought. In other words, you must be an imitator of your prophet *(payghambar)* in the knowledge and gnosis of any station that you are in, and do not neglect his *Sharī'a* . . .[37]
>
> Don't let your caution slip, in other words, don't neglect the *Sharī'a* because anyone who neglects it will certainly be sorrowful since "renunciation of caution and discretion is poor opinion."[38]
>
> Know that the wise men have said that man's expediency is to respect the claims of the Verifier of the Truth and not to step outside the bounds of imitation *(ḥadd-i taqlīd)* and admit one's own incapacity and ignorance and know for sure that one cannot know in reality God, as God really is, and one cannot recognise in reality things as they really are. When this was understood, the *Sharī'a* was, and is respected. The *Sharī'a* includes conforming to commands, abstaining from prohibited things, being abstinent, not neglecting one point in observing the *Sharī'a*, speaking truthfully and behaving correctly.

> Once the *Sharī'a* is respected, the wayfarer knows that the perfection of man is that he reaches the human level and becomes completely clean of blameworthy qualities and unpleasant character traits and he becomes adorned with laudable qualities and pleasant character traits.[39]

Esoteric interpretations of the *Sharī'a* are limited to those who have a great degree of spiritual understanding, such as the Sufi shaykh, which introduces the third step for attaining gnosis of God.

(c) The way of the scholars of Islam (through the study of the Koran and the *ḥadīth*) and the way of the Philosophers (through reason and intelligence) are regarded as a preliminary stage by the Sufis. They hold that there is a superior way to know God, which is surrendering to Him and building faith through performing acts of worship and devotion such as prayer, renunciation and other Sufi practices including the *dhik*, *chilla* (a period of forty day isolation for spiritual contemplation) and the recital of litanies. All of these activities must be performed under the guidance of the Sufi shaykh, if they are not, then they have no value because only the Sufi shaykh can recognise the significance of the effects and spiritual visions that may result from such practices.

The aim of these activities is to recognise the self, for man is the purpose of God's creation, since all of God's attributes and character traits can be witnessed through man. If he perfects himself and manifests the appropriate attribute at the right time, he is like a mirror for God. This is why many Sufis quoted the *ḥadīth*, "I [God] was a hidden treasure and I desired to be known," and "God created Adam in His own form." Adam, is of course, the archetype of all humans and therefore each person is made in God's image, having the potential to manifest all the character traits in the correct manner. From this perspective, one can understand why Nasafī states:

> O dervish, there is a sign for understanding the magnificence and greatness of man, and if you find that sign in yourself it is clear that you have understood what a man is. That sign is that hereafter you must search in yourself for whatever you are searching. If you are searching for God's essence and attributes, then search in yourself. If you are searching for the First Intelligence and the First Spirit (which is the Attributed Spirit) then search in yourself. If you are searching for Satan and the Devil, then search in yourself. If you are searching for the Resurrection and the Reckoning and the Straight Path then search in yourself. And if you are searching for the water of life then search in

yourself – pass the darkness of nature until you arrive at the water of life. O dervish! I say all of this and I know for sure that you do not understand what I am saying.

I travelled in search of Jamshid's world reflecting chalice
I did not rest during the day and I did not sleep at night.
I listened to the description of Jamshid's chalice from a wise man.
I was the world reflecting chalice![40]

The path to felicity, which is composed of renunciation and gnosis of God, is encapsulated by Nasafī to reflect a simple formula known to millions of Muslims: "There is no god, but God."

O dervish! Renunciation and gnosis of God is the testimony of Islam. The testimony of Islam is negation and affirmation. Negation is the renunciation of idols and affirmation is the gnosis of God. Fortune and fame are two great idols and they have lead astray and they lead astray many people. They are the deities of creatures and many creatures worship fortune and fame. You must have no doubt about the reality of this situation described in this discourse. Whoever has renounced fortune and fame and has cast aside love of this world from his heart has completed the negation and whoever has obtained the gnosis of God has completed the affirmation. This is the reality of "There is no god but God."[41]

The testimony of Islam has been the source of inspiration for Sufis throughout history. For Ibn 'Arabī, the testament of Islam could be formulated in the idea of "He/not He," which reflects the negation (there is no god) and affirmation (but God). In other words, everything in the world possesses existence, but this existence is limited in comparison to that of God. For example, man is limited in terms of the duration of his life and also in the talent he possesses, whereas God is eternal and knowing and powerful over everything. Thus, in some respects, man resembles God in that he can manifest the appropriate character traits but in other respects he cannot be compared with God, Whose essence is unknowable, that is He/ not He, or "there is no god, but God."

The public utterance of the testimony of Islam makes an adult a Muslim, but for Nasafī, however, being a real Muslim is not so easy:

Whoever has not carried out renunciation and does not have gnosis of God has never said the testimony of Islam.[42]

Nasafī own views are reflected in the discourses of the People of Unity:

> O dervish! The People of Unity say this in a better, more pleasant way. They say that the meaning of the testimony of Islam is negation and affirmation but the negation is not seeing the self and the affirmation is seeing God.[43]

In fact, this is a similar way of expressing Ibn 'Arabī's "He/not He." The incomparability *(tanzīh)* of the self with God is contrasted with the similarity *(tashbīh)* of the self with God. Real Muslims are able to witness the unity in these opposites and the reward of undertaking renunciation and having gnosis of God is the felicitous life, which for Sufis is a life here and now and also in the next world.

> The testimony of Islam, prayer, fasting have a form and a reality, and you have been uninformed of these realities and you have been content in the form. It is a great shame if you do not reach these realities. Renunciation and gnosis of God are like a tree, for the gnosis of God is the root of this tree and renunciation is the trunk. All the good attributes and pleasant character traits are the fruit of this tree. The root of this tree is the heart and the trunk is manifested from the heart. However much the root becomes stronger, the trunk also becomes stronger, until renunciation reaches a point where this world, the next world and the existence of the wayfarer are obliterated and God alone remains. O dervish! God alone always existed and God alone always exists, but the wayfarer was blind but he sees at the hour when he reaches the reality of the testimony of Islam.[44]

II. THE SUFI PATH

(i) The Order *(ṭarīqa)*

By the thirteenth century, Sufism developed within a range of different orders *(ṭarīqa)* which were brotherhoods of Sufis having a common spiritual "family tree." This spiritual ancestry *(silsila)* was traced back through various shaykhs to the Prophet Muḥammad. According to Sufi tradition, at Muḥammad's death, the spiritual virtue *(baraka)* was passed on to his successors (many orders cite 'Alī b. Abī Ṭālib as the first link in the *silsila*). With the growth in the number of shaykhs possessing *baraka*, the *silsilas* often became complex and in addition, the growth in the numbers of shaykhs who initiated disciples into Sufism resulted in a differentiation among the orders in ascetic disciplines and spiritual practices by which one could come close to God (such as the silent *dhikr* and the vocal *dhikr*).

The extent to which Nasafī was affiliated to a Sufi order is unclear. Although he claims in his works that he served under Sa'd al-Dīn Ḥammūya, there is no letter of *ijāza*[45] which would indicate that Ḥammūya was indeed Nasafī's shaykh. In fact, Nasafī's "formal" connections to a Sufi order has been questioned to the extent that he has been called a "free-thinker."[46] Although it is clear that Sa'd al-Dīn Ḥammūya was initiated into Najm al-Dīn Kubrā's circle of Sufis which came to be known as the Kubrāwiyya order, in his later life it seems that Ḥammūya was "poorly received" by other Kubrāwī Sufis, which may have been a result of his "heterodox" Sufism and his close association with Ibn 'Arabī and his Damascene circle.[47] If Ḥammūya was not completely integrated into the Kubrāwiyya circle then it is possible that Nasafī may also have been on the fringe of this order. From this perspective, the passages in Nasafī's texts which are severely critical of Sufism make more sense.[48] So the real situation concerning Nasafī's affiliation with the Kubrāwiyya is not clear, but presented on the next two pages are two possible *silsilas*[49] which link Nasafī with Muḥammad.

One reason which supports the belief that Nasafī was affiliated with the Kubrāwiyya order is the fact there are many similarities in the basic beliefs held by both Nasafī and also the order as a whole. This order was greatly inspired by the teachings of Junayd of Baghdad (d. 910), and there are several references within Najm al-Dīn Kubrā's *Fawā'iḥ al-jamāl wa fawātiḥ al-jalāl* to Junayd.[50] Junayd listed eight principles which he considered essential in the Sufi path. These were purity, silence of the tongue, seclusion and avoidance of people, fasting, continual *dhikr*, negation of thoughts, inclination for the association of pure people (such as the shaykh), and finally contentment with God's command. Najm al-Dīn Kubrā offered the same eight principles adding two of his own: the renunciation of sleep and observing the Sufi rules concerning consumption of food and drink.[51] Nasafī also lists ten actions of the "People of the Path," which reflect the influence of Junayd and Najm al-Dīn Kubrā. The ten are: the search for God, the search for a wise man (shaykh), desire for the shaykh, obeying the commands of the shaykh, renunciation, God-fearingness, speaking little, sleeping little, eating little and seclusion.[52]

Distinctions have been made by Sufis themselves and also western scholars between the "sober" and "drunken" forms of Sufism. This is particularly the case with reference to Junayd's form of Sufism,[53] since he is known to have been critical of Bāyazīd Basṭāmī's descriptions of

I.

'Azīz al-Dīn Nasafī

Sa'd al-Dīn Ḥammūya, d. 1252

Ṣadr al-Dīn Abū'l Ḥammūya, d. 1220

'Imad al-Dīn 'Umar b. Ḥammūya, d. 1181

Mu'īn al-Dīn Abū 'Abdallāh Muḥammad ibn Hammūya d. 1135

Abū 'Alī al-Faḍl al-Fārmadhī, d. 1084 — Khiḏr

Abū'l Qāsim al-Gurgānī, d. 1076 — The Prophet

Abū 'Uthmān Sa'īd al-Maghribī, d. 984

Abū 'Amr M. b. Ibrāhīm al-Zajjāji, d. 992 (or 959)

Al-Junayd ibn Muḥammad, d. 910

Sarī al-Saqaṭī, d. 867

Ma'rūf al-Karkhī, d. 815

Mūsā al-Riḍā (Eighth Imam), d. 818 — Dāwūd al-Ṭā'ī, d. 781

Shī'-ite Imāms — Ḥabīb al-'Ajamī, d. 737

Ḥasan al-Baṣrī, 643–728

'Alī b. Abī Ṭalib

The Prophet

mystical experience. Nasafī also regarded the "sober" form of Sufism as a higher stage than the drunken form. The latter, which is characterised by the ecstatic comments such as "I am the Truth," or "Glory be to Me how great is My majesty," is necessary although it does not represent the ultimate degree of spirituality:

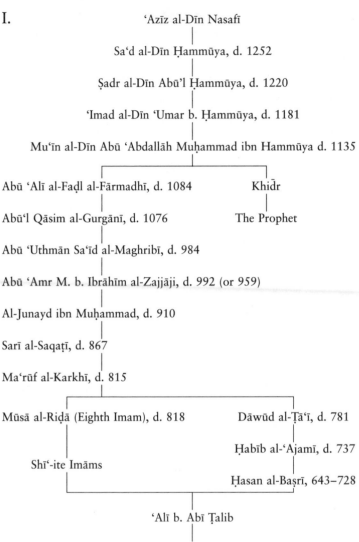

II.

'Azīz al-Dīn Nasafī

Sa'd al-Dīn Ḥammūya

Najm al-Dīn Kubrā

'Ammār Bidlīsī | Ismā'īl al-Qaṣrī

Abū Najīb al-Suhrawardī

Aḥmad al-Ghazālī

Abū Bakr al-Nassāj

Abū'l Qāsim al-Gurgānī

Iraqian Tradition

Junayd

Shī'ite Imāms

> When they return from the ascent, some wayfarers are sober and some are drunk because they have tasted from cups full to the brim of pure wine and their wine bearer was their God. For this reason, those who are weaker do not look after their manifest dimension and they behave drunkenly and they neglect the manifest dimension of the Holy Law.[54]
>
> And whoever has become a lover and manifests his love remains dirty and does not become clean because that fire which entered by means of his eyes has left by means of his tongue, and the heart remains only half burnt. Thereafter, the heart can do nothing, neither a task of this world nor a task of the next world nor a task of the Lord.[55]

In *Bayān-i tanzīl*, Nasafī remarks that drunkenness is at the beginning and middle of the station of unity with God, and the wayfarer cannot but make such ecstatic utterances. However, sobriety is at the very end of the station and is the more mature relation between man and God.[56] When Nasafī makes critical remarks about Sufism, he is not complaining about those Sufis who are drunk, for they cannot help their state, rather he is condemning those who use Sufism and make claims to advance themselves.

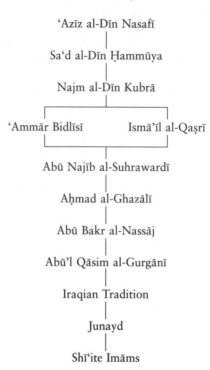

Aside from being a "sober" order, the Kubrāwiyya also became known for its psycho-analysis of light colour in mystical visions. The details of such phenomena were described by Najm al-Dīn Kubrā and also by 'Alā' al-Dawla Simnānī.[57] In Nasafī's works, there is no such exegesis of colours, indeed, one is struck by the dryness of Nasafī's treatises when compared with the poetic and imaginal nature of Najm al-Dīn Kubrā's *Fawā'iḥ*. (Of course, one has to remember that the objectives of the two were different; Nasafī was concerned with explaining the beliefs of the *'Ulamā'*, Philosophers, Transmigrationists and Sufis, while Kubrā was detailing his own visionary experiences).

Nasafī's links with "institutionalised" Sufism certainly go as far as believing in the necessity of the shaykh and performing the Sufi devotional practices under his guidance. Spiritual wayfaring is impossible without these two, and therefore the remainder of this chapter will investigate in more detail Nasafī's explanation of the shaykh and devotional practices.

(ii) The Sufi Shaykh

The importance of the Sufi shaykh in actualising gnosis of God is paramount in Nasafī's theosophy. The difference between the shaykh and the wayfarer is that the former has already completed the spiritual wayfaring and thus possesses the spiritual blessing *(baraka)*[58] from his own shaykh. *Baraka* is the blessing bestowed by God upon the individual, and since Muḥammad is thought to have received God's blessing, so too others believed that Muḥammad passed on this *baraka* to those around him who were worthy of it. The initiation into Sufism and the transmission of *baraka* was not bestowed upon everyone because the gnosis of Sufism could not be understood by all members of the community, and the beliefs and ecstatic utterances *(shaṭḥiyyāt)* could easily be mis-interpreted by the common people and also the *'Ulamā'*. Therefore, the novices were bound to the commands of the shaykh by an oath of loyalty *(bay'a)*, and they were not supposed to divulge these secrets to the uninitiated or unsympathetic.

> The tradition of the beloved ones [i.e. the shaykhs] was that the community which enjoyed association with them saw its protection in whoever had preparedness, did not divulge secrets and preserved dignity. They surrendered to him [the shaykh] for protection and declared that they would not betray this protection but keep it secret from those who were not of the community.[59]

In addition, if the Sufi shaykh was accused of deviating from Islam, he was able to defend the "orthodoxy" of his beliefs and practices by referring to his *baraka* and the *silsila* as the ultimate authority (since it had been passed down to him from Muḥammad via his own shaykh). To repeat, it is through *baraka* that one comes close to God. In some cases, the *baraka* was received not from the living shaykh of a particular order, but from the spirit of an Islamic mystic who had died many years previously. This was the case of a Khwājagānī Shaykh, 'Abd al-Khāliq Ghujdawānī (d. 1220), who was initiated into Sufism by the spirit of Abū Ya'qūb Yūsuf Hamadānī (d. 1140).

The shaykh possessing *baraka* was one of the most important components in Nasafī's theosophy. In a typical comment, Nasafī explains:

> Know that association has strong effects and great qualities, in evil and good. The reason that any wayfarer arrives at the destination and achieves his aim is because he has association with a wise man. The reason that the wayfarer does not arrive at the destination and does not achieve his aim is because he has not had such association. The task [of Sufism] requires association with a wise man. All the ascetic discipline and spiritual effort and the rules of courtesy and conditions which have been set in the Sufi path *(rāh-i taṣawwuf)* are so that the wayfarer becomes worthy of the association with a wise man. When the wayfarer becomes worthy of association with a wise man his task is complete.[60]
>
> O dervish, if a wayfarer has association with a wise man for one day, even one hour, and he is prepared *(musta'ad)* and worthy of this association, this is better than being engaged in a hundred years or a thousand years of ascetic discipline and spiritual effort.[61]

Finding a suitable Sufi shaykh was not an easy task because by the thirteenth century, Sufism had become so popular in the Islamic world that there were many "shaykhs," and some of them had reached this spiritual position in society without truly deserving it. Nasafī refers to this several times:

> People must have great caution at the beginning and not become the disciple of any person even if they are good and sound, since shaykh-hood and leadership and the taking of disciples is a different task. I myself do not speak the discourses of those people who are the People of Idle Talk. O dervish, I have seen many who have claimed such things for themselves and they make claims of shaykh-hood and they have made shaykh-hood a trap of fortune and fame. God preserve everyone from the association of such people.[62]
>
> O dervish, my intention of this wise man or searcher of the Truth is not these inactive religious scholars *('Ulamā')* and not these impure

shaykhs. These religious scholars and shaykhs are a thousand times more imitating, lost and further from God Most High than you are. Despite this remoteness from God, they regard themselves as near to Him, and as a result of extreme ignorance and darkness, they regard themselves as wise men, and they see themselves as existing with light. Each time they read the verse: "It is like the depths of darkness in a vast deep ocean, overwhelmed with billow, topped by dark clouds, depths of darkness, one above the other,"[63] they apply these words to the Chinese and Indians but never to themselves.[64]

Nasafī describes the difficulty of finding a suitable shaykh:

O dervish, you will not find this wise man or this Verifier of the Truth in mosques, preaching from the *minbar* or reciting *dhikr*. You will not find him in the religious schools giving lessons, and you will not find him among the people of high office among the bookish people or among the idol worshippers. You will not find him in the Sufi *Khānaqāh* prostrating himself with the People of Imagination and self-worshippers. Out of these three places for worshipping God, there may be one person out of a thousand working for the sake of God. O dervish, the wise man and Verifier of the Truth and the men of God are hidden and this hiddenness is their guardian, their club, their fortress, their weapon. [This hiddenness] is the reason why they are clean and pure. He that is not hidden is a plot and a trick of Satan. O dervish, their exterior is like the exterior of the common people and their interior is like the interior of the élite. They do not give access to any leader or chief and they have no claim to be leader or leaders. Each one is busy with something or someone according to his need and they earn their own living through their own business, fleeing from the wealth of kings and tyrants. They do not seek anything in excess and if something falls to them without effort or exertion which they do not need, they give it away. They spend most of their time in retreat and seclusion, and they do not enjoy interaction with this world, and they are opposed to company with the lords of high position. If it is useful, they spend their time in association with the dear ones and the dervishes.[65]

The kind of wise man that Nasafī would have approved of can be ascertained by the references that he makes to other mystics in his works. These include Ibn 'Arabī, Ṣadr al Dīn Qūnawī, Shaykh Shihāb al-Dīn 'Umār Suhrawardī,[66] Abū Ḥāmid Ghazālī[67] and 'Ayn al-Quḍāt Hamadānī.[68] Presumably the shaykhs of the Kubrāwiyya order were also held in high esteem, such as Najm al-Dīn Kubrā, Najm al-Dīn Rāzī and Sa'd al-Dīn Ḥammūya.

Nasafī describes the ideal shaykh with reference to the views of Shaykh Shihāb al-Dīn Suhrawardī:

. . . know that when one man is overtaken by the Truth's divine attraction *(jadhb)* and that person arrives at the level of love in the love of God, it is more likely that he will not return from that level but will live and die there. Such a person is called the object of divine attraction *(majdhūb)*. There are some people who return and they are aware of themselves and they are called the divinely attracted wayfarers *(majdhūb sālik)* if they engage in wayfaring and complete the wayfaring. If a person performs the spiritual wayfaring first of all and completes it and then the divine attraction of the Truth overcomes him, such a person is called a wayfarer of divine attraction. If a person performs the spiritual wayfaring and completes it, but the divine attraction does not overtake him, then such a person is called a wayfarer *(sālik)*. So there are four kinds; the divinely attracted one, the divinely attracted wayfarer, the wayfarer of divine attraction and the wayfarer.

Shaykh Shihāb al-Dīn Suhrawardī said in his *'Awārif al-ma'ārif* that there should be one group of shaykhs and leaders among these four and they are the divinely attracted wayfarers, and the others should not be shaykhs or leaders.[69]

The reason that the *majdhūb* is not considered as a suitable shaykh is because he cannot be held responsible for his words or actions in the state of being overtaken by divine attraction. Such ecstatic utterances not only aroused the opposition of the *'Ulamā'* but also could not be understood by novices who wished to follow the Sufi path. Thus it is necessary that the shaykh is someone who has both traversed the path and can recognise the different stations and states and understand all the pitfalls and dangers, and has also received divine grace.

It has already been mentioned that it was not easy for novices to identify "legitimate" Sufi shaykhs and therefore Nasafī describes four qualities that are found in a genuine shaykh.

The first is that they [the Shaykhs] are pious and forbear and they keep the customs and traditions and ways, and they are very careful in nourishment, clothes and place of living. They keep their distance from dubious property, bequests and taxes, the property of kings, the property of the followers of titles and tyrants . . . Accepting what is legal and having caution in nourishment and clothing and places to live has many good qualities which people do not know except for the Perfect Ones. And accepting what is illegal and not having caution in nourishment and clothing and places to live has many bad qualities which people do not know except for the Perfect Ones.

The second is that they flee from fortune and fame; they do not like these two since they are the cause of all sin. The indication of the person who has renounced fortune is that he has none, and he does not accept it even if it is given to him. He is not arrogant with anyone, but is humble and he does not associate or sit with the People of Titles and the People of this World.

The third is that they never speak of their soul's purification or make claims of themselves. That is, they do not speak about their own obedience to God and their own purity. They do not describe their own sacrifices and munificence, but they talk about their own faults and deficiencies, and the perfection and states of others. They speak of injustices that they themselves have caused and of the justices caused by others.

The fourth is that they do not speak too much, and they do not speak of that matter which is not asked of them. They give brief answers to questions. If in truth they do not know that matter then they say, "I do not know," and they do not answer in a dubious and inexact way.

So every person who trains people should have these four internal indications in him and many people will benefit from association with him. It is unlawful for the person who does not have these four indications to train people since association with him will harm them, and he may cause innumerable faults in them.[70]

Once the appropriate shaykh has been found, it is incumbent upon the novice to persuade the shaykh of his genuine desire to follow the Sufi path.

When you have found one [a shaykh], pay attention and serve him and regard him dearly, and see association with him as the cause of all your blessings and surrender to him. You should empty your existence of your ego and your opinion, and you should fill your non-manifest dimension with him and his will and his love, even if he distances you from himself and drives you away. He cannot endure social interaction and association with everyone. Be inseparable from him and try to be in such a way that he cannot refuse you. When you have been accepted, you have found the correct path and you have become one of the Saved People *(ahl-i najāt)*.[71]

Having been accepted by the shaykh, the Sufi novice commences a commitment to wayfaring *(sulūk)*. There are six essential conditions for wayfaring,[72] all of which are connected with the relationship between the novice and the shaykh. These conditions are as follows:

i. The novice must find a shaykh.
ii. During the course of his life he must not love anyone as much as he loves the shaykh.
iii. The novice must obey all of the shaykh's commands.
iv. All the thoughts and opinions that the novice has must be rejected.

v. On the basis of the two previous points, the novice must never complain or deny the shaykh. This is because the novice cannot recognise what is good or bad or what is obedience or disobedience. Therefore the simplest policy for the wayfarer is to carry out all the shaykh's commands without complaint or denial. This is the case even if it means doing certain things which appear to contradict the *Sharī'a:*

> . . . [the wayfarer should not] act on the basis of his own opinion or idea, even if it is the obligatory prayer *(namāz-ī farẓ)*, [and he should not act] without the command of the guide *(hādī)* since whatever the wayfarer does on the basis of his own opinion is the cause of his remoteness, and whatever he does according to the command of the guide is the cause of his nearness.[73]

Not all Sufis would have agreed on this point, that is, that the shaykh may cause the wayfarer to temporarily refrain from following the *Sharī'a* (as in not performing the obligatory prayers). However, the genuine shaykh always has a valid reason for doing this, and he himself continually follows the manifest (and non-manifest) dimensions of the *Sharī'a*, for the first quality of the genuine shaykh is that he "keeps the customs and traditions and ways."

vi. The novice must remain constant upon the path.

This commitment and surrender by the wayfarer to the shaykh has two conditions:

> The first condition is that the disciple, in the association of his shaykh, is just like the community in the association of its prophet[74]; and the second condition is that the shaykh speaks with the disciple in accordance with his station.[75]

The ideal period to commence this commitment to the shaykh is at the age of twenty. Nasafī comments that the first twenty years of man's life is the period when his body becomes mature, and in the next twenty years his spirit becomes mature.[76] This ascetic discipline and spiritual effort under the shaykh continues for twenty years:

> In these twenty years, [the wayfarer] must never be relaxed and without religious effort for an instant . . . O dervish! A person who is accounted as one of the People of the Holy Law does not waste his life if he serves a perfect teacher for twenty years which is the time for wayfaring. [If he does this] then there will be no knowledge pertaining to the manifest dimension that is unknown to him. [Likewise] a person who is accounted as one of the People of the Way does not waste his life

> if he has the association of a perfect shaykh for twenty years which is the time for wayfaring. If he does this, no knowledge of the real knowledge will remain unknown to him.
>
> The unfortunate person and dweller of Hell is he who is accounted as one of the People of the Holy Law and has been busy in these twenty years – which is the time for wayfaring – in the position of judgement or teaching. The appropriate way for a person to be engaged in the position of judgement or teaching is to remain in the service of a perfect shaykh for twenty years. It is also appropriate if such a person then becomes engaged in shaykh-hood or being a preacher. If he renounces all of this after forty years despite these titles, he is perfect.[77]

Although the period of religious effort and spiritual discipline is limited to twenty years, the association with a wise man lasts for a life time:

> The dervishes must never be without religious effort and ascetic discipline until they are forty years of age, and when the fortieth year has passed they must not perform religious effort and ascetic discipline in an excessive way, but they must not be without it until they become sixty years old. When the sixtieth year passes, they must not perform much religious effort and ascetic discipline. After the sixtieth year they must continue with association, the People of the Heart cannot live without association.[78]

(iii) Devotional Practices

From this point, Nasafī proceeds to describe the customs *(adab)* of wayfaring, the striking feature of which is the predominance of prayer in the everyday life of the wayfarer:

> Know that the first custom of wayfaring is continually being ceremonially pure, and each time that ablutions are made, two cycles of prayer of thanks are performed. After the first cycle, after the opening chapter of the Koran, [the wayfarer] must read, "If one does a sinful thing or wrongs himself in any way and afterwards implores Allah's forgiveness, he will find God Forgiving and Compassionate."[79] At the second cycle, [the wayfarer] must read: "Those who commit an indecency or wrong themselves but remember God and pray forgiveness for their sins – and who shall forgive sins but God? – and do not persevere in the things they did and that wittingly, their recompense is forgiveness from their Lord."[80]
>
> The second custom is to divide the times of day and night. That is, [the wayfarer] should establish a fixed litany *(wird)* for each particular time of day so that his life is not wasted; a litany for worship, a litany for food and a litany for sleep.

The third custom is the prayer repeated during the night *(namāz-i tahajjud)*. That is, in the second half of the night, [the wayfarer] must perform twelve cycles of the "*witr*" prayers (voluntary prayers). Some, after reading the opening verse of the Koran at the end of the *namāz-i tahajjud* recite this verse: "And as for the night, keep vigil a part of it, as a work of supererogation for thee; it may be that thy Lord will raise thee up to a laudable station."[81] Others, at the end of the *namāz-i tahajjud*, after the opening verse of the Koran, recite the *sura* "We have sent down,"[82] and some read from "By the sky and the nightly-visitant,"[83] to the end of the Koran in the *namāz-i tahajjud*.

The fourth custom is the mid morning prayer *(namāz-i chāsht)*. That is, each day at sun rise, [the wayfarer] must perform two cycles for the sunrise prayers *(namāz-i ishrāq)* and at mid morning he must perform twelve cycles for the *namāz-i chāshtgāh*.

The fifth custom is the prayer of the penitents *(namāz-i awwābīn)*. That is, [the wayfarer] must perform twelve cycles between the evening prayer and the prayers before sleeping.

The sixth custom is continual *dhikr*.

The seventh custom is recognising thoughts *(khāṭir)*. That is, there are four kinds of thought; merciful *(raḥmānī)*, angelic *(malakī)*, egoistic *(nafsānī)*, and satanic *(shayṭānī)* and there is an indication for each one.[84]

The eighth custom is reading something from the discourses of the shaykh.

The ninth custom is accepting service in the *khānaqāh*.

The tenth custom is sitting everyday for a period in the association of dervishes and listening to their discourses.

The eleventh custom is the declaration of incidents *(mājarā)*. That is, if a dervish tells a discourse or does something that vexes another dervish, the vexed dervish must not keep it in his heart but explain the incident in a kind way before all the dervishes and the dervish who has caused the incident.

The twelfth custom is religious effort and ascetic discipline.[85]

Thus the Sufi's wayfaring is based upon devotion to God and not a moment passes when he is engaged in a task which does not involve him thinking about God. Half of the above customs (if one considers *dhikr* as a form of prayer) are established upon prayer, the frequency of which conditions the wayfarer's life towards complete devotion. Indeed, prayer is portrayed as consisting of half of wayfaring *(sulūk)* in another work:

O dear friend! the reality of wayfaring is two steps; proceeding from veils and reaching stations. A veil is whatever [the wayfarer] has to remove from himself and a station is whatever he has to actualise for himself. So whoever has been completely cleansed of blameworthy attributes and unpleasant character traits has passed all the veils; and

> whoever becomes completely described by praiseworthy attributes and pleasant character traits has reached all the stations. Whoever has passed the veils has produced purity and whoever has reached all the levels has performed prayers, since the reality of purity is distinction *(faṣl)* and the reality of prayers is connection *(waṣl)*.[86]

This description of prayer in terms of connection *(waṣl)*, that is, connection with God, is important to note because it reflects the Sufi belief that it is through prayer that the wayfarer witnesses God. What the *mi'rāj* was for the Prophet Muḥammad, so too, the prayer is for the wayfarer.

With regards to prayer, the Islamic mystics of Nasafī's era believed that there were particular times when its effects (such as the possibility of experiencing a mystical vision or witnessing God) were very strong. Nasafī himself comments:

> When the sun rises, the prayers of dawn are recited twice and when the prayers of dawn have been performed, a time is reserved for the complete recital of the morning prayers until the sun rises high. And then once it has risen, [the wayfarer] performs the mid-morning prayer twelve times. When this is completed he may become occupied with whatever he wishes. So from the start of the morning until this point, not one word concerning this world has been spoken and he has not left the place of prayer. The Sufis hold this time very dear because many divine graces have been found during this period.[87]

Such careful attention to the details and times of prayer, as has already been shown, has a basis in the Koran. Muḥammad directed his community concerning the time of prayer in the following way, "Perform the prayer at the sinking of the sun to the darkening of the night and the recital of dawn; surely the recital of dawn is witnessed."[88] In the following verse, prayer during the night is advocated: "And as for the night, keep vigil a part of it, as a work of supererogation for thee; it may be that thy Lord will raise thee up to a laudable station."[89] The Sufi orders complied in these commands, and some zealous orders went to extremes in performing them. For example, the Sufis of the *Shadhiliyya* order used to drink coffee to keep themselves awake during their litanies and vigils.[90] By the thirteenth century, the Sufis believed that they had discovered the reason why the night and early morning were set aside by Muḥammad for prayer. It was considered that during these times, man's five external senses were incapacitated and did not work so efficiently. The Sufis held that while man's senses were incapacitated, the "internal senses" had a better chance to perceive what the external senses blocked. This included the possibility of witnessing God. Hence, Nasafī's exhortation that after service to a wise man, there is nothing better than eating little, speaking little and sleeping little becomes clear[91] for this is considered as one of the ways to incapacitate the external senses.

Other practices which are associated with prayer include the *dhikr* (which was discussed in the previous chapter). Nasafī's descriptions of the different forms of performing the *dhikr* have been noted by M.I. Waley, so it is not necessary to repeat them here.[92]

(iv) Contemplative Discipline, the Mastering of One's Soul and Other Sufi Practices

There are other Sufi practices which cannot be classified as devotional because they are concerned with the individual's examination of his own thoughts and actions. For example, "contemplative vigilance" *(murāqaba)* is the attention paid by the Sufi to all his thoughts and actions, including the *dhikr*, to ensure that he is concerned only with God.[93] Vigilance over thoughts *(khawāṭir)* is a major element in contemplative practices and Nasafī describes four kinds of thought of which the Sufi must be able to distinguish; divine *(raḥmānī)*, angelic *(malakī)*, egotistical *(nafsānī)* and satanic *(shayṭānī)*.[94]

Special attention is paid to the *khāṭir* when the wayfarer undergoes a period of seclusion *(chilla)*[95] during which time he also engages in prayer, *dhik* and *fikr*. Recognition of the *khawāṭir* is necessary because they are an indication of the position the wayfarer has made on the path, and frequently they can give an indication of his spiritual station and also if any obstacles remain in the way. Nasafī mentions that during the *chilla*, it is necessary to negate the *khawāṭir*, even those of a divine nature. If a *khāṭir* does arise and it cannot be put aside, then it is necessary for the wayfarer to present it to the shaykh, who can explain it in order that it does not obstruct the wayfarer's path.[96]

The *chilla* is instrumental in mastering the wayfarer's soul or spirit, ideally leading to human perfection. For a period of forty days the wayfarer is engaged in devotional and ascetic practices, adhering to his shaykh's rules. One of these rules as described by Nasafī is the implementation of a strict diet:

> O dear friend! It is necessary that the wayfarer eats once every day, any time which is better and more suitable for him. It is [also] necessary

> that on that particular occasion, he eats "pure" food *(ṭa'ām-i laṭīf)*. The quantity of food differs for each wayfarer; he must eat an amount that does not make him full, because being too full is not pleasant, yet he must not become a slave to eating an extremely small amount which may cause his strength to fail, for this is not pleasant either.[97]
>
> One shaykh may give an amount of food each night of less than fifty *dirham*, and another may give more. Our shaykh ordered a loaf of bread worth forty *dirham*, a piece of meat worth forty *dirham* and a bowl of stew *(āb-i gūsht)*. I suffered if I did not eat, and now it is clear that he was right . . . some ate forty mouthfuls during the first night [of the *chilla*] and they ate one mouthful less each night so that they ate only one mouthful by the last night. Others ate one *man* [about three kilograms] during the whole *chilla* and [some] ate the equivalent of seven *dirham* each night. Others did not eat meat at all during the whole period of the *chilla*.[98] Our shaykh said that all of this was unimportant because performing [the *chilla*] is [more] important. The meaning of decreasing food and how much each person eats pertains to the shaykh.[99]

Thus Nasafī advocates the middle way between excessive fasting and excessive eating in order to control the *nafs*. Some Sufis prior to Nasafī are said to have starved to death whereas others are known to have enjoyed lavish spreads.[100] The importance that Sufis attached to eating the proper food in correct amounts can be seen in the comment by 'Alā' al-Dawla Simnānī that "the mystics advancement on the path is four sixths worship of God through observing the [lawful nature] of the morsel, one sixth recollection [dhikr], and one sixth following the guidance of the master."[101] In addition to offering advice to dervishes concerning the quantity of food to be eaten during the *chilla*, Nasafī also gives instructions on how the wayfarer should behave when he participates in the communal meals of the *khānaqāh*:

> The dervishes must be present and sit politely at meals and they must not eat anything greedily. They must respect the elders and not sit above them, nor should they start eating before them. Moreover, they must not look at anyone else's plate, rather, they should look at their own. They should eat in small morsels, chewing well, and they may take another morsel after swallowing the first. If it happens that the dervishes eat from one dish, then each dervish must eat from the part facing him and not stretch across the other dervishes. If something falls from his hand, he must pick it up with his left hand and not put it in his mouth, but place it to one side. The dervish must not refuse food in front of the other dervishes. If they do not want food then they must keep themselves busy. Before starting the meal, the dervish must wash his hands, and he must wash his hands and mouth when the meal is over.[102]

The foregoing passage is significant because it reveals the importance of the communal nature of Nasafī's Sufism (not to mention the concern for selfless behaviour and purity). This attention to communal Sufism is highlighted in Nasafī's discussion of disputes among the dervishes:

> If a dervish makes a remark or does something which causes the others to suffer, the [dervish] who has been made to suffer must not keep the problem in his heart. He must disclose tactfully whatever has taken place to the dervish who has caused the suffering, before the other dervishes. If he has a clear answer, in such a way that it is accepted by the other dervishes, then he explains until the problem is solved for the [accusing] dervish. If he has no clear answer, then he should not draw out the explanation but he should quickly apologise and beg forgiveness. He should rise up and go to wherever the shoes are stored and stand there with his hands placed together with his head hung low until the accusing dervish rises and the other dervishes arise in unison with him. Then the two dervishes embrace and become happy. Then all the others in accord with the two dervishes embrace one another and they sit down again.[103]

It is clear from such comments that Nasafī was intimately involved in life within the *khānaqāh*. In other words, he was not merely a speculative Sufi, but he was also actively engaged in the practice of Sufism in the company of other Sufis. Of course, this does not prove his affiliation to the Kubrāwiyya order, but it does appear to be the case that Nasafī was genuine in stating that one should first go the *madrasa* and then go to the *khānaqāh*.

One of the activities that took place within the confines of the *khānaqāh* and which became a major point of controversy within the Islamic community, was the *samā'*. The *samā'* is "sacred music and dance" in which the individual opens himself "to an influence, to a vibration of suprahuman origin 'made sound' in order to awaken in us the echoes of a primordial state and to arouse in the heart a longing for union with its own Essence."[104] Both the philosophers within the Islamic world and Sufis had noticed the effects that music had upon the mood of the human soul. Nasafī underlines this idea in the following passages:

> All humans share in a feeling of release from hearing singing voices *(aṣwāt)* and melodies *(alḥān)* but some not only feel released [but] pleasant singing voices and melodies cause unveiling in some and cause sadness in others. Because of this, one person [has] asked, "What are the effects of *samā'*?" It is said that it depends upon the listener because pleasant singing voices and melodies are like raindrops and the listeners

> are like plants, or we say that singing voices and melodies are like sunlight and the listeners are like minerals, and although in truth, the sunlight is one thing, it reveals something in each mine.[105]
>
> If a dervish weakens in religious effort or ascetic discipline, or if there is an illness in his mind, he must quickly become busy in curing it, arranging for suitable oils, pure food and temperate air. A cure that can help him is a pleasant voice. One of the dervishes who has a pleasant and sad *(hazīn)* voice should occasionally sing for him. If it does not cause trouble for anyone, and if the dervishes are weary, that weariness is eased away by one of the dervishes singing something at an expedient time and at an agreed place where there are no common people present. It is permissible if he sings along with a tambourine. There are some wayfarers for whom states are produced during the *samāʿ* and innumerable benefits and openings come to them from those states. It is expedient for such people to engage in *samāʿ* if the time, place and brothers are all appropriate.[106]

Some jurists, such as Ibn Abi'l Dunyā (d. 894) condemned singing and music since they held that it stimulated the "soul inciting to evil." The Sufis themselves had mixed feelings towards the *samāʿ* because it acted upon both the sensual and spiritual. The Naqshbandiyya order forbade participation in the *samāʿ* since they saw its dangers were stronger than its benefits.[107] Other Sufis, including Saʿd al-Dīn Ḥammūya deemed it permissible[108] and Abū Ḥafṣ Suhrawardī recognised that the matter depended upon the individual.

> Music does not give rise, in the heart, to anything which is not already there: so he whose inner self is attached to anything else than God is stirred by music to sensual desire, but the one who is inwardly attached to the love of God is moved, by hearing music, to do his will.[109]

For this reason, participation in the *samāʿ* requires the permission of the shaykh who understands the true nature of each of the dervishes. The shaykh is able to determine which individuals are suitable to participate and those who are not able to appreciate the spiritual nature of the *samāʿ*. By Nasafī's era, it appears that the *samāʿ* had degenerated somewhat, or at least, the ecstatic states of the Sufis (during which clothes were rent and dancing breast to breast was known to occur)[110] had been misinterpreted by the common people. Nasafī is cautious about the Sufis engaging in *samāʿ* when the common people are present and he gives this warning:

> O dervish! It is the custom of these times that the élite and common people sit together and perform the *samāʿ*, but this is neither the dervish

> way, nor the tradition of the shaykhs. It is one of the customs and habits of the common people. The shaykhs have said that the dervishes must not go to this *samā'*. According to this helpless one, the People of Discernment should not be present in this *samā'* because learned people do not do childish things. Playing is the pastime of children.
>
> O dervish! The dervish must certainly keep the *samā'* for the appropriate time, place and brothers so that it is in line with the tradition of the shaykhs.[111]

Nasafī also gives guidelines for how one should behave during the performance of the *samā'*, such as whether or not one should stand up and whether it is permissible to remove one's turban, and these instructions are the very same as those offered by Abū Ḥāmid al-Ghazālī.[112]

The speculative and practical form of Sufism that Nasafī advocates places the wayfarer in the middle ground, for he does not encourage excessive ascetic disciplines and religious effort, nor does he permit free licence to the self:

> Don't be a slave to [either] too much prayer and fasting or to excessive pilgrimage *(ḥajj)*, but perform God's ordinances *(fariẓa)* accordingly. Don't be a slave to either remembering too many words or story telling. And don't be a slave to understanding much wisdom but be satisfied with the required amount.[113]

By following this path, the wayfarer will find that gradually the self (that he once knew) is transformed. The "dropping off" of concerns pertaining to the body and mind is an unveiling which reveals the real self beyond the ego. God may even reward the wayfarer by bestowing a *ḥāl* upon him, and it may be the case that he realises the unity between himself and his Lord. This, the ultimate mystical experience is the subject of the next chapter.

Notes

1 Koran, 10: 65.
2 See L. Massignon, art. "Taṣawwuf," *Encyclopaedia of Islam* (Leiden: E.J. Brill).
3 The full *shahāda* is "There is no god but God and Muḥammad is the messenger of God."
4 *Maqṣad-i aqṣā*, p. 266
5 See Margaret Smith, *Rābi'a the Mystic* (Cambridge: Cambridge University Press, 1928).
6 Ibid, p. 30.

7 This description is found in al-Ghazālī, *Mishkāt al-anwār*, translated Gairdner, pp. 60–61.
8 The *shaṭḥ* of Bāyazīd Basṭāmī (d.ca. 845).
9 The *shaṭḥ* of Husayn Ibn Manṣūr al Ḥallāj (d. 922).
10 In *Maqṣad-i aqṣā*, p. 277, Nasafī attributes this *shaṭḥ* to Abū Bakr al-Shiblī (d. 945).
11 In *Maqṣad-i aqṣā*, p. 277, Nasafī attributes this *shaṭḥ* to Abū'l-'Abbās Qaṣṣāb.
12 *Bayān-i tanzīl*, fol. 7a line 3 – 7b line 6.
13 See Chittick, *Faith and Practice*, p. 13–14.
14 *Kashf al-ḥaqā'iq*, p. 202.
15 *al-Insān al-kāmil*, p. 290–291.
16 Koran, 19: 71.
17 The *Tubba'* tree occurs in sura 44: 37.
The *Zaqqum* tree is described in sura 37: 62–66. "We have appointed it as a trial for the evildoers. It is a tree that comes forth in the root of Hell; it spathes are as the heads of Satans, and they eat of it and of it fill their bellies, then on top of it they have a brew of boiling water, then their return is unto Hell."
18 *Kashf al-ḥaqā'iq*, p. 180–181. The imagery of the tree is also found in the Koran: "A good word is as a good tree – its roots are firm, and its branches are in heaven. It gives its produce every season by the leaves of its Lord. So God strikes similitudes for men, haply they will remember. And the likeness of a corrupt word is a corrupt tree – uprooted from the earth, having no establishment. God confirms those who believe with the firm word, in the present life and in the world to come." (Koran, 14: 30)
19 *Kashf al-ḥaqā'iq*, p. 105.
20 Nasafī, *Kitāb-i tanzīl*, fol. 71b line 18 – fol. 72a line 6.
21 For an account of the Mongol invasion and the atrocities they committed see 'Alā al-Dīn 'Ata al-Malik Juwainī, *History of the World Conqueror*, trans, J.A. Boyle. See also chapter 1.
22 *al-Insān al-kāmil*, p. 193.
23 *Maqṣad-i aqṣā*, p. 228.
24 *Kashf al-ḥaqā'iq*, p. 104–105.
25 *Maqṣad-i aqṣā*, p. 222.
26 Ibid.
27 *Manāzil al-sā'īrīn*, p. 331.
28 *al-Insān al-kāmil*, p. 138.
29 Ibid.
30 *Maqṣad-i aqṣā*, p. 223.
31 Ibid, p. 223.
32 *al-Insān al-kāmil*, p. 48.
33 *Kashf al-ḥaqā'iq*, p. 203–204.
34 Koran, 4: 79.
35 Koran, 13: 35.
36 *Maqṣad-i aqṣā*, p. 251.
37 *Manāzil al-sā'īrīn*, p. 455.
38 Ibid, p. 455–6.
39 *Maqṣad-i aqṣā*, p. 285–86.

40 Ibid, p. 282. The poem is attributed to Shaykh Rūzbihān Baqlī (1128–1209), see M. Hillman's comments in M. Boylan's *Hafez: Dance of Life* (Washington: Mage Publications, 1987), p. 102.
41 Ibid, p. 224.
42 *Maqṣad-i aqṣā*, p. 224.
43 Ibid, p. 224–225.
44 Ibid, p. 225.
45 "*Ijāza-nāma*" (literally, letter of permission) was given by a Sufi master to a disciple which in effect was the disciple's certificate to teach the gnostic wisdom that he had learnt under the guidance of the Shaykh. The "*ijāza-nāma*" given to Sa'd al-Dīn Ḥammūya by Najm al-Dīn Kubrā exists to this day in the Suleymaniye Library in Istanbul. See J.J. Elias, "The Sufi Lords of Bahrabad: Sa'd al-Dīn and Ṣadr al-Dīn Ḥamuwayi," *Iranian Studies*, volume 27, numbers 1–4, 1994, p. 55–56.
46 Professor H. Landolt delivered a lecture in September 1995 at the third European Conference of Iranian Studies at Cambridge University entitled "A free-thinker among the Sufis: the case of 'Azīz-i Nasafī."
47 See J.J. Elias, "The Sufi Lords of Bahrabad," p. 73.
48 For example, there are explicit criticisms of some of the so-called Sufi Shaykhs in the introduction to *Kashf al-ḥaqā'iq*, in a discussion concerning the wise man. It is said that one will not find him in the *khānaqāh*, prostrating himself with the People of Imagination and self-worshippers. (*Kashf al-ḥaqā'iq*, p. 28).
49 These *silsilas* are based on those in J.S. Trimingham's *The Sufi Orders in Islam* (Oxford: Oxford University Press, 1971). See pages 262 and 31. See also H. Landolt's comments on Ḥammūya's *silsila*, "Sa'd al-Dīn Ḥammū'ī," *Encyclopedia of Islam* (second edition, 1995), vol. VIII, p. 703.
50 Najm al-Dīn Kubrā, ed. F. Meier, *Fawā'iḥ al-jamāl wa fawātiḥ al-jalāl*, ed. F. Meier (Wiesbaden: Steiner, 1957), 6, 80, 93, 109, 127, 148.
51 Najm al-Dīn Kubrā, *al-Sā'īr al-ḥā'īr* (Tehran: Naqsh-i jahān, 1361).
52 *Maqṣad-i aqṣā*, p. 215.
53 See J. Baldick's comments in *Mystical Islam* (London: I.B. Taurus, 1989), p. 45–46.
54 *al-Insān al-kāmil*, p. 109.
55 Ibid, p. 118.
56 *Bayān-i tanzīl*, fol. 7a line 3 – 7b line 6.
57 See Najm al-Dīn Kubrā, *Fawā'iḥ al-jamāl wa fawātiḥ al-jalāl*, and J.J. Elias's "A Kubrāwī treatise on mystical visions: the Risāla-yi Nūriyya of 'Alā ad-Dawleh as-Simnānī," *The Muslim World*, 83 no. 1, January 1993.
58 See G.S. Colin, art. "Baraka," *Encyclopedia of Islam*[2].
59 *Kashf al-ḥaqā'iq*, p. 9.
60 *Maqṣad-i aqṣā*, p. 220–221.
61 Ibid, p. 221.
62 Ibid, p. 226–7.
63 Koran, 24: 40.
64 *Kashf al-ḥaqā'iq*, p. 28.
65 Ibid, p. 28–29.

66 Suhrawardī's *'Awārif al-ma'ārif* is also mentioned by name in *Maqṣad-i aqṣā*, p. 226.
67 Nasafī cites Ghazālī in *Kashf al-ḥaqā'iq*, p. 125.
68 Nasafī cites 'Ayn al-Quḍāt in *Kashf al-ḥaqā'iq*, p. 114.
69 *Maqṣad-i aqṣā*, p, 226.
70 *Kashf al-ḥaqā'iq*, p. 129.
71 Ibid, p. 27–28.
72 *al-Insān al-kāmil*, p. 95.
73 *Kitāb-i tanzīl*, fol. 73b, lines 17–19.
74 This reflects the *ḥadīth*, frequently quoted by Sufis, that "The Shaykh in his group is like a Prophet in his people." See Furūzānfar, no. 224.
75 *Kitāb-i tanzīl*, fol. 77b, lines 1–3.
76 Ibid, fol. 75a, lines 3–5.
77 *Kashf al-ḥaqā'iq*, p. 130.
78 *al-Insān al-kāmil*, p. 129.
79 Koran, 4: 110.
80 Koran, 3: 135. (A slightly adapted version of Arberry's translation).
81 Koran, 17: 79.
82 Koran, 97: 1.
83 Koran, 86: 1.
84 The indications of thoughts are discussed in note 94 below.
85 *Kashf al-ḥaqā'iq*, p. 132–133.
86 *Kitāb-i tanzīl*, fol. 74a, lines 9–14.
87 *al-Insān al-kāmil*, p. 121.
88 Koran, 17:78.
89 Koran, 17:79.
90 A. Schimmel, *Mystical Dimensions of Islam*, p. 254.
91 *al-Insān al-kāmil*, p. 129.
92 M. I. Waley, "Najm al-Dīn Kubrā and the Central Asian School of Sufism," *Islamic Spirituality II*, ed. S.H. Nasr (New York: Crossroad, 1991).
93 See M.I. Waley, "Contemplative Disciplines in Early Persian Sufism," in *Classical Persian Sufism*, ed. L. Lewisohn, pp. 535–38.
94 *Kashf al-ḥaqā'iq*, p. 133, see also *al-Insān al-kāmil*, p. 105. The indications of these thoughts were described by other Sufis such as Qushayrī (d. 1074) and Najm al-Dīn Kubrā. For Qushayrī see M. Sells, *Early Islamic Mysticism* (New York: Paulist Press, 1996), pp. 142–145. Najm al-Dīn Kubrā described these thoughts in *al Sā'īr al-Ḥā'īr*, edited by Mas'ūd Qāsimī (Tehran: Naqsh-i jahān, 1361), p. 35–37, and also in *Fawā'iḥ al-jamāl wa fawātiḥ al jalāl*, [25].
95 For Nasafī on *chilla*, see *Kashf al-ḥaqā'iq*, p. 134–35.
96 *Kashf al-ḥaqā'iq*, p. 135.
97 *Kitāb-i tanzīl*, fol. 74b, lines 14–17.
98 This was the position advocated by Shihāb al-Dīn al-Suhrawardī *(al-maqtūl)*. In his *Ḥikmat al-ishrāq* he states, "Before beginning [to read] this book, one should engage in ascetic practices for forty days and refrain from eating meat." (Persian translation by S.J. Sajjādī, Tehran University Press, 1978, p. 403). One may also refer to Sahl al-Tustarī who commanded that his disciples did not eat meat except on Fridays so

as to regain strength for worship (see Böwering, *The Mystical Vision of Existence in Classical Islam*, p. 78).

99 *Kashf al-ḥaqā'iq*, pp. 134–35.

100 See Schimmel, *Mystical Dimensions of Islam*, pp. 115–17.

101 J.J. Elias, "A Kubrawi Treatise on Mystical Visions," *The Muslim World*, Vol. 83, No.1 (1993), p. 76.

102 *al-Insān al-kāmil*, p. 128.

103 *al-Insān al-kāmil*, p. 125.

104 J.L. Michon, "Sacred Music and Dance in Islam," *Islamic Spirituality: Manifestations*, ed. S.H. Nasr, pp. 474–475.

105 *Bayān-i tanzīl*, fol. 16a lines 9–13.

106 *al-Insān al-kāmil*, p. 126.

107 A. Schimmel, *Mystical Dimensions of Islam*, p. 180.

108 Sa'd al-Dīn Ḥammūya composed the following:

When the heart attends the spiritual concert (samā'), it perceives the Beloved
And lifts the soul to the abode of the divine mysteries.
The melody is the steed of thy soul; it raises it up
And takes it joyful to the world of the Friend.

Cited by S.H. Nasr, "The Influence of Sufism on Traditional Persian Music," *Studies in Comparative Religion*, 1972, Vol. 6, no. 4, p. 227.

109 M. Smith, *Readings from the Mystics of Islam* (London: 1950).

110 See Schimmel, *Mystical Dimensions of Islam*, p. 181.

111 *al-Insān al-kāmil*, p. 126–27.

112 See Abū Ḥāmid al-Ghazālī's section on *samā'* in *Kīmīyā-yi sa'ādat*, edited Husayn Khadīwjam (Tehran: Markaz-i intishārāt-i 'ilmī wa farhangī, 1361/1983), in particular pp. 497–8.

113 *Zubdāt al-ḥaqā'iq*, p. 116–117.

5

Visionary Experience and Unity with God

I. TYPES OF VISIONS AND MYSTICAL EXPERIENCE

The aim of Sufism is felicity and the greatest felicity for Sufis is witnessing God. By Nasafī's era, the wayfarer followed the Sufi path and engaged in practices such as *dhik, fikr, chilla* and *samā'* along with other devotional acts which were means to the end, that is, they were tools for polishing the mirror of his heart. For the Sufi, a transparent heart could reflect the knowledge of the spiritual world and thus he could come close to God. As he progressed along the path and achieved a greater degree of proximity to God, he discovered "imaginal" signs and indications manifested in his heart. These signs matched his experiences or states, thus the manifestation of an inner sign without the inner experience or feeling was interpreted as a hallucination, thus signs were witnesses of what the wayfarer was.[1] Frequently appearing in the form of coloured lights, or *photisms*, the imaginal signs were discussed by the Sufis of the Kubrāwiyya order, such as Najm al-Dīn Kubrā, Najm al-Dīn Rāzī and 'Alā' al-Dawla Simnānī.[2] The visions of these Sufis were remarkably similar in that each one portrayed a seven-fold hierarchy of photisms, however, the ranking of colours (which symbolised a particular spiritual level) differed for each of the three mystics. The seven-fold hierarchy represented the seven heavens referred to in the Koran[3] and it was these seven heavens that Muḥammad had to pass to reach God during his "night ascent."[4] Likewise, the Sufi had to traverse seven levels of being until he was able to encounter his Lord.

Nasafī does not discuss photisms or a seven-fold hierarchy, however, he does describe various kinds of visions and spiritual occurrences that the wayfarer may experience. In this chapter, the different mystical visions and experiences included in Nasafī's works will be presented, revealing his acceptance of all beliefs as genuine expressions of reality. This is followed by an examination of how Nasafī regarded the ultimate spiritual station and vision of God, and this is compared with the explanations of Najm al-Dīn Kubrā and Ibn 'Arabī, thus enabling us to see if Nasafī's version of Sufism was representative of the age.

(i) The Journey to God Represented Through Symbols

The works of thirteenth century masters such as Najm al-Dīn Rāzī and 'Azīz Nasafī depict the spiritual ascent through images of the stars, moon and sun. It is not surprising that mystics witness such images because these are symbols which occur in the Koran, and Sufis spend many hours in contemplation of the esoteric meanings of verses in which these symbols appear. For example, Nasafī refers to the sixth *sura* of the Koran which concerns the Prophet Abraham, to explain the reality of the hierarchy of spiritual existents:

> . . .there are three angels in *Malakūt* which are the leaders of angels and they are called the Great Angels. Of these three, one is in such a way that the body of existents comes from him, and this Great Angel has four rows of angels, each row having several thousand angels which are busy in obedience and submission to God. These are the terrestrial angels, so each particle of earth has an angel with it. Abraham's first glance was upon this Great Angel and this is the meaning of: "When the night covered him over, he saw a star, he said 'This is my Lord,' but when it set he said, 'I love not those that set.'"[5]
>
> Of these three angels, one is bigger than the first angel, and the life of the existents comes from it. And this angel has nine rows of angels, and in each row there are several thousand angels and they are occupied in obedience and submission to God and all these angels are equal. Abraham's second glance fell upon this Great Angel: "When he saw the moon rising in splendour he said, 'This is my Lord,' but when he saw the moon set he said, 'Unless the Lord guide me, I shall be among those who go astray.'"[6]
>
> There is another Great Angel which is bigger than these two, and this Great Angel has ten rows of angels and in each row there are several thousand angels each yearning for God Most High and Holy and they are absorbed in the Lord of creatures, and this Great Angel is not informed about the earth or heaven. Abraham's third glance fell upon him, and this is the meaning of: "When he saw the sun rising in splendour he said, 'This is my Lord, this is the greatest of all.' But when the sun set he said, 'O my people! I am indeed free from your guilt of giving partners to God.'"[7] This angel guided Abraham to the Lord of creatures so that he was liberated from association of others with God, and when he attained the world of unity he said, "For me, I have set my

face firmly and truly towards Him who created the heavens and earth, and I shall never give partners to God."[8]

The reason that Abraham's glance fell upon *Malakūt* is set out in the verse, "So also did we show Abraham the power and the laws of the heaven and earth that he might have certitude."[9]

Half a century prior to Nasafī, Najm al-Dīn Rāzī portrayed a similar account of Abraham's mystical encounters and he related these visions to the mystic's ascent and the condition of his heart. His exegesis of visions of the sun, moon and stars matches the ontological hierarchy of *Jabarūt*, *Malakūt* and *Mulk* that Nasafī so often describes.

As for those lights that are seen in the form of heavenly bodies, – stars, moons and suns – they derive from the lights of spirituality that appear in the sky of the heart, in accordance with its degree of purity. When the mirror of the heart becomes as pure as a star, the light of the spirit becomes apparent to the amount of a star . . . it sometimes happens that the soul attains such purity that it appears to be like the sky, and the heart is seen in it like the moon. If the full moon is seen, the heart has become completely pure; if it is less than full, a degree of impurity remains in the heart. When the mirror of the heart attains perfect purity and begins receiving light of the spirit, that light will be witnessed in the likeness of the sun. The brightness of the sun is in proportion to the degree of the heart's purity, until a point is reached at which the heart is a thousand times brighter than the external sun. If the moon and the sun are witnessed together, then the moon is the heart, illuminated with the reflection of the light of the spirit, and the sun is the spirit.[10]

(ii) Visions of the Next World

Visions of the sun, moon and stars are not the only form of "imaginalisation," for Nasafī describes another type of vision which enables the mystic to witness the state of the spirit after natural death:

Observing the states after death is a great task for the wayfarer. People are ignorant about this reality, if they were not, surely they would make an effort and endeavour in order for these states after death to be revealed to them, so that they could witness the station which they will return to after separation from the body.[11]

Know that the ascent for Sufis means that the spirit of the wayfarer leaves the body in a healthy and wakeful state. And the state that will be revealed to [the wayfarer] after separation from the body is now revealed to him before death. He surveys Heaven and Hell and he arrives at the level of the eye of certainty from the level of knowledge of certainty, and he sees whatever he has understood.[12]

Our Shaykh stated, "My spirit spent thirteen days in the heavens and then returned to my body. And during those thirteen days my body was like that of a dead man and had no concern for anything. Others who were present said that my body had been in such a way for thirteen days." And another dear one stated, "My spirit remained there for twenty days and then came back to the body." And another dear one said, "My spirit spent forty days and then returned to the body." He remembered everything that he saw in those forty days.[13]

(iii) Encounters with Spirits, Future Events and Dreams

Once the heart has become mirror-like, it is able to reflect knowledge that has come from the spiritual world, an example of this includes communication with the spirits of dead people, such as the Friends. Nasafī describes the process of pilgrimage to tombs:

> If [the wayfarer] pays a pilgrimage to the tomb of a Friend, and requests help from the spirit of the Friend, it will be obtained. The manner of paying pilgrimage and praying is in this way; he must walk around the tomb and concentrate, freeing his mind from everything, thus making the mirror of the heart clean and pure so that his spirit can encounter the deceased through the grave. Then, if the wayfarer desires knowledge or wisdom, the solution to [his] problem will be manifested on his heart in that very hour. If he has the receptivity for discovering it and if his request is for help and assistance, not only will his important affairs be resolved sufficiently, but the approval of the prayer will also be manifested in his other affairs after the pilgrimage. This is because the spirit of the deceased has favour with God and that spirit asks that the important affairs of the wayfarer are resolved in a sufficient manner. If the deceased spirit has not found favour near God but has favour near God's esteemed ones, he asks of them that God resolves the important affairs sufficiently.[14]

In addition to this, the mirror of the heart can reflect images about the states of living people and the states of future events:

> There are some people who can tell the names of whoever they see or whoever they have not seen. Moreover, they can tell the names of that person's parents and kinsmen and tribe even though they are not informed of those peoples' past and present circumstances.[15]
>
> There are some people who see in their sleep the occurrence of a thing even before it has taken place in this world. Other people witness the occurrence of a thing even before it has taken place while they are awake. There are several types [of vision]: either a form becomes illustrated outside of the mind and describes a past or future circumstance, or a picture appears upon their heart. This is the reality

of revelation *(waḥī)*, inspiration *(ilhām)*, a thought *(khāṭir)* and intuition *(firāsat)*.[16]

The witnessing of visions, as mentioned earlier depends upon dulling the five external senses, and this occurs naturally for most people during sleep.

> . . .the invisible world has levels and from level to level there are many differences, and the non-manifest dimension of the wayfarer also has levels and from level to level there are many differences. The first level [of the non-manifest dimension of the wayfarer] can extract from the first level [of the invisible world] and the last level [of the non-manifest dimension of the wayfarer] can extract from the last level [of the invisible world]. The knowledge and insight of the wayfarer are also obtained in this way, and veridical dreaming *(khwāb-i rāst)* is one example of this. Ecstasy *(wajd)*, spiritual occurrences *(wārid)*, inspiration *(ilhām)* and divine knowledge *('ilm-i ladunnī)* are expressions for this reality. This reality does not pertain to infidelity *(kufr)* or Islam. Each person who makes his heart clear will find these effects and such meanings are discovered in the dreams of many people, but occurs less in wakefulness because the senses are incapacitated in dreams. And the obstructions which are produced by means of the senses and by means of anger and appetites, are lessened. For this reason, the non-manifest dimension [of the wayfarer], at that hour, is able to acquire knowledge from that world. So isolation and seclusion, the wayfarer's ascetic discipline and spiritual effort are for the sake that during wakefulness, his body can be like that of the person who is asleep, perhaps cleaner and purer.[17]
>
> When the senses are incapacitated by means of sleep, at that time the heart finds suitability with the heavenly angels in the same way as two clear mirrors which are opposite one another. The reflection of the angel's knowledge will appear on the heart of the sleeper . . . This dream can be interpreted and explained. And this is the meaning of veridical dream, and this dream is one part of the forty-six parts of prophecy.[18]

It is interesting to note in the foregoing passage that Nasafī admits that making the heart mirror-like is not confined to Muslims, thus the opportunity of witnessing visions and having mystical experiences such as communicating with the spirits of the living and the dead is open to non-Muslims:

> O dervish, this manifestation of reflections does not depend on unbelief *(kufr)* or belief *(islām)*, it depends upon a heart which is plain and without colouring. This manifestation of reflections appears in the complete and the incomplete and in the pious and in the lewd person.[19]

Moreover, this form of knowledge is not confined to humans:

> And apart from wayfarers there also exists a people whose hearts have been made plain and are not tarnished, and it is also manifested upon their hearts. And some say it is even manifested for animals. Some of the animals inform people before the arrival of each calamity or fortuity which comes to this world. Some people understand and some do not understand.[20]

Najm al-Dīn Rāzī also indicates that non-Muslims can witness mystical visions, yet he stipulates that they cannot reach the same degree of gnosis that Muslims enjoy. Indeed he classifies visions into two varieties; the first is the mystical vision of the spirit, and the second is the mystical vision when God reveals himself to the mystic in the form in which the mystic can comprehend Him as the Real God.[21]

(iv) The Different Levels of Mystical Experience as Manifested Through Visions

The distinction that Najm al-Dīn Rāzī draws between two forms of mysticism enables him to discount non-Muslims, for they cannot see the "lights of the attribute of unity" and therefore cannot transcend the human state. The reason that Rāzī gives for the inability of followers of other religions (Hindus, Christians and Philosophers) to reach the ultimate stage is because their practices are deficient. For example, the "extreme mortification of the soul" can only lead to a certain degree of unveiling, and they cannot know whether or not they have been lead astray in their journey by their own ego since they do not see the necessity of having a shaykh.[22]

Nasafī also divides mystical experience into two different kinds:

> O dervish, life, knowledge, desire, power, hearing, seeing and speech are the attributes of the First Intelligence, and creation, giving life and instruction are the actions of the First Intelligence. No one except for God knows the greatness and splendour of the First Intelligence. Many great men among the eminent shaykhs have arrived at this First Intelligence and have been obstructed by it because they have seen its attributes and actions, and have not seen anything greater than its decree or found anything above its command: "When He decrees a thing He need only say 'Be,' and it is."[23] They believed that perhaps it was God, and they worshipped it for a while until the favour of the Truth Most High came to them and they saw a decree greater than that of the First Intelligence and a command above that [of the First Intelligence] "And Our command is but one, as the twinkling of an

> eye."[24] At that time it became clear for them that it was God's caliph, it was not God, but it was the locus of manifestation of God's attributes and actions.[25]

In the foregoing quotation, the first realisation of the shaykhs is the unity of existence seen in the First Intelligence (that is, *Jabarūt*). The superior realisation is the unity of existence which stretches from man to the level of God beyond the First Intelligence which is the level of *Aḥadiyya*. In the Sufi tradition, this level transcends man's experiences and therefore it can only be considered theoretically.

With this perspective in mind, we can now return to the question of whether non-Muslims can enjoy the same range of mystical experience as Muslims. As we have seen, Najm al-Dīn Rāzī denies this possibility, and although Nasafī does not say so explicitly, it seems that he does not share the same opinion. This is revealed by his discussion of the discourse of the Indians *(ahl-i hind)* which describes human perfection in exactly the same way as the discourses of the Muslims, which draws inspiration from the Light verse of the Koran.[26]

> . . . understanding this discourse is very important, for the ascetic disciplines and spiritual effort of the Indians are included as the foundation of this discourse. In other words, this discourse is extremely good and many problems are resolved by understanding it.[27]
>
> The world is made of two things, light and darkness, in other words, a sea of light and a sea of darkness. These two seas are mixed together and it is necessary to separate the light from the darkness in order for the attributes of light to be manifested. Indeed, this light can be separated from the darkness within a given creature, because there are workers in the creature's body . . . The alchemy that man performs is that he takes the "soul" of whatever he eats; in other words, he takes the select and quintessence of food. In this way, light is separated from darkness in such a way that light knows and sees itself as it is. Only the Perfect Man can do this.[28]
>
> O dervish! It is not possible to completely separate this light from darkness because light cannot exist without darkness . . . Light must be with darkness just as a lamp in a niche, so that its attributes may be witnessed. When the light ascends in levels and each one of the workers completes its task, so that the light reaches the brain, it is like a lamp in a niche. The reality of man is the lamp.[29]
>
> When this lamp becomes strong and pure, the knowledge and wisdom which is hidden in its essence becomes more apparent.
>
> O dervish! From beginning to end, this discourse has been an explanation of the journey of the Indians.[30]

So non-Muslims can also witness God by following their own divine laws and engaging in spiritual exercises. This conclusion reflects

Nasafī discussion concerning man's perfection and its relationship with the "four times", for each of the four moments carry the specific qualities of the heavens and stars which determine the characteristics of each individual. It is possible for the "four times" to bring the same qualities to one person in each climate, whereby individuals outside of the *Dār al-Islām* (the Islamic world) can attain perfection.

Nasafī was not the first Sufi to believe that non-Muslims could witness God. For example, Shihāb al-Dīn Suhrawardī *(al-maqtūl)* explained that divine wisdom or mystical intuition manifested itself in pre-Islamic sages. According to Suhrawardī, two chains of divine wisdom were united in himself: the first of these came from Hermes and was passed on through the Greek sages including Empedocles, Pythagoras, Plato and Aristotle; the second chain commenced with Zoroaster and was then given to Iranian sages such as Jāmāsf, Farshāwashtar and Buzurgmihr.[31]

This ecumenical position in Sufism accords with verses in the Koran which express tolerance towards other religions: "To each among you We have prescribed a Law and an open way. If God had so willed He would have made you a single people but His plan is to test you in what He hath given you; so strive as in a race in all virtues. The goal of you all is God. It is He Who will show you the truth of the matters in which ye dispute."[32]

The Kubrāwī exegesis of visions played an important part in the development of *'irfān* during the twelfth and thirteenth centuries in Iran and Central Asia. There are two reasons which may explain the formulation of the particular techniques and methodologies in the Sufi orders. Firstly, it was a reaction to the popularity that Sufism enjoyed during this period, and secondly it was a way to recognise the correct spiritual station of Sufis, some of whom mistakenly thought that they had reached the ultimate station and whose "Ḥallājian" *shaṭḥiyyāt* incurred the wrath of the *'Ulamā'*.

The great appeal of Sufism was indeed a problem because it resulted in lay people desiring a "popular" form of Islamic mysticism which in reality obscured the essence of Sufism. Indeed, Nasafī himself was opposed to such a "vulgarization" of Sufism as his comments concerning the Sufis and the common people sitting together for *samā'* (see previous chapter) indicate. His concern about the popularisation of Sufism is mirrored in Trimingham's observation that "the practical goal of Sufism for the majority came to be the attainment of ecstasy *(wajd = faqd al-iḥsās)*, 'loss of consciousness.' This is not the *wajd* (encounter with God) of the Sufis; it was in fact a degeneration which the early masters of Sufism had perceived and warned against when dealing with the question of *samāʿ*." For the masses, ". . .loss of consciousness is regarded as 'union,' an emotional identification of seeker and sought. To some this experience became a drug for which soul and body craved. For the ordinary lay member, participation in the ritual of *dhikr*, which for him occasionally leads to the trance-ecstasy, provides at lowest a release from the hardships of everyday existence, and, at a higher level, some measure of freedom from the limitations of human life and a glimpse at transcendental experience."[33] Nasafī hinted at this problem outlined by Trimingham:

> And "inviting ecstasy" *(tawājud)* is an expression for a person who is not an ecstatic but [for a person] who makes himself resemble an ecstatic *(wājidat)*, since inviting ecstasy is the same as feigning illness.[34]

II. THE VISION OF GOD

In the previous section, it was shown that a correct interpretation of the wayfarer's visions reveals his proximity to God, thus the stars, moon and sun represent *Mulk*, *Malakūt* and *Jabarūt*. *Jabarūt* is the level of God's knowledge of things, and this level is the wayfarer's ultimate aim because at this station he understands that there exists a higher level still. This is God's essence which was called *Aḥadiyya* by Farghānī and termed "the invisible, invisible, invisible world," by Nasafī. In chapter two, the Sufi idea of reaching God's essence was discussed and it was established that attaining the essence is only a metaphor because man can witness nothing other than God's face. In this section, the reasons behind this are re-investigated by concentrating upon Nasafī's views concerning the ultimate spiritual station, and in addition, his beliefs are also compared with those of Najm al-Dīn Kubrā and Ibn 'Arabī to show the "orthodoxy" of his position within the Sufi world.

Most Sufis held that it was impossible for any individual to reach and know God's essence, yet the author of *Kashf al-ṣirāṭ* (who may have been Nasafī)[35] describes the views of two groups of Sufis who differ on this issue. According to the author of *Kashf al-ṣirāṭ*, one group of Sufis believe it is not possible to know God's essence:

> Know that each person has an interpretation *(taʿwīl)* for the *ḥadīth*: "Whoever knows himself knows his Lord," and also for the *ḥadīth*: "God created Adam upon His own form." Some, including Ḥujjat al-Islām Shaykh Shihāb al-Dīn Suhrawardī, 'Ayn al-Quḍāt and Shaykh Yūsuf Hamadānī hold that it is not possible for men, Prophets and

> Friends to know in truth God Most High just as God Most High is. They say that the interpretation of the *ḥadīth:* "Whosoever knows himself knows his Lord," is that it is not possible for anyone to know the self as the self really is because one cannot recognise the Truth Most High as the Truth Most High is. So the knowledge of the Truth is actualised from the knowledge of the self according to this mode. Likewise you should also understand the interpretation of the *ḥadīth:* "God created Adam upon His own form." It is not possible to recognise both in reality. In addition, it has been said that the world of man is the conceptualisation of the form of a thing and it conforms to the known *(ma'lūm)* in the mind *(dhihn)*. So it is necessary that the known is seen *(mubṣar)* or heard *(musma')* by this person, or its conceptualisation is possible. If such a thing is not the object of sensory perception *(maḥsūs)* it is necessary that there is no genus *(jins)* or similarity *(mānand)* for it. So how is it possible to conceptualise a thing for which there is no like *(mithl)*, genus or species *(naw')* and is not the object of sense perception? It is not possible to conceptualise the Real One *(aḥd-i ḥaqīqī)*. So knowledge of the reality of His essence is not possible. There is no path for intelligence to the reality of His essence but there is a path for intelligence to His existence and attributes through signs and indications. His excellency the Messenger said: "Think about God and not the essence of God," and he also said, "The person who speaks of God's essence is foolish."[36]

The other group of Sufis claim that it is possible to go beyond this stage and reach God's essence:

> Others, including Shaykh of Shaykhs Sa'd al-Dīn Ḥammūya, Ibn 'Arabī, Ibn Sab'īn and Imām Aḥmad Ghazālī – may God sanctify their spirits – hold that is possible for man to know in reality the Truth Most High just as the Truth Most High is, by the servant's becoming wise *(dānā)* of the Truth. They say that Muḥammad's knowledge of the Truth was just as the Truth Most High's knowledge of the Truth Most High. They also say that no one recognises himself just as the self is except Muḥammad. So the meaning of this *ḥadīth* [He who knows himself knows his Lord] is obvious *(ẓāhir)* according to them, for the person who recognises himself just as the self is, recognises the Truth Most High just as the Truth is.
>
> So you have understood the meaning of the [foregoing] *ḥadīth* and you have understood the meaning of the *ḥadīth* that "God created Adam upon His own form," in other words, upon the form of instruction *(ṣurat-i ta'līm)* or the form of free disposal in the world *(ṣurat-i taṣarruf fī 'ālam)* or in a form transcendent of direction. Some have said that the meaning of this *ḥadīth* is obviously clear and people have fallen into error as a result of this clarity. The meaning of this *ḥadīth* is that whoever recognises himself recognises his Lord because there is no more than one existence. The Unitarian *(muwaḥḥid)* is the

> person who understands and sees one thing and if he sees or knows two things he is an associator of others with God *(mushrik)*. So on the basis of this thinking that existence is one, whoever recognises himself also recognises his Lord.[37]

The beliefs of the second group of Sufis do not follow the "orthodox" interpretation of Sufism where man witnesses God's face in everything but cannot reach His essence. In works aside from *Kashf al-ṣirāṭ*, Nasafī explains the highest spiritual station as the level where man sees God's essence as it is manifested through His infinite faces. This station is the subject of the following section.

Variegation *(talwīn)*, Stability *(tamkīn)* and Creative Power *(takwīn)*

Nasafī's standpoint regarding the highest spiritual station in relation to attributes is representative of Sufism in the thirteenth century, although the terminology that individual Sufis employed to describe this underlying reality differed. As stated above, Nasafī uses the word stability *(tamkīn)* to denotate the pinnacle of spiritual achievement:

> When [the wayfarer] ceases reflection and inspiration presents itself, and inspiration becomes dominant over him, he passes from the world of intelligence and reaches the world of love. When he ceases from inspiration and witnessing presents itself, he passes from the world of love and reaches the station of stability *(maqām-i tamkīn)* and in [the station] of stability, he becomes attributed with whatever attribute he desires.
>
> So at first the *dhikr* is dominant over the wayfarer, then reflection is dominant, then inspiration and then witnessing, and finally he reaches the station of stability, and he becomes pure from any variegation. In other words, at first the attributes of the wayfarer become dominant over his existence and each day, perhaps each hour, an attribute becomes dominant over him. But when the wayfarer passes from the station of variegation *(talwīn)* and reaches the station of stability, his existence becomes dominant over his attributes, and the indication of the station of stability is that he can actualise whatever station or attribute that he desires, that is, he can choose, and all attributes are his property. If he desires he engages in the *dhikr*, and if he wants he can be busy in reflection, if he doesn't want he does not engage himself in the *dhikr* or reflection, he has made himself ready for inspiration so that he can be informed of past and future events. In other words, the mirror of his heart has been polished from the illuminations of both worlds, so that the reflection of whatever occurs or will occur in this world will become apparent upon his heart. If he wishes he can put the past and future to one side and enjoy his moment.

> As long as the wayfarer is in the station of variegation, sometimes grace *(fayḍ)* is dominant over him, and sometimes expansion *(basṭ)* and sometimes the word *(kalām)* is dominant over him; sometimes silence and sometimes familiar talk *(ikhtilāṭ)* is dominant over him; sometimes seclusion *('uzlat)* and sometimes anger *(qahr)* and sometimes kindness *(luṭf)* is dominant over him. All of these come regardless of the wayfarer's desire but when he reaches the station of stability, they all come at his desire. Through his words and actions, he is a doctor and cure for peoples' states, and he is a king with regard to his own state because he can be any way that he desires.
>
> O dervish! Until the wayfarer reaches the station of stability he is not free from slavery and has not reached freedom. The People of Heaven are kings because while they were in the station of variegation, they were slaves to their appetites and their attributes were anger and incapacity, but when they arrived at stability, they became kings over their appetites and the master over wrath and the lord of all their attributes.[38]

For Nasafī, the wayfarer in the station of stability is similar to God; just as God can create anything that He desires and manifest whatever He desires, so too can the perfect wayfarer be a master of his self and "create" or display whatever attribute he desires. In this station, the spirit of such a wayfarer is like pure light and his body is like a prism which separates all the colours from this pure light, in other words, he has become attributed with all the Godly character traits and he knows the appropriate occasion for their manifestation.

Najm al-Dīn Kubrā expresses the same reality that Nasafī describes although the terminology that the former uses is a little different. His views are stated clearly in his discussion of *walāyat*, or Friendship:

> Three levels are possible for the wayfarer in the station of Friendship, and all of his Friendship is condensed in those three levels. The first level is variegation *(talwīn)* and the second level is stability *(tamkīn)* and the third level is "bringing to be" *(takwīn)*. To use another expression, the first level is knowledge, the second level is state, and then it is annihilation from that state in the changer of states. We also say that the first level is disengagement then it is solitariness and then unity, or we can say that the first level is fear and hope and then contraction and expansion and then it is familiarity and awe; [39]

Najm al-Dīn Kubrā offers many alternatives for explaining this one reality, however, the first definition is the important one for our discussion. Here Friendship of God is explained in terms of *talwīn*, *tamkīn* and *takwīn*. *Takwīn* occupies the top rung, and this is another way to describe Nasafī's view of *tamkīn*. In Najm al-Dīn Kubrā's triad of *talwīn*, *tamkīn* and *takwīn*, *takwīn* is related to the Arabic *kun*, or "Be," which is the divine command. The perfect wayfarer is attributed with this power to manifest whatever attribute he desires and (just as in Nasafī's depiction of the situation) this desire does not come into conflict with God's desire because

> when the Friend of God enjoys a form of this reality and is clothed in these garments, he does not have any desire himself because he has annihilated his desire and established it in His desire. Each time he establishes his annihilated desire in the desire of the Truth Most High, his desire is the desire of the Truth. God Most High does not desire a thing unless the servant desires that very thing, and the servant also does not attach his desire to anything unless the Truth Most High desires that very thing, just as the Beneficent Truth says: "but desire, you shall not, unless God desires, the Lord of the two worlds."[40,41]

Several years before Najm al-Dīn Kubrā was conveying this message to his followers in Central Asia, Shihāb al-Dīn Yaḥyā Suhrawardī was also explaining the same idea in the form of the station of *kun* for the Prophets and Friends: "In this station they are able to create and fix for themselves the suspended exemplars *(muthul mu'allaq)* in whatever form they desire. This station is that very station of *kun*."[42] As we have seen, the ultimate station for Najm al-Dīn Kubrā is *takwīn* where the wayfarer has the power to manifest any attribute he desires; Nasafī's system fully accords with this although he names it stability *(tamkīn)*. Ibn 'Arabī uses a similar term, "stability in variegation" *(al-tamkīn fī'l-talwīn)* – although he is explaining the same situation from a slightly different perspective. Stability in variegation portrays the ultimate vision of God, the moment when the wayfarer realises that he can never witness the essence of God but always contemplates a face of God. He is stable in witnessing everything as God, but the variegation is due to the fact that God's faces are infinite in number.

> In existence, the "reality" is variegation. He who is stable in variegation is the Owner of Stability. The heart longs to witness this reality. God made the heart the locus of this longing to bring the actualisation *(taḥsīl)* of this reality near to man, since there is fluctuation in the heart. God did not place this longing in the rational faculty, since reason possesses delimitation. If this longing were in the rational faculty, the person might see that he is fixed in a single state. But since it lies in the heart, fluctuation comes upon him quickly. For the heart is between the fingers of the all-merciful, so it does not remain in a single state in the reality of the situation. Hence it is fixed in its fluctuation within its state in accordance with its witnessing of the way the fingers cause it to fluctuate.[43]

One of Ibn 'Arabī's favourite sayings is that God's self-disclosure never repeats itself,[44] thus, whatever the wayfarer sees, it is a brand new face of God which is unique to that wayfarer and to that moment. In this way neither the wayfarer, nor God becomes bored: "God does not become bored that you should become bored."[45] In the same way that not one attribute is dominant over the wayfarer, so too the wayfarer does not become tied or limited to one face of God. This is Ibn 'Arabī's "station of no station," for no one particular station is dominant over the wayfarer.[46] Nasafī describes a similar idea after presenting the six different stations of the Friends in the first chapter of *Kitāb-i tanzīl*:

> O dear friend! The stations of the Friends are no more than these six stations, and a person should not think that these six stations are in order and that the wayfarer completes the first station and then goes on to the second station, because it is not in this way. At the end of journeying, each wayfarer is in one of these stations and one of these stations has became his aim and he remains there. There are few wayfarers who are informed of all six stations, and until the wayfarer discovers the information of these six stations and sees the correctness and corruption of each one – not through imitation *(taqlīd)* and supposition *(gumān)* but through unveiling and contemplation – he will neither reach the end point of the journey nor be informed of the extremity of the journey nor recognise the truth from the false nor understand God.[47]

From another perspective, the "station of no station" is the "station of bewilderment." This is because the wayfarer has one eye of *tashbīh* and one eye of *tanzīh*, that is, one eye focused upon God's incomparability and the other eye on God's similarity, the result can only be confusion, becoming cross-eyed, perplexity and bewilderment. The station of bewilderment is also described by Nasafī.

> O dear friend! The final task of the wise man is bewilderment in the gnosis of God and the gnosis of the world. And the greater [his] bewilderment, the greater his gazing *(niẓāra kardan)* because wisdom is the cause of bewilderment, and bewilderment is the cause of gazing. So for the person whose wisdom is greater, his bewilderment will be greater. And for the person whose bewilderment is greater, his gazing will be greater. Gazing without complaint is a sublime station and a magnificent task.[48]

The wayfarer keeps on gazing because he witnesses God's face in everything. It is not the same as beholding God's essence, for no-one has the preparedness to do this. Nasafī explains this reality through the Koranic story of Moses requesting to see God.

> Moses was at this station when he desired to see God. The Truth Most High said, "You cannot see Me,"[49] He did not state "I will not show Myself to you."[50]

The wayfarer sees God's essence in as much as it is revealed through the signs of the world, but he can never truly reach God's essence.

Likewise, Najm al-Dīn Kubrā posited bewilderment as the final spiritual station, and his description of the mystic's vision graphically reveals the oscillation between *tanzīh* and *tashbīh*:

> When the wayfarer reaches bewilderment after fulfilling his purpose by means of the manifest and non-manifest signs and the self-disclosure of the attributes and essence, his longing for Him increases and the sky and earth are like a prison, a battlement or a fortress for him in which he is imprisoned.[51]

Thus *tanzīh* is witnessed here, but at this point things begin to change until *tashbīh* becomes apparent:

> When he decides to find a way to escape and be released and free, the veils of the signs and indications of the sky and earth, face him, and all the things on the earth – ranging from fire, light, animals, plants, rocks, clay, and everything which is existent from them – bring themselves level with him. Now the divine signs concord with him in bewilderment, and sometimes they share his anxiety and discomfort and their crying voices are heard. Sometimes they call him to themselves and sometimes he hears their individual voices [which say], "Come to me and look at the wonders that have been concealed in me." Yes, all of them are wonders, even the weed of the earth or the particles of the sky. Sometimes his changing spiritual state and spiritual aspiration reaches the extent that he witnesses God's signs in himself or he witnesses himself inside of them, or he feels that the stars are falling into him, or the sky is descending upon him, or he feels the taste of the sky in his inside, or he witnesses himself upon the top of the sky and at the same time he is looking at the earth.[52]

The signs of God are a veil, but whether they hinder or help the wayfarer depends upon how he looks at them. Veils can hide something, and in this respect, they represent a *tanzīh* position, and since it is impossible for the wayfarer to reach the essence of God, he will always be faced by veils. However, if the wayfarer realises that the veils reveal something about God, then he will pass from one veil to another, enjoying the knowledge that he can obtain from each one. Najm al-Dīn Kubrā's portrayal of *tashbīh* continues:

> Sometimes the earth rises in companionship with him and is like a friend and associate and it speaks with him and declares, "Behold me and the wonders in me and see how God Most High is generous to you, since you can walk upon me. I am your mother and greater than you and look upon what a foundation I am based upon!"[53]

It is interesting that Najm al-Dīn Kubrā's visionary experiences included such discussions with the earth. His visions were inspired by the Koran which states: "We shall show them Our signs upon the horizons and in themselves."[54] For many Sufis, the earth (or horizon), is considered from one perspective as the most distinguished element that God created.[55] Nasafī himself says that the first substance that God created was earth and the last thing is intelligence,[56] all things are created through the earth, even Adam, who is made of earth and of God's spirit.[57] In Najm al-Dīn Kubrā's visionary portrayal, the earth is the mother and that which God breathed into man (i.e. the spirit) is the father. Thus in the state of bewilderment, the wayfarer recognises that he is composed of two seemingly conflicting substances: earth and spirit, density and subtlety, darkness and light. This is another reflection of the *tanzīh* – *tashbīh* relationship, which appears contradictory until the wayfarer reaches station of bewilderment where all opposites are fused together. Like Najm al-Dīn Kubrā, Nasafī also describes the earth and spirit, or elements and natures, in terms of mothers and fathers:

> This sea of light is called father and this sea of darkness is called mother, and the fathers and mothers place their arms around each others neck and embrace, and the kingdoms are born from them.[58]

Earth is considered a distinguished thing because it has the preparedness to receive the spirit. Having received the spirit, the earth reaches its perfection in two ways: through the macrocosm and through the microcosm. Thus God has two mirrors in which he can witness himself. Earth, the primal element is a non-composite and can neither be corrupted nor decay, thus it is relatively eternal. [59]

Najm al-Dīn's visionary descriptions of bewilderment continue, revealing that the wayfarer flashes from *tashbīh* to *tanzīh* and from *tanzīh* to *tashbīh* like a coin spinning in the air. In the previous section, the earth is witnessed in a *tashbīh* manner, but then suddenly it flips to a *tanzīh* nature:

> Sometimes the earth under his feet resembles a billowing ocean with waves crashing around him, and he is set upon that stormy ocean but he

> does not drown. This ocean becomes corporealised in a form for him when he does not listen to the discourse of the earth, or if he listens, he will be in a state where he enters the station of bewilderment and he constantly looks at that until a group of spiritual ones who live in the earth attack him, but since he has fortified himself in the garrison of truthfulness and freedom they cannot defeat him. In the end everything on the earth is vanquished in his circle of power.[60]

Najm al-Dīn Kubrā concludes his section on bewilderment and its effects in the following way:

> The main aim of discussing this reality is that each time the changing spiritual state of the wayfarer reaches the extremity of strength, and his spiritual aspiration *(himmat)* ascends to the highest rung, he can enjoy the effect of that very spiritual state through the faces of the signs and indications.[61]

The vivid unveilings experienced by Najm al-Dīn Kubrā graphically portray the Islamic concepts of *tanzīh* and *tashbīh* which were explained in chapter two. This dual nature of God is confirmed in much of the Sufi literature of the twelfth and thirteenth centuries. (Another example includes the extraordinary visions described in what amounts to a spiritual autobiography by Rūzbihān Baqlī).[62] Unfortunately, Nasafī does not reveal the character of his visions, however, as has been shown earlier, he does provide wayfarers with an answer to the seemingly contradictory nature of Islamic visionary experience, which is the *tanzīh-tashbīh* relationship.

III. SPIRITUAL PERFECTION AND CREATION

Related to this discussion of the ultimate spiritual station of bewilderment, and already alluded to above, is the capacity of wayfarers to use the attributes given to them to "create," that is, creation not in the sense of manifesting the appropriate attributes or character traits, such as generosity or wrath, etc., but creating objects on a corporeal plane and causing effects in the world of sense perception. The word for this creative power or *himma*, is found in the Koran and has been translated as "purpose" and "design."[63] By the twelfth and thirteenth centuries, *himma* had become a technical term of the Sufis. For example, the great Persian poet Niẓāmī (b. 1140) refers to *himma* in his *Makhzan al-asrār* (1166) when he describes how Maḥmūd of Ghazna (969–1030) fell sick while besieging an Indian city. Niẓāmī explains that the cause of the sickness was the efforts of three Hindu ascetics who had combined their *himma* in an attempt to make Mahmūd leave India.[64] The Sufi "theoreticians" of the same period, including Ibn 'Arabī, Shihāb al-Dīn al-Suhrawardī *(al-mutqūl)*, Najm al-Dīn Kubrā and Nasafī, all discussed the significance of *himma* in their works.

Himma is manifested at the stage of human perfection where the Perfect Man assumes the noble character traits:

> People may apply the word "state" and mean by it the servant's becoming manifest in the attribute of God by engendering *(takwīn)* things and producing effects through his Resolve *(himma)*. This is the becoming similar *(tashabbuh)* to God which is called assuming the character traits of the names *(al-takhalluq bi'l asmā')*.[65]

The ability to "create" an effect in this world through *himma* depends upon the strength of the individual's concentration:

> Every man creates by his fancy in the Imaginative faculty that which has existence nowhere else, this being a common faculty. The gnostic however, by his Concentration *(himma)* creates that which has existence beyond the origin of Concentration, indeed, the Concentration continues to maintain its existence, which depletes it in no way at all. Should the attention of the gnostic be deflected from the maintenance of what he has created, it will cease to exist, unless the gnostic commands all planes (of existence), in which case such deflection does not arise, since (at all times) he is present on some plane or another.[66]

Najm al-Dīn Kubrā also employs the word *himma* in several of his works[67] but his most interesting explanations appear in his *Fawā'iḥ al jamāl wa fawātiḥ al jalāl*, where *himma* is posited as the highest level:

> The end of love *(maḥabba)* is the beginning of passionate love *('ishq)*, and love belongs to the heart and passionate love belongs to the spirit and the mystery *(sirr)* connects *(yajmu'u)* the dearest ones, and *himma* is the effect of [this] connection.[68]

Kubrā states that each time the wayfarer's desire becomes strong and he has preparedness and constancy in searching for the Truth, then a link is created between the possessor of *himma* and his desired object. This connection is like a chain which is drawn between two things, or it is like a spear between a combatant's hand and the breast of his enemy, or it is like an arrow, or it is like a light than shines from the sun to the earth.[69] As a result of this connection, the wayfarer's *himma* is now able to create. The progress of the wayfarer's *himma* from beginning to end is summarised by Kubrā:

> The traveller is a horseman and *himma* is the horse. There is a beginning and end for *himma*; the beginning is desire, then searching, then connection *(rabṭ),* then free disposal *(taṣarruf),* then being *(al-kawn). Himma* is power, and the mystery *(sirr)* unites with the *himma* and the power of the Truth.[70]

This creation through the "hand of *himma*" is found when the wayfarer has a pure heart and when his hands do not reach towards this or that. Then another hand appears which participates in his affairs and performs tasks that ordinary hands are incapable of undertaking.[71] Kubrā gives the example of his being able to feel his own Shaykh's shadow and *himma* within him. He thought that his shaykh had left the city but he realised that he had returned because the shaykh's shadow and *himma* felt like a heavy mountain upon him so that he was not able to move in any direction. Kubrā told those around him to go out and greet the shaykh. Those who were present were amazed to see Kubrā's shaykh riding towards the city in the distance.[72]

This ability to cause things to occur or appear in the visible world from the invisible world cannot be realised by the common people. However, those who have a pure heart and a connection with God are able to actualise the things that appear in the invisible world. Thus, they are able to fly, walk on water, pass through fire without injury, in fact they have the power of free disposal *(taṣarruf)* through their *himma*.

One of the distinctive features of Kubrā's theosophy is its attention to the lights and colours that the wayfarer sees throughout the spiritual journey. Therefore, it is of little surprise that Kubrā describes a particular "vision" which is related to *himma*. These lights, colours and visions are induced by the continual practice of *dhikr*. Unlimited space and broad expanses of land around oneself may be seen as well as colours ranging from green, red, yellow and blue. The colours are representative of a spiritual state: green indicates the life of the heart, while fire in a pure form free from turbidity is a sign of the life of *himma,* and the reality of that *himma* is power *(qudrat)*. If there is turbidity in the fire which causes the wayfarer discomfort, he is witnessing the fire of the soul and Satan. Blue is an indication of the life of the soul and yellow is a sign of the wayfarer's weakness and inability.[73]

Since Nasafī is associated by some to the Kubrāwiyya order, one might expect to find similar descriptions of lights and visions within his works. Although he does discuss visions, there is not a single reference to such coloured lights or fire. Despite this, Nasafī follows in the tradition of Ibn 'Arabī and Najm al-Dīn Kubrā by portraying a spiritual station which reflects the effects of *himma*. In *Kitāb-ī Tanzīl*, Nasafī discusses one station for the Friends which presents the idea of creation at every moment in time when God replaces something which was existent in the west and replaces it with something similar in the east. This is one way of explaining the miracles of Prophets and charismatic powers of the Friends, or in other words, the *himma* of the Friends.

> . . . forms are annihilated every moment and something similar to that becomes existent and the senses do not perceive that because of the extreme speed. Now know that if a fixed *(mu'ayan)* form in a fixed time in the east becomes non-existent, in that very fixed time something similar to that becomes existent in the west. Is it not a marvel *('ajab)*, for how is it possible that whatever is existent in the east at a fixed time becomes non-existent and something similar to that becomes existent in the west? Why is it impossible for whatever is existent in the east [suddenly] to become non-existent there and become existent in the west? It is God that becomes manifested with these forms and the east, west, south, north, over and under are the same for God because God's light is expanded, unlimited and infinite. This is the meaning of the manifestation of angels and Gabriel, the Throne of the Queen of Sheba *(takht-i bilqīs)*, Khiḍr, the Invisible Shaykh, miracles and charismatic powers.[74]

The possession of *himma* is one of the distinguishing features of the hierarchy of the three hundred and fifty six Friends who oversee the world (to be discussed in the next chapter). Nasafī's explanation of the abilities of these individuals resembles that of Najm al-Dīn Kubrā:

> Their charismatic powers and power are in such a way that earth, water, air, fire, desert and mountains do not obstruct their vision, and they can see and hear the words of the People of the West when they themselves are in the east. If they want they can travel to the west from the east in an hour. Land, sea, mountain or plain are the same to them, and water and fire are equal. There are many of these charismatic powers *(karāmat)* and powers *(qudrat)* which belong to them. Although each one of the three hundred and fifty six are wise *(dānā)*, esteemed *(muqarrab)*, the possessor of *himmat*, the possessor of power *(ṣāḥib-i qudrat)* and one whose prayers are answered *(mustajāb al-da'wat)*, the Pole *(quṭb)* is wiser and more esteemed than them all and his power and *himmat* is greater. The person who is nearer to the Pole is wiser and more esteemed.[75]

In *al-Insān al-kāmil*, however, Nasafī is more reticent in confirming his belief in this station. This is somewhat strange because in other places he discusses the miracles of the Prophets and the charismatic powers of the Friends.

> O dervish, this is the eighth Heaven and according to the helpless one, it is the last Heaven and there is no other than these eight. But some say that there is another Heaven other than these eight, and there is a tree in this Heaven and it is called the Tree of Power. When the wayfarer reaches the eye of certainty *('ayn al-yaqīn)*, – that is, until this point he has known the knowledge of certainty *('ilm al-yaqīn)* – he sees the eye of certainty which is the existence of God . . . But the understanding of this helpless one does not reach this ninth Heaven of which this group has related and I have not seen anyone among them nor among their peers. I have only heard very much [about them].
>
> Know that some say that there is a group and God gives them whatever they desire, and everything that is necessary appears for them; and in whatever they fix their *himmat*, [that thing] accords with their *himmat*: "Many a dusty and dishevelled one clad in rags, to whom men pay no head, will have his oath fulfilled when he swears to God."[76] In other words, they have the wisdom to perfection and power to perfection and *himmat* to perfection. All of their desires are actualised and everything comes about in the way that they desire because they have died the voluntary death before the natural death and they have passed on from this world and they are in the next world. For example, if these people want rain to come, in the moment that it passes through their minds, clouds appear and rain begins to fall. If they do not want rain to fall, in the instant that it passes through their minds the clouds disperse and disappear. If they want someone to fall sick, that person becomes sick instantly; and if they want a sick person to become healthy, in an instant that person becomes healthy. In all things it is in this way. In addition, it is said that this group can journey from the east to the west in one hour and can come from the west to the east in one hour. They can walk upon water, fly in the air or walk upon fire if they want. People can see them if they want and people cannot see them if they want, and everyday their food is ready and cooked for them without the effort or endeavour of any person.[77]
>
> O Dervish! Today as I am writing this, I do not have this [power] and my acquaintances do not have this, and despite this, its [reality] cannot be denied. It may be that God Most High will give and grant this to me since He is capable in everything.[78]

There are several possible explanations for Nasafī's hesitance regarding the ninth heaven and the Tree of Power. Firstly, one has to consider that there was always danger to Sufis from the secular rulers or those members of the *'Ulamā'* who favoured a more exoteric interpretation of Islam. Reference was made in chapter one to the dangers faced by followers of Ibn 'Arabī in Egypt during the generation after Nasafī. It has also been suggested that Shihāb al-Dīn al-Suhrawardī was executed as a result of the political implications of his esoteric beliefs.[79] (Although the word *himma* is not used in his *Ḥikmat al-ishrāq*, Suhrawardī describes sages who possessed illuminationist wisdom within them and who could make anything appear before them at will, such as food, shapes and beautiful sounds and other things).[80] Another reason lies in the reluctance of masters of charismatic powers and *himmat* to demonstrate their power to the common people. In *Kitāb-i tanzīl*, Nasafī himself comments that it is necessary for Prophets to manifest prophecy and miracles but it is not necessary for the Friends to show their Friendship and charismatic powers. In fact the Friend sees charismatic powers as a trial and a test and they are anguished and afraid at their manifestation. This is because some of the "Friends" desired that the common people look at them and the charismatic power, and thus recognise them. Such a person is not a Friend, rather, he is "a demon, a deviator of others, in other words, he puts on the clothes of the good and pious and attracts people to himself and in this way actualises fortune and fame."[81]

In *Zubdat al-ḥaqā'iq*, Nasafī also is cautious about *himmat:*

> The thought and plans of humans have effects but the *himmat* and wishing of humans have no effect . . . if human *himmat* and wishing had effects then no one would be incapable and poor, they would all be capable and rich. If action *('amal)* is united *(jam')* with human *himmat* and wishing *(khwāst)* then tasks are completed through that *himmat* and action.
>
> If one recognises sickness and killing as an effect of one's *himmat* and says that this is my action *(fi'l)* then in fact this claim is a lie and this claimant is a liar. But it is possible if God Most High frees one of His Friends from sickness through prayer and *himmat* and intercession *(shafā'at)* or makes one of His enemies sick or kills him. Indeed there have been many such cases. But the reality *(ma'nā)* is that it is the Truth's action. But when this action of the Truth is manifested through the prayer and intermediary of one of the Friends, that is called "charismatic power," and "intercession." In other words, God Most High bestows upon the Friend the acceptance of prayer, intercession and charismatic powers.[82]

The meaning behind this passage is that *himmat* ultimately comes from God, and the Friend who has reached the highest spiritual station does not desire to do anything that God does not desire. At this point, the *himmat* of the Friend on the one hand and God's desire on the other are the same, leaving the question of who is actually exercising *himmat* somewhat ambiguous. Are the Islamic mystics who describe "monistic" experiences actually stating that they are identical with God? The problem of identity between the mystic and God may best be explained with reference to the mirror imagery which so often occurs in Sufi texts. The pinnacle of the mystical experience has been interpreted by J.J. Elias:

> It is no longer possible to differentiate God as He witnesses Himself in the mirror from the mirror as it bears witness to God. They are like two bright lights reflecting back at each other. The beauty of God is reflected and witnessed by the mirror, which then reflects this beauty back to God Who witnesses the perfect reflection of His own beauty as identical to His beauty. In other words, God witnesses the same image of Himself in the mirror as the mirror witnesses in God.[83]

Is the mirror identical to God? Who exercises the power of *himmat* – man or God? This ambiguity is beautifully expressed by Maḥmūd Shabistārī (d. ca 1339) in his *Gulshān-i rāz*. Shabistārī discusses God's essence in the form of the beauty spot on the beloved's face which is reflected in the heart of the lover.

> *I know not if her beauty spot is our heart's double, its projected image,*
> *or the heart the image and facsimile of her face's fascinating beauty spot.*
> *Has the heart, as a reflection or facsimile of that face come forth*
> *or was her image therein projected so palpably?*
> *Is the heart within her face or her face within the heart?*
> *An intricate enigma, ineffable, invisible to me as well!*[84]

The answer to the problem of identity between God and the spiritual wayfarer must be affirmative and negative. It is affirmative in respect of the fact that it is God's image that is reflected in the heart of the wayfarer, but it is also negative because the reflection is only one form, that is, it is only a self-disclosure of God in the form that the heart is capable of reflecting. At this point it is necessary to recall Nasafī's warning in his introduction to *Kitāb-i tanzīl* that the pure essence and Holy Face of the Truth is so great that an individual's intelligence cannot encompass Him and the extremity of man's knowledge is that point where he knows that he cannot know God as God really is.[85]

In chapter three it was described how "contemplation" is the ultimate epistemological level that the wayfarer can reach. In a state of contemplation, the wayfarer has returned to the world after witnessing a state of absolute unity of existence. In this world He realises that everything is a sign of God and he sees the unity in multiplicity. At this point, he knows that God is both transcendent from His creation and at the same time He is also immanent. One should speak neither of an "Allah transcendent" nor an "Allah immanent." This position, which is generally representative of Ibn 'Arabi's so-called school of the Unity of being *(waḥdat al-wujūd)* was severely criticised by some Sufis, including Shaykh Aḥmad Sirhindī (1564–1624). According to one modern commentator of Sirhindī, Ibn 'Arabī was censured by Sirhindī because the former "expounded the doctrine *(of waḥdat al-wujūd)* in the light of his experience of oneness and identity. Though he did not stay at the stage of 'pure union' and moved ahead, he did not move sufficiently enough and affirm the complete transcendence of God and His absolute difference."[86] Sufis such as Ibn 'Arabī and Nasafī indeed did move on from 'pure union' since they returned to this world and through contemplation witnessed God's incomparability and similarity. They could not "affirm the complete transcendence of God and His absolute difference" because this would have been a distortion of what they perceived to be the real ontological and epistemological relationship between man and God.

Sirhindī believed the ultimate situation was one of servanthood *('abdiyat)*, which affirmed God's incomparability, whereas he held that the *wujūdīs* saw unity *(tawḥīd)* as the pinnacle of spiritual realisation.[87] Indeed, Nasafī does view unity as the final spiritual level, equating unity *(tawḥīd)* with contemplation *('iyān)*:

> . . .when the wayfarer reaches the station of unity *(maqām-i tawḥīd)*, which is the ultimate station of the wayfarers, he reaches his perfection and becomes mature *(bāligh)*. . .[88]
>
> Know that there are four kinds of maturity:
> One [kind] is the maturity of surrender *(bāligh-i islām)* which is the station of imitation *(taqlīd)* and compliance *(inqiyād)*. In this station, the wayfarer says with his tongue that God is one.
>
> Another [kind] is the maturity of faith *('īmān)* which is the station of reasoning *(istidlāl)* and knowledge *('ilm)* and in this station the wayfarer knows in his heart that God is one.
>
> Another [kind] is the maturity of certitude *(īqān)* which is the station of assurance *(itminān)* and tranquillity *(ārām)* and it is in this station that the wayfarer sees that God seems to be one *(khudā'ī-rā gūya yikī mī-bīnad)*.
>
> Another [kind] is the maturity of contemplating *('iyān)* which is the station of the unveiling of obscurities *(kashf-i ghiṭā')* and the rending of the veil *(shaqq-i shaqāq)* and it is in this station that the wayfarer sees that God Most High is one . . . and this maturity of contemplation is the perfection of man and the ultimate station.[89]

So although Nasafī posits unity *(tawḥīd)* as the ultimate spiritual level in the foregoing, it has been shown in other places that his explanation of unity in terms of contemplation indicates that it is a situation where the wayfarer has returned to the world after experiencing "absolute unity" and sees both God's incomparability and also His similarity through His places of manifestation in the world. Likewise, Ibn 'Arabī did not claim that unity was the highest spiritual level as Sirhindī appears to be saying. Rather, perfection is described as servanthood *('ubūdiyya)* and manliness *(rajūliyya)* or in other words, incomparability and similarity.[90]

The mystical experiences that Nasafī describes are both theistic and monistic but the language that is available to us in the West has been determined culturally by a tradition which is theistic. While it includes terms for the monist, as yet there is still no word for the *tanzīh/tashbīh* position. Perhaps Corbin did the best thing by creating his own terminology, such as "theo-monist."[91]

Notes

1 H. Corbin, *The Man of Light*, p. 78.
2 Ibid, pp. 61–144.
3 Koran, 2: 29, "It is He who created for you all that is in the earth, then He lifted Himself to heaven and levelled them seven heavens; and He has knowledge of everything."
4 For Muḥammad's night ascent M. Sells, *Early Islamic Mysticism* (New York: Paulist Press, 1996), pp. 47–56.
5 Koran, 6: 76.
6 Koran, 6: 77.
7 Koran, 6: 78.
8 Koran, 6: 79.
9 Koran, 6: 75.
10 Najm al-Dīn Rāzī, translated H. Algar, op. cit., p. 296.
11 *al-Insān al-kāmil*, p. 108.
12 Ibid.
13 Ibid, p. 109.
14 Ibid, pp. 236–7.
15 *Kashf al-ḥaqā'iq*, p. 106.
16 Ibid, p. 107.
17 *al-Insān al-kāmil*, pp. 89–90.
18 Ibid, p. 246. The forty-six parts of prophecy refer to a *ḥadīth*, see Wensinck, *Concordance et Indices de la Tradition Musulmane* (Leiden: E.J. Brill, 1936–1969), Vol 1, 343, s.v. juz')
19 Ibid, p. 243.
20 Ibid, p. 174.
21 Najm al-Dīn Rāzī, translated H. Algar, op. cit., p. 289.
22 Ibid, p. 239.

23 Koran, 36: 82.
24 Koran, 54: 50.
25 *al-Insān al-kāmil*, p. 225.
26 Koran, 24: 35.
27 *al-Insān al-kāmil*, p. 24.
28 Ibid.
29 Ibid, p. 25.
30 Ibid, p. 26.
31 H. Ziai, "The Source and Nature of Authority," op. cit., p. 324.
32 Koran, 5: 51.
33 J.S. Trimingham, *The Sufi Orders of Islam*, p. 200.
34 *Kashf al-ḥaqā'iq*, p. 174.
35 The passage in *Kashf al-ṣirāṭ* is similar to a discussion found in *Kashf al-ḥaqā'iq*, p. 159–160.
36 *Kashf al-ṣirāṭ*, Veliyuddin 1767, fol. 208b, line 13 onwards.
37 *Kashf al-ṣirāṭ*, Veliyuddin, 1767, fol. 209a, line 14 onwards.
38 *Kashf al-ḥaqā'iq*, p. 141–142.
39 Najm al-Dīn Kubrā, ed. F. Meier, [174]. There is also a Persian translation of this work by Najm al-Dīn al-Kubrā, trans, Muḥammad Bāqir Sa'ādī Khurāsānī see *Fawā'iḥ al-Jamāl wa Fawātiḥ al-Jalāl* (Tehran: Intishārāt-i marwī, 1368). This passage appears on pages 242–243.
40 Koran, 81: 29.
41 Najm al-Dīn Kubrā, Arabic [175], (Persian translation p. 244).
42 Suhrawardī, *Ḥikmat al-ishrāq*, op. cit., p. 387.
43 Ibn 'Arabī, *al-Futūḥāt al-Makkiya* (II 532.30) trans. Chittick, *The Sufi Path of Knowledge*, p. 108.
44 Ibn 'Arabī, *Futūḥāt* (I 266.9), translated Chittick, *The Sufi Path of Knowledge*, p. 103.
45 A *ḥadīth* quoted several times by Ibn 'Arabī in the *al-Futūḥāt al-Makkiya*, see for example the discussion in (III 254.23, 255.8), translated Chittick, *The Sufi Path of Knowledge*, p. 101.
46 See Chittick, *The Sufi Path of Knowledge*, p. 376–379.
47 *Kitāb- tanzīl*, fol. 51a, lines 11–16.
48 Ibid, fol. 38b, lines 1–4.
49 Koran, 7: 143.
50 *al-Insān al-kāmil.*, p. 116.
51 Najm al-Dīn Kubrā, Arabic [185], Persian p. 254.
52 Ibid.
53 Ibid.
54 Koran, 41: 53.
55 For example, Ibn 'Arabī comments, "The earth . . . gives all benefits from its own essence and is the locus of every good. Hence it is the mightiest of corporeal bodies. In its movement it vies with no moving thing, since none of them leave the earth's location. Each pillar manifests its authority within the earth while it is patient, the receptive, the fixed, the stable." Quoted by S. Murata, *The Tao of Islam*, p. 140.
56 *Kashf al-ḥaqā'iq*, p. 57.
57 Koran, 32:7–9.

58 *al-Insān al-kāmil*, p. 164.

59 It is possible to interpret the following passage about the earth in two different ways. The first belittles earth while the other praises it due to its non-composite, non-corruptible nature:

> when many of the Great Ones had seen the calamities and catastrophes in this universe, and had witnessed much torment and various vexations in this world and the next world, they said 'I wish I had never been born from my mother, I wish I were earth,' since there is no level lower than earth and they desired that level. (*al-Insān al-kāmil*, p. 231).

"I wish I were earth" is an allusion to the Koran, 78: 41: "O would that I were dust."

60 Najm al-Dīn Kubrā, Arabic [185], Persian, p. 255.

61 Ibid.

62 See C. Ernst, *Rūzbihān Baqlī*. The second chapter of this work entitled "The Inner Structure of Sainthood," pp. 17–110, neatly portrays this *tashbīh-tanzīh* dynamic.

63 This appears several times in Arberry's translation of the Koran, for example 9: 74 (London: Allen & Unwin, 1955).

64 Niẓāmī, *Makhzan al-asrār*, Matba'a Armaghān, Tehran, 1313, 1099–1101. For an English translation see Gholām Hosein Dārāb's *The Treasury of Mysteries* (London: Arthur Probsthain, 1945), p. 90.

65 Ibn 'Arabī, *al-Futūḥāt al-Makkiya*, II 385.12, translated Chittick, *The Sufi Path of Knowledge*, p. 265.

66 Austin, *Ibn al-'Arabī: The Bezels of Wisdom*, p. 102.

67 For example, see Najm al-Dīn Kubrā's *Ila'l-hā'im al-khā'if min lawmat al-lā'im* (Tehran: Sāzmān i intishārāt-i kayhān, 1364), p.57.

68 Najm al-Dīn Kubrā, *Fawā'ih al jamāl wa fawātiḥ al jalāl* [84].

69 Ibid [106].

70 Ibid [106].

71 Ibid [182].

72 Ibid [155].

73 Ibid [13].

74 *Kitāb-i tanzīl*, fol. 47a, lines 8–16.

75 *Manāzil al-sā'irīn*, p. 318–319.

76 *Ḥadīth*. Also quoted by Najm al-Dīn Rāzī, translated H. Algar, op. cit., p. 242. According to Algar, this *ḥadīth* is recorded by al-Ḥakīm, and also by al-Ghazālī in *Iḥyā 'Ulūm al-Dīn*, III, 270.

77 *al-Insān al-kāmil*, pp. 305–307.

78 Ibid, p. 308.

79 See H. Ziai, "The Source and Nature of Authority: A Study of al-Suhrawardi's Illuminationist Political Doctrine," op.cit, pp 304–344.

80 Suhrawardī, *Ḥikmat al-ishrāq*, op. cit., p. 374.

81 *Kitāb-i tanzīl*, fol. 64, lines 12 64b line 2.

82 *Zubdat al-ḥaqā'iq*, p. 69.

83 J.J. Elias, *The Throne Carrier of God*, p. 96.

84 Trans. Lewisohn, *Beyond Faith and Infidelity*, p. 198.

85 *Kitāb-i tanzīl*, fol. 38a, lines 9–13.

86 Muhammad Abdul Haq Ansari, *Sufism and Shari'ah* (Leicester: The Islamic Foundation, 1986), p. 94.
87 Ibid, p. 15.
88 *Kashf al-ḥaqā'iq*, p. 123.
89 Ibid, p. 125.
90 Chittick, *The Sufi Path of Knowledge*, p. 366.
91 For this term see H. Corbin, *History of Islamic Philosophy*, translated L. Sherrard (London: Kegan Paul International, 1993), pp. 294–95.

6

The Perfection of Man: The Concepts of Friendship and Prophecy

I. THE SPIRITUAL ASCENT

Achieving human perfection is viewed by Sufis as a journey or a spiritual ascent which reaches a pinnacle with the Prophet Muḥammad, the last messenger of God and Seal of the Prophets. This perfection is comprised of three elements, for according to a Sufi axiom attributed to Muḥammad: "The Law is my words, the Way is my works and the Reality is my states."[1] In other words, the Law is knowledge, the Way is putting the knowledge into practice and the Reality is the inward states and stations that the wayfarer may enjoy on the Sufi path.[2] This is the simplest guide for the wayfarer:

> At first, the wayfarer must study and learn whatever is necessary from the Holy Law. Then he must perform and comply with whatever is necessary from the Way until the reality becomes manifest from the lights in accordance with the wayfarer's effort.[3]

Although Muḥammad is the example of perfection for Sufis, from one perspective the sealing of Prophecy means that there can be no other legislating messenger and this (according to Ibn 'Arabī) is "a terrible blow" for the Sufis or Friends because it implies the impossibility of experiencing total and perfect servitude.[4] In other words, the Sufis cannot attain Muḥammad's level of spiritual perfection, yet as it will be shown in this chapter, from another perspective, the relationship between Prophecy *(nubuwwat)* and Friendship of God *(walāyat)* is interpreted in such a manner that it is possible for the Friends to reach the Prophet's spiritual level.

Nasafī was one Sufi who highlighted the importance of the relationship between Prophecy and Friendship:

Once in the district of Nasaf, in fact in the [whole] area of Transoxania, the topic of whether or not the attribute of Friendship is stronger than the attribute of Prophecy was widespread. Some people thought that this debate over the Friends and the Prophets was the only topic of discussion. When I came under the service of Shaykh of Shaykh's, Sa'd al-Dīn Ḥammūya, we also discussed this subject. Now after his death, his followers are also discussing the Prophets and Friends.[5]

Nasafī sets out a spiritual hierarchy (which is accepted by the *'Ulamā'* and Philosophers) and which clearly distinguishes the station of Prophecy from that of Friendship of God. For example, the station of the Seal of the Prophets is four stations higher than that of the Friend. This hierarchy is set out below:[6]

Spirit	Reason for Ascent	Station
9. Seal of the Prophet	Receives final set of Holy Laws and annuls previous Laws.	The Throne
8. Men of Resolution	Receives a new Holy Law and the previous Holy Law is annulled.	The Stool
7. Messengers	God gives the Messenger a Holy Book.	Seventh Heaven (Saturn)
6. Prophets	God gives revelation to be sent to the people, and miracles.	Sixth Heaven (Jupiter)
5. Friends	As a result of gnosis, God gives love and inspiration.	Fifth Heaven (Mars)
4. Gnostics	Knows and sees things as they are.	Fourth Heaven (Sun)
3. Ascetics	Turns away from this world and renounces the pleasures of this world.	Third Heaven (Venus)
2. Worshippers	Worships very much on the basis of confirming the Prophets	Second Heaven (Mercury)
1. Believers	Confirms the Prophets	First Heaven (The Moon)

With Muḥammad, the cycle of Prophecy came to a close and on the basis of the above chart, this means that individuals can progress no higher than the fifth spiritual station (the Messengers and Men of Resolution are the higher ranks of the Prophets). This "orthodox" representation of the Islamic spiritual hierarchy in which the Friends occupy a lower position than the Prophets is clearly established by the author of *Kashf al-ṣirāṭ*. In this work, humans are classified into four categories, reflecting the Koranic verse 4: 71, "And whosoever obeys God and the Messenger shall be with those whom God has blessed; the Prophets, the truthful, the martyrs and the righteous." The righteous are those people in the station of submission *(islām)*, the martyrs (also called the gnostics) are those in the station of faith *(īmān)*, the truthful (also named the Friends) are those in the station of excellence *(iḥsān)* and the Prophets are in the highest station of witnessing *('iyān)*.[7] Yet Sufis such as Tirmidhī and Ibn 'Arabī hint of a secret that spiritual progress is possible for the Friend to the extent that one can reach the same level as the Prophets. The forcible disclosure of such a secret, according to Ibn 'Arabī, would shake God's Throne.[8]

On discussing the spiritual hierarchy outlined above, Nasafī suggests that the relationship is not as simple as it appears at first sight. To begin with, he gives the views of the *'Ulamā'* who endorse these nine levels and claim that the spirits are created before bodies thus having a fixed station and therefore the spirit of each person cannot progress beyond that fixed station. The Philosophers also agree that there are nine levels, but hold that the spirits are created with the bodies and therefore the spirits can ascend depending upon the degree of wisdom and purity attained during life on earth. Nasafī does not say whether the people of Unity accept this nine-fold division, however, he remarks that there is no limit to the progress of the human spirit because

> . . .if man could live for a thousand years, and during this time he was busy in education, review, ascetic discipline, religious effort and *dhikr*, each day he would understand and discover something which he had not known or discovered the previous day through wisdom, for God's wisdom and knowledge has no limit. . .
>
> According to the People of Unity, perfection in a human does not exist because whatever perfection a human attains, he is still relatively incomplete in relation to his preparedness and in relation to God's knowledge and wisdom. Therefore a man who is said to be perfect is relatively perfect. According to the People of the Holy Law and the Philosophers, perfection exists.[9]

These remarks of the People of Unity that man's spirit has no limit and therefore can ascend to the pinnacle of the spiritual hierarchy, is endorsed in another section of *al-Insān al-kāmil*:

> A group among the Sufis also say that the Seals ascend as far as the Throne, that is, the Seal of the Prophets and the Seal of the Friends. This group sees Friendship of God as the superior level, but how can the level of Friendship be higher than the level of Prophecy? We have explained this discussion in *Kashf al-ḥaqā'iq*. Anyone who wishes can refer to it there. This group says that Friendship is the heart of Prophecy, and Deity is the heart of Friendship. Prophecy is the Moon when it splits and Friendship is the Sun when it becomes manifest.[10]

The possibility for man to reach the spiritual perfection of the Prophet had been alluded to (or discussed prior to) Nasafī by mystics such as Sahl Tustarī (d. 896), Ḥallāj, Tirmidhī, Rūzbihān Baqlī, Abū Ḥāmid al-Ghazālī and Ibn 'Arabī.[11] To demonstrate both why Friendship is the heart of Prophecy and also why a Friend can reach the spiritual station of a Prophet, it is necessary to analyse the nature of perfection and the Perfect Man.

Qualities of the Perfect Man

In his works, Nasafī describes three qualities which each Perfect Man possesses. Through an investigation of these qualities and then seeing if these qualities apply to the Friend and the Prophet, it is possible to show the differences between the two. In this way, the meaning of "Friendship is the heart of Prophecy" can be explained.

The first quality of the Perfect Man is that he is always existent, both in cosmological terms and also in "reality" within this world. This idea reflects the distinction between the Muḥammadan Reality and the Perfect Man. The Muḥammadan Reality is a term for the first thing that God created, which is both perfect and eternal and is empowered by God to create. A frequently cited *ḥadīth* states: "The first thing created by God was my [i.e. Muḥammad] spirit then He created all the creatures from my spirit."[12] This *ḥadīth* became part of the Sufi tradition, for Sahl Tustarī related how Khiḍr told him that, "God created the light of Muḥammad out of his own light and He gave it form and kept it for a hundred years and each day – which is a thousand years in this world – He looked at this light seven thousand times. And seven thousand lights were created from each glance at this light. So all the existents were created from this light."[13]

The Muḥammadan Reality is then a cosmological reality which is manifested within the world as the Perfect Man. This explains the *ḥadīth*: "I was a prophet while Adam was between the water and clay,"[14] and Nasafī also refers to this *ḥadīth*:

> The origin of human spirits is from the Spirit and the origin of bodies is from Adam's body. Thus, there is no father of spirits except for Muḥammad and there is no father of bodies except for Adam.[15]

Such an interpretation closely resembles that of the Arab poet Ibn Farīd (d. 1233) who had the Prophet say, "There is no living thing that does not derive its life from me, and all desiring souls are subject to my will. Even though I am son of Adam in form, in him I have an essence of my own which testifies that I am his father."[16]

Although Muḥammad's spirit was the first of things to be created, he is the last of a chain of Prophets, and he manifested God's light completely and so he was the epitome of the Perfect Man. Yet it would be wrong to view the Perfect Man and the Muḥammadan Reality as interchangeable as Chodkiewicz has indicated, "the terms *ḥaqīqa Muḥammadiyya* and *insān kāmil* (perfect man) are not purely synonymous, but express differing views of man, the first seeing him in terms of his primordiality and the second in terms of finality."[17] It is possible to see the Muḥammadan Reality and the Perfect Man as a circle, that is, of descent and ascent, which was a familiar motif in all of Nasafī's works.

> . . .the Perfect Man, who in both his descent and ascent, will have passed three heavens and three earths[18] and then is firmly established upon the Throne, that is, he will have come from and returned to the First Intelligence. Thus the circle is completed, the First Intelligence is firmly established upon the Throne and the Perfect Man is also firmly established upon the Throne.[19]

As mentioned above, the Perfect Man is a manifestation of the Muḥammadan Reality, and therefore this quality is not unique to the historical Muḥammad alone. According to Nasafī, Solomon, Khiḍr (see below) and Jesus are all considered Perfect Men.[20] Indeed, Nasafī remarks that the Perfect Man has been known by different names such as Shaykh, Leader, Guide, *Mahdī*, the Wise Man, the Mature, the Perfect, the Perfector, the World Reflecting Chalice, the Cosmos Reflecting Mirror, the Mighty Opium and the Great Elixir.[21] Yet even with the sealing of Prophethood, the Muḥammadan Reality, with its manifestation in the Perfect Man still continues as an actuality in this world.

The second quality of the Perfect Man is that he is the centre of the universe. The Perfect Man is considered the fruit of the tree of creation, and the purpose of God's bestowing existence upon the things is so that Perfect Man will be manifested. The Perfect Man being the centre of the universe can be described with reference to the ancient idea of man being a microcosm of the universe which is called the macrocosm. The early Islamic Philosophers such as al-Kindī and al-Farābī had read such descriptions of the microcosm in Greek philosophy, but it was a group of tenth century Arab thinkers named the Ikhwān al-Ṣafā' (the Brethren of Purity) that developed this concept, in particular, the comparison between man's body with the universe. The similarities between man's soul and the universe were subsequently described by Sufis such as Ghazālī, Ibn 'Arabī and Nasafī. The idea of man as the microcosm being superior to the macrocosm has already been discussed in detail in section three of the first chapter, so it is not necessary to repeat it here.[22]

In brief however, Nasafī describes the relation of the microcosm with the macrocosm which integrates both man's spirit and body. The intelligent man becomes God's caliph in the macrocosm because everything that exists in the macrocosm is created to serve him. In addition, everything in the macrocosm also exists within the microcosm and so it is the task of man to become master of these, making his attributes obedient and subservient to himself. Nasafī describes this in another way, that is, when the Perfect Man separates light from darkness so that all of God's attributes are manifested in the appropriate manner.

> The alchemy that mankind performs is that he takes the soul of whatever he eats. He takes the select and quintessence of those things, that is, light is separated from darkness in such a way that light knows and sees itself as it is. This is not possible except in the Perfect Man.
>
> O dervish! The Perfect Man completes this alchemy and completely separates light from darkness because light does not know or see itself in any other place and it sees and knows itself in the Perfect Man.[23]

The third quality of the Perfect Man as described by Nasafī is that only one exists at any one time.

> This Perfect Man is always in this world and there is only one Perfect Man. This is because all creatures are like one person and the Perfect Man is the heart of that person and creatures cannot exist without a heart. There is not more than one heart, so there is not more than one Perfect Man in this world. There are many wise men in this world, but there is only one heart. Other people are in the process of perfection, each one has its own perfection. When the unique wise man passes away from this world, another person reaches his level and becomes his successor so that this world is not without a heart.[24]

God requires only one Perfect Man in which to display the entirety of His attributes.

> If in all the world one person reaches perfection, this light can see its own beauty and witness its own attributes, names and actions. There is no need for all humans to reach perfection. If all humans reached perfection, then the attributes, names and actions of this light would not be completely manifested, and the order of this world would not exist. It is necessary for each person to have a level and be the locus of

> manifestation of an attribute. Each person has the preparedness for a task in order that the attributes, names and actions of this light become completely manifested and so that the order of the world exists.[25]

From these three qualities of the Perfect Man (that is, his eternal existence, his existing as the heart of existence and the existence of just one Perfect Man), it is now possible to make a distinction between the Prophet and the Friend. This is especially the case regarding the eternal existence of the Perfect Man. Prophecy terminates with Muḥammad, however, the existence of the Perfect Man in this world continues. There is no such obstacle when the concept of the eternal existence of the Perfect Man is applied to Friendship, for Friendship is also eternal. The word "Friend" *(walī)* is one of God's names mentioned in the Koran: "Allah is the Friend of those who believe,"[26] and this name is shared by some of His creatures, again this has a Koranic basis: "Now surely the Friends of God – they shall have no fear nor shall they grieve."[27] Izutsu has made the relevant point that if God's names are eternal, and if man shares a name with God, then it follows that both the Friendship of God and the Friendship of man are eternal. Moreover, God does not call Himself "prophet" or "messenger" which means that the functions of the prophet and messenger are not eternal, but historically limited.[28]

The relationship between Friendship and Prophecy becomes clearer with Nasafī's own definition of the two terms:

> O dear friend! The meaning of "Prophet" in Arabic is "informer", and the meaning of "Friend" *(walī)* is "proximity". So in Arabic, the person who is an informer is a Prophet and the person who is in proximity is a Friend.
>
> O dear friend! At first the wayfarer says that the Friend is the person that God Most High chooses among his servants for Friendship and makes him the near one *(muqarrab)* of His Excellency. He designates him for His inspiration so that he can be certain of God's existence and oneness. This is the meaning of the Perfect Man. A Prophet is the person that God Most High selects from His Friends and designates for His revelation, and He sends him to the creatures so that they are made aware of God and he shows them the path that leads to God. This is the meaning of the Perfecting Man *(insān-i mukammil)*.[29] So a Prophet has two faces, one face is turned to God and the other face is turned to the creatures. He accepts from the Truth and passes on to the creatures. That is, he accepts with the face that is turned to God and he passes on God's orders to the creatures with the face that is turned to them. The name of the face which is turned to God is Friendship and the name of the face which is turned to the creatures is Prophecy.[30]

So the Prophet is also a Friend, and it is through his Friendship that he is a Perfect Man, hence Nasafī's statement that Friendship is the heart of Prophecy. With respect to the Friendship of the Prophet, it is true that the Prophet can be the Perfect Man, satisfying all three conditions mentioned above, but with the termination of Prophecy, Friendship continues in the Friends.

II. THE SUPERIORITY OF FRIENDSHIP OVER PROPHECY

(You are only a warner and the people has its guide)[31]

In then previous section it was shown that through an analysis of the Perfect Man and the Muḥammadan Reality that Nasafī believed the Friends could reach the spiritual station of the Prophets. Moreover, he commented that Friendship was the heart of Prophecy, so now it is necessary to describe the manner in which the superiority of Friendship over Prophecy is manifested.

Knowledge and Friendship

Friendship is a rank which has a closer standing to God and this is reflected in the knowledge of the Friend compared to that of the Prophet in his capacity as Prophet:

> O dervish! According to the people of Unity, the wise men *(dānāyān)* are of three kinds: Philosophers, Prophets and Friends. A Philosopher knows the natures of things, a Prophet knows the natures and qualities of things, and the Friend knows the natures, qualities and realities of things. No one is equal to the Friend in knowledge *('ilm)* and power *(qudrat)*. This is because God has two self-disclosures *(tajallī)*: a common self-disclosure *(tajallī-yi 'āmm)* and a special self-disclosure *(tajallī-yi khāṣṣ)*. The common self-disclosure is an expression for the individual existents and the special self-disclosure is an expression for the Friends, and this is the meaning of: "And it is God, He is the Friend, He gives life to the dead: It is He Who has power over all things,"[32] and this is the meaning of: "God is omnipotent, He knows everything."[33,34]

The knowledge of the Philosopher is of the natures of things, in other words, of things as manifested in the cosmos, while that of the Prophets is the knowledge of revelation which is specific to a historical setting. Nasafī offers another three-fold classification to explain the relationship between the Philosopher, Prophet and Friend. The man of knowledge *('ālam)* is a believer, the man of much knowledge *('alīm)* is a Prophet and the man of most knowledge *('allām)* is a Friend. Nasafī then discusses the differences between Moses (the Prophet) and Khiḍr (the Friend). For Sufis, Khiḍr was the un-named individual that Moses met in verse 18: 65–82 of the Koran. In this story, Khiḍr recognises that Moses is unable to understand his knowledge and therefore he says to Moses: "Surely you cannot have patience with me; and how can you have patience in that of which you have not got a comprehensive knowledge?"[35] However, Khiḍr allows Moses to accompany him on the condition that he does not question him on anything that occurs, and that if Moses asks such questions, then the two would have to separate from each other. Khiḍr and Moses set off, and on their way, Khiḍr makes a hole in the bottom of a boat, kills a young boy and finally fixes a wall of a city where some people had refused them hospitality. For Moses, each of these acts is inexplicable and seems contrary to the actions of a person who follows the Holy Law, and therefore he questions Khiḍr each time. Khiḍr explains that he made the hole in the boat because the king intended to appropriate it from its owners who were poor men. He killed the young boy because his parents were believers and they feared that the boy would become dishonest and ungrateful. Finally, he fixed the wall because it belonged to two orphans and beneath the wall was a buried treasure. Thus, Khiḍr possessed a knowledge of the unseen whereas Moses understood the manifest dimension of things:

> Moses was a Prophet and a man of much knowledge because he had the knowledge of a Holy book. Khiḍr was a Friend and a man of most knowledge and had witnessed the knowledge of the book's word. A word in unseen, thus Khiḍr was a man of most knowledge about the unseen *(ghuyūb)*.[36]
>
> It is related that Moses met with Khiḍr and they spent some time together. One day when they were in the desert, they became hungry. [Suddenly] a gazelle appeared and stood between them. The side of the gazelle which faced Khiḍr was cooked and the side which faced Moses was raw. Khiḍr began to eat but Moses could not eat. Khiḍr said, "O Moses! Bring some fire wood and cook the meat in a pan and eat it!" Moses asked Khiḍr, "Why is your side cooked and my side raw?" Khiḍr answered, "O Moses! I am in the next world and you are in this world. The sustenance of this world is acquired and the sustenance of the next world is ready and cooked. This world is the abode of toil and the next world is the abode of reward. Our provisions are ready and available, but your provisions depend upon striving and effort."
>
> "Whenever Zacharias went into the chamber to her, he found provisions with her, and he said, 'O Mary! Where is this food from?' She answered, 'This is from God, for God gives without stint to whom He will.'[37]"[38]

Moses's lower degree of knowledge (that is, Prophetic knowledge) is useful in a practical sense but it is not sufficient for those who have the capacity to comprehend the realities behind the qualities of things:

> O dear friend! The Prophet is a warner and the Friend is a guide. This is because the Prophet wants to ward off corruption from the creatures and manifest wholesomeness among them, and this is impossible without warning. The Friend wants to remove association of others with God *(shirk)* and manifest unity among the creatures and this cannot be guaranteed without guidance.
>
> Philosophers have made commands and prohibitions, and promises and threats, based upon the natures of things. The Prophets have made commands and prohibitions, and promises and threats, based upon the qualities of things . . . But the Prophets could not say to everyone what the quality is in speaking the truth or lying, in eating lawful food or forbidden food, in honesty or treachery, because not everyone can understand. Moreover, [if the Prophets had done so] then [their] warning would have become long and drawn out, so they gave their warnings in a brief manner. They said that Hell is a place for the person who lies or is treacherous, and there are many torments and punishments there. Likewise, they said that Heaven is a place for whoever tells the truth and remains honest and there is much comfort and happiness there. . .
>
> The Friends say that the removal of corruption from the people and the manifestation of wholesomeness among them is extremely good. But because [the Prophets] made their warnings brief, the good souled pious person and the chaste seeker are always placed in veils and do not reach God, and this is not good.[39]

Even though the Friend has the most knowledge that humans can hope to acquire, they should realise that their knowledge is limited in relation to that of God. The knowledge of the Friend is that of the immutable entities (or to use Nasafī's phrase, "the immutable realities"[40]). Since these are infinite, it is impossible for man to know them as they are, thus any idea of perfection in knowledge is only relative:

> O dear friend! The knowledge of the Philosopher is of the natures of things, and the knowledge of the Prophet is of the qualities of things and the knowledge of the Friend is of the realities of things. Whoever truly understands these three kinds of knowledge is a Philosopher, Prophet and Friend. So perhaps a Philosopher is perfect in wisdom *(ḥikmat)* and has understood God [through wisdom], and perhaps a Prophet is perfect in Prophecy and has understood God [through Prophecy], but it is impossible for a Friend to be perfect in Friendship and have understood God [perfectly through Friendship].[41]
>
> The knowledge which is particular for the Prophet is one thing and the knowledge which is particular for the Friend is another. Although

knowledge is [only] one attribute of God, and power is [only] one attribute of God, knowledge and power have many levels and types in relation to the object of knowledge and the object of power. It is impossible for one person to obtain all the various kinds of power because man's life is short and there are many kinds of knowledge. It is extremely difficult for one person to reach perfection in one kind of knowledge, and in this world there are few people who are perfect in [even] one kind of knowledge. For example, it is difficult for a person to reach perfection in knowledge and know through verification in such a way that nothing remains concealed for him, even if he lived for a hundred years. [It is difficult] to reach perfection and know through verification the knowledge of astrology and the insight of the microcosm and the macrocosm and all the different kinds of knowledge. In this world, there are Philosophers, Prophets and Friends who each have a particular knowledge, so it is not necessary for a person to know all the different kinds of knowledge.[42]

As discussed in chapters three and four, the goal of Sufism is felicity, which is having knowledge of God. This knowledge is intimately related to man's practical effort and is expressed by Nasafī in terms of freedom:

Know that freedom has three ranks:

The first kind is dying from the veils of both fortune and fame and also darkness and appetites, and forgetting the veils of darkness and becoming free from the bonds of darkness' veils.

The second kind is dying from the veils of light which are intelligence, virtue and obedience, and becoming free from their bonds. Prophecy is dying through seeing and becoming free from the bonds of self-conceit, and this is the freedom of the Prophets. Our Messenger, the Master of Prophets said, "Poverty is my pride."[43]

The third kind is dying from oneself and becoming free from the bonds of oneself and this is the freedom of the Friends. The greater Friend and Master of the Wise said, "Die before you die."[44]

O dervish! At this point the wayfarer is freed from Hell and arrives at Heaven, and that dear one stated:

If you want to live, die before death, o friend!
Because Idris [Enoch] become a dweller of heaven from such a death.[45]

III. THE SUPERIORITY OF PROPHECY OVER FRIENDSHIP

It has been shown that the Prophet is also a Friend, but his Friendship is superior to his Prophecy.[46] Yet in another respect, Prophecy is superior to Friendship, which is indicated by the author of *Tabṣirat al-mubtadī'* (Clarification for Beginners) which was composed in the same century as Nasafī's works:

. . .the furthest limit of the stage of Friendship is the beginning of the stage of Prophecy. Hence all the sciences of unveiling bestowed upon the Friend are known by the Prophet but not vice versa.[47]

The important point here is that the Prophet has all the sciences of unveiling bestowed upon him which the Friend has. For Nasafī, however, the Prophet is a Prophet because he informs the creatures about the exoteric dimension of the knowledge that God gives. The Friend remains a Friend because he does not perform this function, but keeps the esoteric knowledge to himself until the time comes when he can divulge it to others. Since it is the Prophet's duty to deliver the exoteric form of knowledge to all people, it is possible to see Prophecy as superior to Friendship. God places this obligation on the Prophets and even the Friend must respect these commands and prohibitions of God. This superiority is revealed in the Koranic story of Moses and Khiḍr, especially in Khiḍr's response to a command of Moses. According to this story, after killing the young boy, Khiḍr reprimand Moses, saying, "Did I not say that you will not be able to have patience with me," Moses replied, "If I ask anything of you after this, keep me not in your company." However, Moses could not restrain himself and asked Khiḍr about his subsequent actions. Hearing these new questions, Khiḍr realised that he had to depart from Moses since the Prophet had previously commanded this.[48] Thus Khiḍr pays respect to Moses, that is, he is a follower of Moses because of Moses's Prophetic capacity.[49]

This story presents some problems because if the Prophet possesses both Prophecy and Friendship, then why was Moses, in his capacity as Friend, unable to understand the esoteric actions of Khiḍr? The answer to this question is that no one can be perfect in Friendship (as Nasafī states several times), so no Friend or Prophet can know everything. Another explanation (although not explicitly discussed by Nasafī) is found in Ibn 'Arabī's understanding of the "solitary ones" *(afrād)* who comprise the individuals of various spiritual ranking (from the *quṭb* to the *awtād* and *abdāl*). The singular of *afrād* is *fard* which is one of the divine names, meaning the Unique. According to Chodkiewicz this "explains the fact that their spiritual level is unknown and why they experience misunderstanding and reproach, for 'they have received a knowledge from God which is known to them alone.' This is illustrated by a reference to the story of Moses and Khiḍr."[50]

For Nasafī, the significance of the relationship between Moses and Khiḍr is that Friendship is recognised as the higher rank from one perspective, and Prophecy is superior from another. He expresses the tension involved in this relationship of each one being a follower of the other thus:

> . . . knowledge about the realities of things is from the lamp of Friendship for the Prophet, and knowledge about the qualities of things is from the lamp of Prophecy for the Friend.[51]
>
> O dear friend! The prophet is a warner and the Friend is a guide. The Possessor of the Holy Law is an Establisher and the Possessor of Realities is an Unveiler. Each Prophet is not a Possessor of a Holy Law, but each Possessor of a Holy Law is a Prophet. Each Friend is not a Possessor of Realities, but each Possessor of Realities is a Friend. An Unveiler is the follower of an Establisher in what is established, and an Establisher is the follower of an Unveiler in what is unveiled. The story of Moses and Khiḍr demonstrated this.[52]

This relationship is fundamental to Nasafī's ideas of the perfection of man after the cycle of Prophecy. A Friend must be a follower of a Prophet in order to preserve the Sharī'a from innovation, thus providing the basis for a stable Islamic community; a Prophet must be a follower of a Friend so that individuals can claim some of the attributes of Prophecy, which means the possibility of achieving the same degree of spiritual unveiling as Muḥammad on his ascent to God. Ibn 'Arabī expressed this point by indicating that in fact Friendship is a form of Prophecy:

> Know that Saintship *(walāyat)* is an all-inclusive and universal function that never comes to an end, dedicated as it is to the universal communication (of divine truth). As for the legislative function of prophecy and apostleship, it came to an end in Muḥammad. After him there will no longer be any law-bringing prophet or community to receive such, nor any apostle bringing divine law.
>
> God however is kind to His servants and has left for them universal Prophecy, which brings no law with it. He has also left to them the power of legislation through the exercise of individual judgement *(ijtihād)* concerning rules and regulations. In addition he has bequeathed to them the heritage of legislation in the tradition "The learned are the heirs of the Prophets." This inheritance involves the use of individual judgement in certain rulings, which is a form of legislation.[53]

Nasafī explained that Shaykh Sa'd al-Dīn Ḥammūya also believed that the Friends could be considered as Prophets:

> Know that Shaykh Sa'd al-Dīn Ḥammūya said that prior to Muḥammad, there were no Friends among the old religions and the

name "Friend" did not exist. All of the esteemed ones were called Prophets, although in each religion there was one person who was a Possessor of a Holy Law. There was no more than one [Possessor of a Holy Law]; the other [esteemed ones] who were called [Prophets] called the people to his religion. So there were many Prophets *(payghambar-ān)* in the religion of Adam who called the people to his religion, and this was the situation in the religions of Noah, Abraham, Moses and Jesus. When Muḥammad came he said, "After me there will be people who will be my followers and they will be the esteemed ones of His Holy Presence. They will be called "Friends" and these Friends will invite people to my religion."[54]

Ibn 'Arabī also makes the important point (mentioned already) that Friendship can only be considered higher than Prophecy on the condition that the two are discussed in the context of Friendship and Prophecy being within the same person:

When the Prophet speaks on matters that lie outside the scope of the law, he is then speaking as a saint and a gnostic, so that his station as a knower (of truth) is more complete and perfect than that as an apostle and law giver. If you hear any of the Folk saying or transmitting sayings from him to the effect that Saintship is higher than Prophecy, he means only what we have just said. Likewise, if he says that the saint is superior to the prophet and the apostle, he means only that is so within one person. This is because in his Saintship he is more perfect than he is as a prophet or apostle. It does not mean that any saint coming after him is higher than he, since one who follows cannot attain to the one who is followed, as regards that which follows him in. were he indeed to affect such a position, he would no longer be a follower; so understand. The Apostleship and Prophecy stem from Saintship and learning.[55]

The sealing of Prophecy means that God's message to the creatures has been perfected. This does not imply that God abandons His creation, since the Perfect Man (who is always in the world) and the Friends (who have the spiritual stations of the Prophets as their inheritors) provide advise and comfort for men and women. Nasafī explains that the Friends are those individuals who follow the Prophets in the Holy Law and who know its esoteric meaning since their faced are turned to God. For this reason, they are considered the heirs of the Prophets. In their Prophetic capacity, the Prophets understand the special qualities of revelation and as Friends they comprehend the realities or esoteric dimensions of such revelations. Hence, the sealing of Prophecy and the end of legislative prophecy is not a "great blow" because non-legislative Prophecy or Friendship, deals with the secrets of religion. In other words, legislative Prophets are limited in explaining the qualities of revelation whereas the Friends are not restricted in this way and may explain the hidden realties. This is what Nasafī appears to be saying in the following:

> Since you have understood that Friendship and Prophecy are the attributes of Muḥammad, know that until now the attribute of Muḥammad's Prophecy was manifested. He stipulated the establishment and manifestation of the form, and in fact, all the Messengers have stipulated the establishment of the form. Prophecy was completed when the form was established and perfected, but now is the time for Friendship to become manifest and for the spiritual realities to appear. The aforementioned Owner of Time is the Friend and when he appears the form is concealed, Friendship becomes manifest and the spiritual realities appear.
>
> Until now, there was discussion in the religious schools about the exoteric knowledge and spiritual realities were concealed since it was the time of Prophecy which stipulates the establishment of the form. When the establishment of the form was completed, Prophecy was also completed. Now it is the time for Friendship to become manifest. When Friendship appears, the spiritual realties become manifest and the form is concealed. Until now, there was discussion of form in the religious schools and now there is discussion of spiritual realities.[56]
>
> Know that the Philosophers are free in expressing knowledge, if they want they train others and they do not train others if they do not want to. The Prophets are compelled in expressing Prophecy for this is the special quality of this station. Whoever is in this station prevents the people from doing anything which has bad qualities and he calls people to do those things which have good qualities. This is impossible without causing bother and vexation to the Prophets, but they endure it all even though it brings them so much trouble. The Friends are free in expressing Friendship. If they want, they can tell people about the reality of things so that God becomes manifest [for them], and they do not tell these things if they do not want to, and this is impossible without unity and guidance.[57]

The relationship between Prophecy and Friendship is complex and this is nowhere more apparent than in the portrayal offered by Sa'd al-Dīn Ḥammūya:

> Know that the beginning of Prophecy is the end of Friendship because the Prophet comes from the Truth to the creatures and the Friend goes from the creatures to the Truth. But in the same way that the end of Friendship is the beginning of Prophecy, the end of Prophecy is the beginning of Friendship. [This is] because the end of the Friend is from form *(ṣurat)* with meaning *(ma'nā)* and the beginning of the Prophet is from meaning with form, so the beginning of that is the end of this, and the end of this is the beginning of that.[58]

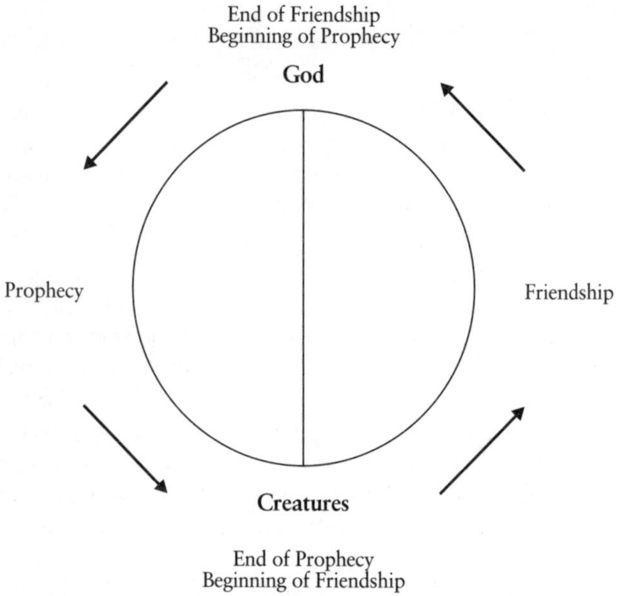

IV. THE FRIENDS AS HEIRS OF THE PROPHETS

The continual existence of the Perfect Man in this world after the sealing of Prophecy raises important questions. Under the name of "Friend", he enjoys the spiritual station of the Prophet and understands the esoteric meaning of God's revelations. This meant that the concept of the Friend, as described by Nasafī and other Sufis of his era, held very important social and political implications. This section will investigate the different interpretations of these Friends and the next section will focus on the political significance of Nasafī's interpretation of Friendship.

The arguments concerning political-religious authority in Islam was focused on the exegesis of a *ḥadīth* which stated, "The learned are the heirs of the Prophets."[59] Nasafī, as one would expect, refers to the Perfect Man (or Friend) as the heir of the Prophets:

> . . . after recognition of and encounter with God, the [Perfect Man] does not see any task or understand any duty as equal to or better than consoling people. He does not hold any comfort greater than saying and doing something so that the people pass their time in this world in an easy way after listening [to him] and taking his advice. Thus they

> become safe from the calamities and misfortunes of this world and they will be saved in the next world. Whoever [causes] such comfort is an heir of the Prophets because the knowledge and deeds of the Prophets are the children of the Prophets. Their legacy passes to their children.[60]

For Sufis, the concept of inheriting from the Prophets dates back at least to the ninth century when Sahl Tustarī discussed the Muḥammadan Light, the source of all creation.[61] Tustarī described a pre-eternal column of light from which everything in existence inherits, although the Prophets inherit in a more comprehensive manner. With the sealing of Prophecy, Tustarī claimed that there existed a Friend who shared in the charisma of the Prophet, which of course, is another way of saying that there is a Friend who is the heir of the Prophet. Three centuries after Tustarī, Ibn ʿArabī developed this idea by focusing upon a tradition in which Muḥammad mentioned 124,000 Prophets and 313 Messengers.[62] For a full manifestation of the Prophetic legacy, the Sufis believed that the number of Friends in this world at any time had to match the number of Prophets.[63] Nasafī also refers to the number of Friends in a similar way, although he has some reservations about the exact number:

> O dervish! The discourse about the Friends is well known and has been written in many books. It is said that there are 124,000, but it is better if the number is not fixed because no one knows the true number. It was said to Muḥammad, "We have spoken to you about the affairs of some."[64] Since the affairs of some were not told to Muḥammad, then no one knows the true number. Of this total, some were "Prophets without a book" *(nabī)* and some were "Prophets with a book" *(rasūl)*. Some were "Men of Resolution" and one was "the Seal." The Seal was Muḥammad.[65]

Nasafī's discussion of the heirs of the Prophets can be divided into two sections. The first represents an interpretation of the Friends known as the "substitutes" *(abdāl)* which was elaborated in more detail by other Sufis including Ibn ʿArabī and Rūzbihān Baqlī (1128–1209). Since Nasafī's description of the *abdāl* is somewhat limited, reference will be made to the beliefs of these mystics in order to clarify its significance. The second discussion of the Friends as heirs of the Prophets centres around Nasafī's position towards Shīʿ-ism. Several contemporary scholars have suggested that Nasafī was sympathetic towards twelver Shīʿ-ism and so it is necessary to address this issue once again.

(i) The Heirs of the Prophets: The *Abdāl*

Although the real number of *Abdāl* cannot be determined, Nasafī describes a hierarchy of three hundred and fifty six individuals:

> Know that there are three hundred and fifty six Friends in this world and there are always three hundred and fifty six present in this world. When one passes away, someone else takes his place. Therefore, there is never less than three hundred and fifty six and they are always in God's court and attending Him. Their tranquillity is through the *dhikr* of God, their knowledge is through witnessing Him and their tasting is through contemplating Him. There are six levels among these three hundred and fifty six: three hundred, forty, seven, five, three and one person.[66]

Nasafī's explanation of the number of Friends was orthodox in the Sufi world, for virtually the same system was described by Hujwīrī (d. 1071) in his *Kashf al-maḥjūb*.[67] Hujwīrī sets out a hierarchy of three hundred individuals named *akhyār*, forty *abdāl*, seven *abrār*, four *awtād*, three *nukabā* and one pole *(quṭb)*.[68] The function of some of these Friends was explained by subsequent Sufis. The seven continually move about and spread the Muslim faith in this world, and the four live at the cardinal points of the compass with reference to Mecca and every night they traverse the universe in thought and inform the Pole of any defects in order that he can remedy them.[69] Another distinction between the ranks of the Friends given by Nasafī (and by other Sufis including Rūzbihān and Ibn 'Arabī) is that they are the heirs of particular Prophets or angels who emphasise certain character traits:

> the three hundred are upon the heart *(bar dil)* of Adam, the forty are upon the heart of Moses, the seven are upon the heart of Jesus, the five are upon the heart of Gabriel, the three are upon the heart of Michael and the one is upon the heart of Isrāfīl.[70]

Yet it appears that Nasafī's spiritual hierarchy does not reach the pinnacle with the *abdāl* who follow the heart of Isrāfīl because he also describes a Friend who is the Seal of the Friends. Nasafī does not mention a Friend being the heir of Muḥammad, but there can be little doubt that he knew of this concept since it was a central theme in the works of Ibn 'Arabī and Sa'd al-Dīn Ḥammūya. The inheritance which the Seal of the Friends receives from the Seal of the Prophets is the same degree of spiritual insight.

> Do not suppose that the Seal of the Friends is additional *(zā'īd)* to the Seal of the Prophets because they are the loci of manifestation of one

reality. But there are two forms *(shikl)* in creation. One is at the beginning of time and the other is at the end of time.

Muḥammad and Aḥmad are two names and they are manifested in one named object *(musammā)*. At the beginning of time it is manifested through the Muḥammadan name, and he invites and calls people from this world to the next world, and at the end of time he is manifested in the Aḥmadan name and he invites the people from the next world to the Lord *(mawlan)* and to the origin of places of creatures and the secret of the Holy Law.

The Seal of the Prophets and the Seal of the Friends are of one art *(ṣan'a)* and their source *(manshā')* is one.[71]

In Ibn 'Arabī's words:

> As for the Seal of the Saints, he is the Saint, the Heir, the one whose (knowledge) derives from the source, the one who beholds all levels (of being). This sainthood is among the excellencies of the Seal of the Apostles, Muḥammad, first of the Community (of apostles) and Lord of Men as being he who opened the gate to intercession.[72]

The idea that the Seal of the Friends is the heir of Muḥammad is implicit in Nasafī's works because he states that the Seal of the Friends is able to reach the same spiritual station as the Seal of the Prophets:

> It is said that each person's spirit can ascend to its original station. In addition, it is said that the spirit of the Seal of the Prophets can ascend to the Throne. A group among the Sufis say that the Seals can ascend to the Throne, that is, the Seal of the Prophets and the Seal of the Friends.[73]

Yet Nasafī makes a distinction between the ascent of the Seal of the Prophets and that of the Seal of the Friends:

> Know that there is another death before natural death for the Prophets and the Friends, that is, they die a voluntary death before natural death, and they can see before natural death what others see after it. They are able to observe the states that exist after death and they can see from the stage of knowledge of certainty to the stage of the eye of certainty. This is because man's body is veil and when the spirit leaves the body, there is no other veil for it. The ascent of the Prophets is of two kinds; either the spirit without the body or the spirit with the body. The ascent of the Friends is of one kind, that is, the spirit without the body.[74]

The question to be asked is what relevance is there for the individual in this doctrine relating to the Friends. The answer is found in how

Ḥammūya (in Nasafī's words) defines the Friend/*abdāl* and how a person is able to join their ranks:

> . . . the three hundred and fifty six people are not called "Friends" but "substitutes" *(abdāl)*.[75]

The term substitute is used because in Nasafī's system, when one of the "Friends" dies, another takes his place. Nasafī explains the situation when the Pole, who occupies the pinnacle of the hierarchy, passes away:

> O dervish! When the Pole departs from this world, one of the three may succeed him, and one of the five may succeed to the position of the group of three, and one of the seven may succeed to the position of the group of five, and one of the forty may succeed to the position of the group of seven, and one of the three hundred may succeed to the position of the group of forty, and one of the individuals of the earth may succeed to the position of the group of three hundred so that there are always three hundred and fifty six in this world.[76]

Theoretically, it is possible for anyone to become a Friend. Of course there are many factors which come into play, such as the "four times" and man's constitution *(mizāj)*. However these factors cannot be known by man and therefore if he engages in ascetic discipline and religious effort and follows the Sufi path, he may just reach his perfection and be admitted into the ranks of the Friends, perhaps even progressing within the hierarchy towards the Throne.

(ii) The Heirs of the Prophets: Nasafī and Shī'-ism

In the middle of the twentieth century, Nasafī was associated by several Western scholars as a Shī'-ite mystic. This idea was advanced by H. Corbin who called Nasafī a "master of Iranian Shī'ite Sufism"[77] and named Ḥammūya a "fervent Shī'ite."[78] Other scholars have noted the Shī'-ite inclinations of the Kubrāwiyya order, pointing to the reverence of Kubrāwiyya Sufis (such as Najm al-Dīn Kubrā and 'Alā' al-Dawla Simnānī)[79] to 'Alī b Abī Ṭālib and the Shī'-ite Imams.[80] Yet despite these claims of Nasafī's Shī'-ism, one is struck by the scarcity of explicit references to this form of Islam within his treatises, and therefore it is necessary to re-investigate the nature of Nasafī's "Shī'ite Sufism". Such a discussion is necessary within the context of the heirs of the Prophets because the Shī'-ites held that their Imams were the heirs of the Prophets.

(a) As one would come to expect by now, Nasafī does not relate his own opinions with regard to Shī'-ism. He is content to present the beliefs of Sa'd al-Dīn Ḥammūya and the following passage has been taken to refer to his belief in twelver Shī'-ism:

> God Most High chose twelve people from Muḥammad's community and made them those who are near to Himself *(muqarrab-i khūd)* and He designated them for Friendship. He made them Muḥammad's deputies *(nayibān)*: "The wise are the heirs of the Prophets."[81] Concerning the truth of these twelve it is said: "The wise in my community are like the Prophets of the children of Israel."[82] According to the shaykh [Sa'd al-Dīn Ḥammūya], the Friends in Muḥammad's community are not more than these twelve. The last Friend, who is the twelfth, is the Seal of the Friends and his name is Mahdī and the Owner of Time.[83]

The foregoing, by itself, is not enough to prove Nasafī's Shī'-ite sympathies. More detailed passages which explain the nature of these twelve members of Muḥammad's community are required if Nasafī is to be associated with Shī'-ism. However there are no such passages in any of Nasafī's known treatises.

(b) Nasafī discusses Shī'-ism within the second chapter of *Kashf al-ḥaqā'iq*, entitled "The Gnosis of Man."[84] In this section, he lists the various Shī'-ite schools of thought, such as the Twelvers, Kaysanis and Ismā'īlīs. This portrayal of Shī'-ism may reflect the importance (or lack of importance) that Nasafī held for the Sunnī/Shī'ite question. In his works the beliefs of the *'Ulamā'* are explained first, followed by those of the Philosophers and finally the discourses of the People of Unity are presented. Thus, it seems that the sections which Nasafī considered as the most relevant are saved till last. Now, the aforementioned discussion pertaining to Shī'-ism in *Kashf al-ḥaqā'iq* is presented within the explanation of *'Ulamā'* belief which comes before those of the Philosophers and People of Unity.

Thus, it may have been Nasafī's opinion that the Sunnī/Shī'-ite question was insignificant when compared with the fundamental message of Sufism. This appears to be the message of the author of *Kashf al-ṣirāṭ* (who may have been Nasafī, as is explained in the appendix). In this work, the author adopts a conciliatory approach on the Sunnī/Shī'-ite conflict by stating that although some Sufis say that Friendship arose from Abū Bakr and other Sufis say it arose from 'Alī, it is better to say that both Abū Bakr and 'Alī were in the station of Friendship and argue no further.[85]

This is the conclusion that Nasafī draws from the *ḥadīth:* "My community will split into seventy-three factions after my death, but all of them will be in the fire except for one."[86] Nasafī's discussion focuses upon why there is no unity in the Islamic community and he cites Abū Manṣūr Māturīdī (d. 944)[87] and Muḥammad Ghazālī as advocated of the Sunnī position and he offers Abū Ja'far Ṭūsī[88] as typical of the Shī'-ite side. Having explained the views of both sides, Nasafī comments that their opinions are regarded as hypocritical *(takalluf)* by the Verifiers of the Truth *(muḥaqqiqān)* and Wise Men *(dānāyān)* because they know that the community is not split into seventy-three sects, rather they see that in one small area there are one hundred conflicting beliefs.[89] The significance of this discussion is of course that Nasafī is repudiating both Sunnī and Shī'-ite sides, a stance which accords with the general spirit of his non-partisan, non-sectarian works, representing perhaps, a belief that the Sunnī/Shī'-ite squabble is irrelevant and misses the essence of Sufism.

(c) The return of the Owner of Time *(ṣāḥib al-zamān)* who is also known as the Mahdī, is a fundamental article of faith for Shī'-ites. Nasafī also discusses the return of the Owner of Time by referring to Ḥammūya's views:

> The locus of manifestation of Prophecy is the Seal of the Prophets and the locus of manifestation of Friendship is the Owner of Time . . .
>
> Shaykh Sa'd al-Dīn Ḥammūya wrote many books regarding the reality of the Owner of Time and he said that he will appear in the time in which we are in now. But this helpless one [Nasafī] believes that the time of his appearance is unknown. O dervish! He will certainly appear since Muḥammad spoke of his appearance and signs, but it is not known when he will appear. As a result of Sa'd al-Dīn Ḥammūya's discourses, many people have become astonished and they swore to themselves, "I am the Owner of Time and those signs concerning his reality will be manifested in me." But they were not manifested in them and they died in this regret and many other people come and die in this regret.[90]

The concept of the Mahdī and his return to this world just before the Day of Judgement is a belief which is affirmed by both Shī'-ites and Sunnīs.[91] Therefore the above quotation is not sufficient to label Nasafī and Ḥammūya Shī'-ite. Yet Ḥammūya's views are interesting in that they may represent a reaction to the turbulent thirteenth century in which there were several Mongol invasions, the capture of Baghdad and the execution of the Caliph, and also the millenarian propaganda of the Ismā'īlīs. Given such circumstances, it would hardly be surprising if both Shī'-ites and Sunnīs were expecting the return of the Mahdī to restore justice to the devastated Islamic community.

Although Nasafī himself claimed contrary to Ḥammūya that the present time may not be the moment for the Owner of Time to appear,[92] it may be the case that he held the return to be very near. The reason for this assumption is due to the fact that in Nasafī's dream mentioned at the start of *Kashf al-ḥaqā'iq*, the Prophet told him not to reveal his treatises until seven hundred years had elapsed since the hegira. At such a time, the various religious schools and beliefs would no longer exist, they would all be replaced by a single belief and then people would be able to study and understand his treatise.

There are two possible explanations of the significance of seven hundred years after the hegira. The first is the idea that the Islamic community is renewed or revived every hundred years. (This is based upon a *ḥadīth* which states: "At the beginning of every hundred years, someone belonging to that time will renew its religion."[93]) The "orthodoxy" of this belief is reflected in al-Ghazālī's reference to this *ḥadīth* in his *al-munqidh min al-ḍalal*.[94] The second possible explanation is related to the return of the Mahdī which may also be connected to the cycles that Nasafī describes in the discourses of the Transmigrationists. The Transmigrationists believed in a series of three cycles. After each period of one thousand years there is a lesser resurrection *(qiyāmat-i ṣughrā)* and after each period of seven thousand years there is a great resurrection *(qiyāmat-i kubrā)* and after each period of forty-nine thousand years there is the greatest resurrection *(qiyāmat-i 'uẓmā)*. With the lesser resurrection, peoples' customs and habits change and the Holy Law of the Prophets are annulled. During the great resurrection, a Prophet finds it easy to establish a new Holy Law whereas in other times it is impossible. With the greatest resurrection, the world is ruined through floods and storms and no life remains on earth until the process of life through plants, animals and humans commences once again.[95] Did Nasafī hold these cycles as his own personal belief and in some way connect the year seven hundred after the hegira with one of the resurrections, and did he somehow associate the Owner of Time with the resurrections? The answer is not clear, but I doubt that they were Nasafī's own beliefs since these discourses appear in the sections of the Transmigrationists.[96]

Even though he was told by the Prophet Muḥammad in his dream that the circumstances of the Islamic community would change after seven hundred years after the hegira, it seems that Nasafī was somewhat sceptical:

> In the opinion of this helpless one, the circumstances will always be just as they are in this very hour. The circumstances will not change one iota, although the conflicts between people may cease in one or two regions.[97]

One may also speculate of the Mahdī or hidden Imam that both Nasafī and Ḥammūya had in mind. Again there are two possible interpretations, the first being a cosmic Mahdī for each individual and the second is the conventional Mahdī who returns to the world prior to the Resurrection. Regarding the first of these, it is interesting that Ḥammūya is reported to have said: "The hidden Imam will not appear before the time when people are able to understand, even from the very thongs of his sandals, the secrets of *tawḥīd*."[98] In other words, the Mahdī or hidden Imam is internalised and appears at any time for the individual who has knowledge of him. Is this the identity of Nasafī's Invisible Shaykh *(shaykh al-ghayb)*?[99] According to 'Allāmah Ṭabāṭabā'ī, ". . .it is the hidden Imam who directs man's spiritual life and orients the inner aspect of human action toward God . . . The Imam watches over men inwardly and is in communication with the soul and spirit of men even if he be hidden from their physical eyes."[100]

Since the hidden Imam appears just before the resurrection, he may be considered as a herald of what is to come. Just like Ḥammūya's internalisation of the Imam, Nasafī describes a belief of the People of Unity, which internalises four possible days of resurrection for each individual. The first day of resurrection is termed the "lesser resurrection" which is when the individual is born and has a life of form *(ḥayat-i ṣūratī)*. The "intermediate resurrection" occurs when the child is able to distinguish right and wrong and commences the life of meaning *(ḥayat-i mā'nā)*. When the individual has belief and attains peace *(sakīna)*, the "greater resurrection" takes place. Finally the "greatest resurrection" is when the individual reaches the world of contemplation *('iyān)* and stability *(tamkīn)*, which is the highest spiritual station as described in chapter five.

The ideas concerning the Mahdī are not specific to Shī'-ism, for the roles of the Sufi Invisible Shaykh and the Mahdī seem very similar once the wayfarer internalises the Mahdī as a spiritual guide. Thus once again, Nasafī's reference to the Mahdī and his dream are not sufficient proof to label him a Shī'-ite.

(d) Another factor which may link Nasafī with Shī'-ism is his belief expressed in the very beginning of *Kashf al-ḥaqā'iq* that he is in a state of infallibility *('aṣmat)* with God. This word is related to *ma'ṣūm*, meaning infallible, which is a state attributed to Shī'ites to the twelve Imams. Nasafī was told by Muḥammad in a dream that he (Nasafī) was infallible. Nasafī then asked Muḥammad the meaning of infallibility and who is infallible:

> The Prophet said, "Infallibility is security *(amānat)* from oneself. Whoever brings his own hand and tongue under control is safe from himself and he becomes infallible since no nuisance or remorse comes to him from them." When you have understood the Prophet's answer and comprehended the meaning of infallibility, now know that infallibility, protection *(ḥifẓ)* and continence *('āfiyat)* share the same meaning. However, the *'Ulamā'* have used each one in a particular place out of courtesy *(adab)*. If this security *(amān)* is with a Prophet, they say that he is in [a state of] infallibility with God. If it is with a Friend, they say that he is [in a state of] protection with God. And if it is with a believer, they say that he is in a [state of] continence with God.[101]

Thus Nasafī gives a meaning to infallibility which "orthodox" Twelver Shī'-ites would find difficult to accept, since it encompasses believers as well as the Imams. The self-attribution of infallibility by individual Sufis was not unique to Nasafī, for Rūzbihān Baqlī indicates that this was one of his characteristics.[102] Infallibility then is not the preserve of the Shī'-ite Imams, but this point may be considered as yet another indication of the similarity or of the close relationship between Shī'-ism and Sufism during this period of Islamic history.

The Shī'-ism of Nasafī or Ḥammūya has yet to be conclusively proven, and recent scholarship has begun to question Corbin's ideas.[103] The reality of Nasafī's and Ḥammūya's beliefs are far from clear and more detailed research needs to be undertaken to determine their positions regarding Shī'-ism. One suspects that there are very strong sympathies with Shī'-ism beyond those of the usual reverence for the Prophet's family[104] and also beyond the general convergence of Sufism with Shī'-ism during the thirteenth century.[105] It is most likely the case that those who wanted to interpret Nasafī's treatises in a Shī'-ite manner could certainly have done so. M. Molé, in his introduction to Nasafī's *al-Insān al-kāmil* states: "Avec sa théosophie de structure ismaélienne et d'affinités dudécimaines, Nasafi apparait comme le représentant d'un ces mouvements shi'ites dont le bouillonement est si caractéristique pour les deux siecles qui séparent l'époque des Mongols de celle des Safavides, et qui préparent le terrain pour le shi-isme safavide."[106]

The convergence between Shī'ism and Sufism became stronger after Nasafī's death and nowhere is this more evident than in the treatises of Ḥaydar Āmulī (d. after 1385) who was well aware of Nasafī's works.[107] Āmulī integrated Ibn 'Arabī's ideas with his understanding of Shī'-ism, for example, he believed that 'Alī b. Abī Ṭālib was the Seal of the Friends, not Jesus.[108]

V. PERFECTION AND ITS POLITICAL SIGNIFICANCE

In chapter four, it was argues that the Kubrāwiyya order favoured a more "sober" version of Sufism. Nasafī also described a perfect wayfarer as one who returned from his encounter with God in a sober state. At this stage, the wayfarer had to become "free" *(āzād)*:

> Know that it has been said that the Perfect Man is the person for whom there are four things to perfection: good words, good acts, good character traits and gnosis. The Free Perfect Man is the person for whom there are eight things to perfection: good words, good acts, good character traits, gnosis, renunciation, seclusion, contentment and anonymity.[109]

Having defined the Free Perfect Man, Nasafī proceeds to classify them into two groups:

> Two groups appear when [the Free Perfect Men] have undertaken renunciation and have become free and released. After renunciation, some choose seclusion, contentment and anonymity and others choose satisfaction, submission and gazing *(niẓāra)*, but the aim of all of them is freedom and release.[110]

Those who choose seclusion, contentment and anonymity know that disunity *(tafraqa)* and confusion *(parākandagī)* come with association with the people of this world. So they are afraid and flee if by chance, something worldly or a worldly person appears before them. In contrast, those who choose satisfaction, surrender and gazing know that man cannot understand in what his fate lies. So if something of this world or a worldly person appears before them they do not flee and they are not afraid because this encounter may be beneficial to themselves or to others.[111] Nasafī himself commented that he had spent time among both groups, but since he perceived advantages and disadvantages in both, he could not decide which one had chosen the best path.[112]

However, in his other treatises, Nasafī seems to give preference to the group which accepts association with worldly people. His own definition of the perfect person is the one who possesses good words, good acts, character traits and gnosis.[113] Although Nasafī states that obtaining gnosis without seclusion is impossible, he also comments that the acquisition of good character traits comes only with association and interaction with people.[114] Thus perfection requires both seclusion and association. Once gnosis and good character traits have been acquired, the task of the Perfect Man is to help others:

> The Perfect Man does not see any obedience better than correcting this world and finding correctness among the people, removing their bad habits and customs, placing good rules and regulations among them, calling people to God, informing them of His magnanimity, greatness and unity, praising the next world very much – informing the people of its eternity *(baqā'ī)* and permanence *(thābat)*, and warning them about this world – describing its changability and impermanence, speaking of the advantages of mendicity *(darwishī)* and anonymity until these two attributes become sweet to them. . .[115]

The idea of there being no better obedience than correcting this world rather than fleeing from it is reconfirmed in other passages:

> As far as possible, do not harm others since there is no disobedience other than causing harm. As far as possible, bring comfort to everything and every person, since there is no obedience other than bringing comfort. Know for sure that whatever a person does, he does that thing to himself. If he is the cause of harm, he harms himself. If he brings comfort, he comforts himself.[116]

However, this guidance for the benefit of worldly people is merely one of advice giving. There is no compulsion involved for the worldly people to accept the recommendations of the Perfect Man since he does not have the political power to enforce his wishes. In any case, making people conform to God's commands and compelling them to be obedient would remove the necessity of God's judgement. Therefore, the Perfect Man advises people and they heed his counsel if they are wise. Concerning the Perfect Man and political power, Nasafī comments:

> . . .this Perfect Man does not possess power *(qudrat)* despite his perfection and greatness, and he lives with unfulfilled desires *(nā-murādī)* yet he passes his time in comfort. He is perfect in terms of knowledge and character traits but he is incomplete in terms of power and desire.
>
> O Dervish! There is a time when the Perfect Man is the possessor of power and he is a ruler *(ḥākim)* or king *(pādshāh)*. However, it is clear that human power is weak and when you look at the reality, man's inability is greater than his power, and his unfulfilled desires are more [numerous] than his fulfilled desires. The Prophets, Friends, kings and sultans have desired many things to be and they were not, and they desired many things not to be and they were. So it is clear that all people, from the complete to the incomplete, from the wise to the ignorant, from kings to subjects are incapable and helpless and live their lives with unfulfilled desires. When some of the Perfect Ones saw that man does not have the power to fulfil his desires and that power cannot be obtained through his own effort or endeavour and that it is necessary to

live with unfulfilled desires, they knew there was nothing better for man than renunciation, and there was no obedience equal to freedom and release, so they renounced everything and became free and released.[117]

In addition, the Perfect Man does not actively seek political power nor the approval of those around him:

> O Dervish! Do not suppose that the Free Person does not have a house and lodging or garden and orchard, for he may own them. He may be a ruler or king, but he is not happy if kingship is given to him and he is not sad if it is taken away from him. The coming and going of kingship is the same for him and the rejection and acceptance by the people is [also] the same for him. He does not say, "I want to be rejected," if they accept him. And he does not say, "I want to be accepted," if they reject him.[118]

There was no real consensus among Sufis regarding contact with secular rulers, for several leading shaykhs are known to have had connections with the secular leaders of society. One famous example is Shaykh 'Ubayd Allāh Aḥrār (1403–1490) of the Naqshbandiyya order who considered it necessary to keep contact with the rulers and influence them to protect Islamic Law and the community.[119] However, Sufis affiliated to the Kubrāwiyya order are generally regarded as distancing themselves from the worldly corruption that comes with power and kingship.[120]

> O dear friend! Do not eat or accept anything derived from the fortune of the court of kings because their fortune hardens the heart. And do not eat or accept anything derived from the fortune of religious bequests *(waqf)* because the fortune of religious bequests blackens the heart.[121]

Nasafī followed a hard line with rulers and connections with political power:

> O Dervish! The Wise Man, the Verifier of Truths and the Men of God are beneath domes[122] which are their keepers and guards and become their fortress and armour and are the cause of their cleanliness and purity . . . O Dervish! Their manifest dimension is like the manifest dimension of the common people and their non-manifest dimension is like the non-manifest dimension of the élite. They do not give access to any leader or chief and they do not make claims of leadership or lordship. Each one is engaged in an occupation which is necessary to him and their occupation is their means of livelihood. They flee from the fortune of kings and tyrants.[123]

Nasafī's personal advice to his dervishes is that they need to be aware that the love of leadership is inherent in the soul of all men. Therefore the remedy is to oppose the soul and renounce this love from the heart and become free:

> O Dervish! The love of being a king, minister, master, director, leader, shaykh, preacher, judge or teacher of a religious school and others like these, are all the doorways to Hell. The ignorant person is he who tries every day to make these doorways wider and larger for himself. The wise man is he who tries to block these doorways or else make them more narrow for himself. Closing off the doorways to Hell for oneself is the renunciation of fame.
>
> O Dervish! There is no world without these [kingship, etc], and it is necessary for these positions to exist in this world. But it is not necessary for you to occupy these positions. When the wayfarer relinquishes these cruel wildernesses and renounces leadership, he is released. The wayfarer remains in a state of terror as long as he has not relinquished these cruel wildernesses and there is no security for him.[124]

Nasafī's non-political world view may be explained in several ways. Firstly, if he was a Shī'-ite, or else associated with Shī'-ites, he may have found it expedient to conceal his ideas. Although little is known of the particular religious environment in which Nasafī lived, it is probable that the orthodox Sunnī *'Ulamā'* who were in the majority would not have favoured the passages in Nasafī's works which express a certain "Shī'-ite" leaning. In addition, some Ismā'īlīs believe that Nasafī followed their path[125] and if this is the case then it is likely that Nasafī would have attempted to conceal his ideas given that the Mongols came to the Middle East on the pretext of wiping out the threat of the Assassins. Nasafī's vision of Sufism, however, contained no explicit threat to the rulers. Such a threat was to emerge with the combination of Sufism and Shī'-ism as propounded by certain descendants of Shaykh Ṣafī al-Dīn (1252–1334) who eventually succeeded in creating the Safavid state. Aside from the danger that Sufis faced from secular rulers, they also had to be careful in their relations with the *'Ulamā'*. Although Nasafī pays respect to the *'Ulamā'* and believed that the wayfarer should attend the *madrasa* before entering the *khānaqāh*, his Sufi views which were similar to those of Ibn 'Arabī could have resulted in problems for him. As mentioned in chapter one, the possession of Ibn 'Arabī's books in Egypt in the fourteenth century was prohibited and any person advocating his ideas was threatened with execution.

Notes

1 A popular *ḥadīth* among Sufis, see Schimmel, *Mystical Dimensions of Islam*, p. 99.
2 See Chittick, *The Sufi Path of Love* (Albany: SUNY Press, 1983), p. 10.
3 *al-Insān al-kāmil*, p. 3.
4 R. Austin (translated), *Ibn al-'Arabī: The Bezels of Wisdom*, p. 168.
5 *Manāzil al-sā'irīn*, p. 316.
6 *al-Insān al-kāmil*, pp. 52–67.
7 *Kashf al-ṣirāṭ*, Veliyuddin, no 1767, 218–219.
8 See M. Takeshita, *Ibn 'Arabī's Theory of the Perfect Man and its Place in the History of Islamic Thought* (Tokyo: Institute for the Study if Languages and Cultures of Asia and Africa, Tokyo University of Foreign Studies, 1987), p. 159.
9 *al-Insān al-kāmil*, p. 30.
10 Ibid, p. 110.
11 M. Takeshita, op. cit.
12 Quoted by Nasafī, *Kashf al-ḥaqā'iq*, p. 103. See B. Furūzānfar, op. cit., pp. 113–14.
13 Quoted by Nasafī, *Maqṣad-i aqṣā*, p. 276. See also Chodkiewicz, *Seal of the Saints*, p. 65–66.
14 Quoted by Nasafī, *Kashf al-ḥaqā'iq*, p. 104.
15 Nasafī, *Kashf al-ḥaqā'iq*, p. 104.
16 Chodkiewicz, *Seal of the Saints*, p. 67.
17 Ibid, p. 71.
18 That is, *Mulk*, *Malakūt* and *Jabarūt*.
19 *al-Insān al-kāmil*, p. 190.
20 Ibid, p. 5. See also *Maqṣad-i aqṣā*, p. 217.
21 *al-Insān al-kāmil*, p. 5.
22 See chapter II, III. For Nasafī's summarised treatment of this discussion, see *al-Insān al-kāmil*, p. 142–43.
23 Ibid, p. 25.
24 Ibid, p. 5. It is interesting that Ibn 'Arabī also described the Perfect Man as being the heart of the universe. "Through the Perfect Man appeared the perfection of the image. He is the heart to the body of the universe. The universe is the expression for everything other than God. It [the heart] is the Well-Visited House of God, since it contains him. He says in a *ḥadīth*, 'Neither my earth nor my heaven contains me, but the heart of my pious slave contains me.'" See Takeshita, p. 114.
25 *al-Insān al-kāmil*, p. 250.
26 Koran, 2: 257, cited by Nasafī in *Kashf al-ḥaqā'iq*, p. 186.
27 Koran, 10: 62.
28 T. Izutsu, *Sufism and Taoism* (Berkeley: University of California Press, 1983), p. 264.
29 The Persian of this word is ambiguous because it can read either *insān-i mukammal* (which means the Perfected Man, i.e. perfected by God) or *insān-i mukammil* (which means the Perfecting Man, i.e. perfecting the

creatures). From the text, it seems that the Perfecting Man is the correct reading. See also F. Meier's comments in "The Problem of Nature in the Esoteric Monism of Islam," p. 186.

30 *Kitāb-i tanzīl*, fol. 61b, line 6–15.
31 Koran, 8: 7, cited by Nasafī, *Kashf al-ḥaqā'iq*, p. 102.
32 Koran, 42: 9.
33 Koran, 28: 12.
34 *Kashf al-ḥaqā'iq*, p. 58–9.
35 Koran, 18: 67–68.
36 *Kashf al-ḥaqā'iq*, p. 59.
37 Koran, 3: 37.
38 *al-Insān al-kāmil*, pp. 307–8.
39 *Kitāb-i tanzīl*, fol. 62b, line 3 – fol. 63a, line 2.
40 *Manāzil al-sā'īrīn*, p. 365.
41 *Kitāb-i tanzīl*, fol. 62a, lines 15–19.
42 Ibid.
43 *Ḥadīth*, Furūzānfar, op. cit., no. 54.
44 *Ḥadīth*, Furūzānfar, op. cit., no. 352.
45 *Kashf al-ḥaqā'iq*, p. 104.
46 "Friendship is more powerful than Prophecy concerning the reality of Prophecy." *Kitāb-i tanzīl*, fol. 61b, line 15.
47 *Tabṣirat al-mubtadī'* translated by Chittick in *The Faith and Practice of Islam*, p. 88.
48 Koran, 18: 75–6.
49 See also R. Austin, *Ibn al-'Arabī: The Bezels of Wisdom*, p. 260.
50 Chodkiewicz, *Seal of the Saints*, p. 107.
51 *Kitāb-i tanzīl*, fol. 62b, lines 1–3.
52 Ibid, fol. 63a, lines 10–12.
53 Austin (translated), *Ibn al-'Arabī: The Bezels of Wisdom*, p. 168.
54 *Manāzil al-sā'īrīn*, p. 320.
55 Austin (translated), *Ibn 'Arabī: The Bezels of Wisdom*, p. 168–69.
56 *Maqṣad-i aqṣā*, p. 246.
57 *Kashf al-ḥaqā'iq*, p. 103–4.
58 Sa'd al-Dīn Ḥammūya, *al-Miṣbāḥ fī'l-taṣawwuf*, p. 137.
59 Reliable *ḥadīth*, quoted by Najm al-Dīn Rāzī, translated by H. Algar, op. cit., p. 445. Algar has found this *ḥadīth* in the collections of Bukhārī, Muslim, Abū Dā'ūd and Ibn Ḥanbal.
60 *al-Insān al-kāmil*, p. 6.
61 See G. Böwering, *The Mystical Vision of Existence in Classical Islam* (Berlin/New York: Walter De Gruyter, 1980), p. 65.
62 See Schimmel, *And Muḥammad is His Messenger* (Chapel Hill: The University of North Carolina Press, 1985), p. 56. See also Chodkiewicz, *Seal of the Saints*, pp. 53–54.
63 Chodkiewicz, *Seal of the Saints*, pp. 54 & 84.
64 A reference to the Koran 40: 78, "And certainly We sent apostles before you: there are some of them that We have mentioned to you and there are others whom We have not mentioned."
65 *Manāzil al-sā'īrīn*, p. 323.
66 *Manāzil al-sā'īrīn*, p. 317.

67 The only difference between Nasafī's explanation and that of Hujwīrī is that in Nasafī's scheme there is a group of five individuals whereas in Hujwīrī's system there is a group of four rather than five. See Hujwīrī (translated Nicholson) *Kashf Al-Mahjūb of Al Hujwiri*, (Gibb Memorial Series, no. 17. 1911; reprint London: 1959), p. 214.

68 Ibid. In addition, Nasafī's hierarchy resembles that of Rūzbihān Baqlī. The Latter added four more individuals, making three hundred and sixty, "God has three hundred and sixty eyes each day and night," Rūzbihān Baqlī, *Sharḥ-i shaṭḥiyyāt*, edited H. Corbin (Tehran: Department D'Iranologie de L'Institute Franco-Iranien, 1966), p. 367. These four other individuals are identified as Idris, Khiḍr, Elijah and Jesus who were carried off alive from death. In fact, the spiritual hierarchy offered by Rūzbihān was much more comprehensive than Nasafī's. The former mentions twelve thousand hidden Friends in Turkestan, India, Africa and Ethiopia, four thousand in Anatolia, Khurāsān and Iran, four hundred in Shatt Bahar, three hundred in North Africa and Egypt, seventy in Yemen, Ta'if, Mecca, the Hijaz, Basra and Batiyih, forty in Iraq and Syria, ten in Mecca, Madina and Jerusalem, seven who travel and fly around the world, three individuals (one in Fārs, another in Anatolia and another in Arabia) and finally the Pole. Rūzbihān, op. cit., p. 10.

Ibn 'Arabī's hierarchy is by far more detailed and complex than Nasafī's and Rūzibihān's, for he lists eighty four different classes of spiritual men, thirty-five of these have a constant number at any given time (see Chodkiewicz, *Seal of the Saints*, p. 103).

69 Carra de Vaux, "Walī," op. cit., p. 1109–1111.

70 *Manāzil al-sā'īrīn*, p. 319. Rūzbihān states: "There is a connection *(paywasta)* between God and those of the earth. There are three hundred people whose hearts resemble *(mānad)* Adam's heart, forty people whose hearts resemble Gabriel's, five people whose hearts resemble Michael's, three people whose heart resembles Isrāfīl's and one person whose heart resembles Azā'īl's." Rūzbihān, op. cit., p. 52–3.

In Ibn 'Arabī's system, the first of these follows in the footsteps of Abraham, the second follows Moses, the third follows Aaron, the fourth follows Idris, the fifth follows Joseph, the sixth follows Jesus and the seventh follows Adam. The pinnacle of these thirty five is the Pole, followed by two Imams and four *awtād* and seven *abdāl*. See Chodkiewicz, *Seal of the Saints*, p. 103.

71 Ḥammūya, *al-Miṣbāḥ fī'l-taṣawwuf*, p. 98.

72 Austin (translated) *Ibn al-'Arabī: The Bezels of Wisdom*, p. 67.

73 *al-Insān al-kāmil*, p. 110.

74 Ibid, p. 107.

75 *Manāzil al-sā'īrīn*, p. 322.

76 Ibid, p. 317.

77 H. Corbin, *History of Islamic Philosophy*, p. 69.

78 Ibid, p. 298.

79 See J. J. Elias, *The Throne Carrier of God: The Life and Thought of 'Alā ad-dawla as-Simnānī*, pp. 54–55 & 123. However, the fact that individual Sufis held the Prophet's family in esteem did not necessarily mean that they were advocates of Shī'ism.

80 H. Halm, *Shiism*, translated J. Watson (Edinburgh University Press, 1991), p. 74. See also M. Molé, "Les Kubrawiya Entre Sunnisme et Shiisme Aux Huitieme Siecles de l'Hégira," *Revue des Études Islamique* 52 (1961): 61–141.
81 *Ḥadīth*, Bukhārī, *'Ilm* 10, Ibn Dā'ūd, 'Ilm 1, Ibn Māja, *Muqaddima* 17.
82 This is variant of the previous *ḥadīth*.
83 *Manāzil al-sā'īrīn*, pp. 320–21.
84 *Kashf al-ḥaqā'iq*, for the discussion of Shī'-ism see page 82.
85 *Kashf al-ṣirāṭ*, Veliyuddin no. 1767, fol. 236a.
86 *Ḥadīth* quoted by al-Ghazālī in *Faith and Practice of al-Ghazālī* (al-munqidh min al-ḍalal), op. cit., p. 18.
87 See D. B. MacDonald, "Māturīdī" *E.I.*[1], vol V.
88 See R. Strothmann, "Al-Ṭūsī" *E.I.*[1], vol VIII.
89 *Kashf al-ḥaqā'iq*, p. 16.
90 *Maqṣad-i aqṣā*, p. 245–46.
91 A. A. Sachedina, *Islamic Messianism* (Albany: SUNY Press, 1981), p. 69.
92 Another example is found in *Manāzil al-sā'īrīn*, p. 321:

> One day I said, "O Shaykh! Is it expedient to propagate about the reality of one who has not yet come? Perhaps it may not be so [i.e. the moment of his appearance]." The Shaykh was very much vexed so I did not pursue the matter and did not speak of it.
>
> O Dervish! Whatever the Shaykh spoke about was a result of [his] gnosis, but many people were harmed by these discourses and many were perplexed. I mean that in my lifetime, I have seen several people in Khurāsān, Kirmān and Fārs who claimed to be the Owner of Time . . . But [their claims] were not true and they died in deep regret and many other people come and make this claim and they also die in deep regret.

93 See A. J. Wensinck, *Concordance et Indices de la Tradition Musulmane* (Leiden: E. J. Brill, 1992), 1:324; Abū Dā'ūd, *Malāhim* 1.
94 See al-Ghazālī in *The Faith and Practice of al-Ghazālī*, op. cit., p. 81.
95 *Manāzil al-sā'īrīn*, p.415–16.
96 F. Meier seems to be saying that these were Nasafī's own personal beliefs, "The Problem of Nature in the Esoteric Monism of Islam," op. cit., p. 182.
97 *Kashf al-ḥaqā'iq*, p. 3.
98 Cited by H. Corbin, *History of Islamic Philosophy*, p. 71.
99 *al-Insān al-kāmil*, p. 241. Najm al-Dīn Kubrā also mentions the Shaykh al-ghayb. For Kubrā, the *Shaykh al-ghayb* is not the eschatological figure in the exoteric Shī'-ite tradition who appears before the Resurrection. Rather he is the wayfarer's guide to the inner spiritual journey. The reality of the *Shaykh al-ghayb* is in fact the reality of the wayfarer himself:

> "Know that there is a witness *(shāhid)* for the traveller and he is called the Invisible Shaykh. The traveller is taken to heaven and he is made manifest there. The reason that he [the *Shaykh al-ghayb*] is his witness, [is because] he [the shaykh] is he [the traveller] because

the traveller moves and rests through the moving and resting of the Shaykh." *Fawā'iḥ al-jamāl wa fawātiḥ al-jalāl* [69].

"The first spiritual opening is through the eye, then through the face, then through the breast, then through the whole body, and this is called "the man of light" and what is in front of you is named the "leader of the people" and he is also called the Invisible Shaykh." *Fawā'iḥ al-jamāl wa fawātiḥ al-jalāl* [66].

100 'Allāmah Sayyid Ṭabāṭabā'ī, translated S. H. Nasr, *Shi'ite Islam* (Albany: SUNY Press, 1977). p. 214.

101 *Kashf al-ḥaqā'iq*, p. 4–5.

102 C. Ernst, *Rūzbihān Baqlī*, p. 48.

103 J. J. Elias has mentioned a treatise entitled *Risāla fī zuhūr khatm al-walāya* (Treatise on the Appearance of the Seal of Friendship) in which the Seal is not the Shī'-ite Mahdī (as one might suppose from reading Nasafī's works) but Jesus, which is more in line with Ibn 'Arabī's discussion of the Seal of the Friends of God. Indeed, Elias has also suggested 'Alā' al-Dawla Simnānī made a criticism of Nasafī's "misinterpretation" of Ḥammūya's beliefs regarding the nature of Friendship. See "The Sufi Lords of Bahrabad," Iranian Studies, 27, no. 1–4, 1994, p. 71–72.

104 For example, Ibn 'Arabī comments on an interpretation of a *ḥadīth* in which the Prophet asked God to "pray for Muḥammad and for the family of Muḥammad as You prayed for Abraham and the family of Abraham." See Y. Friedmann, *Prophecy Continuous* (University of California Press, 1989), p. 72. See also V. Danner who states, "We have only to recall that the early Shī'-ite Imams of the first century or so of Islam were also authorities in Sunnism and in Sufism precisely because they were the most prestigious of the Prophet's descendants." In "The Early Development of Sufism," *Islamic Spirituality: Foundations*, edited S. H. Nasr, (London: SCM Press, 1985), p. 246–7.

105 See H. Corbin, "De la Philosophie Prophétique en Islam Shī'ite," *Eranos Jahrbuch* 1962 (Zurich, 1963), p. 75, and H. Halm, *Shiism*, pp. 72–74.

106 M. Molé, *Kitāb al-Insān al-kāmil*, p. 26.

107 Āmulī refers to a "student" of Ḥammūya, see H. Landolt, "'Azīz-e Nasafī Et La "Monisme Ésotérique," op. cit., p. 167.

108 Sayyid Ḥaydar Āmulī, *Inner Secrets of the Path*, translated Assadullah ad-Dhaakir Yate (Dorset: Zahra Trust, 1989), p. 125.

109 *al-Insān al-kāmil*, p. 8.

110 Ibid, p. 9.

111 Ibid, p. 9.

112 Ibid, p. 10.

113 Ibid, p. 4.

114 *Kitāb-i tanzīl*, fol. 76b, lines 13–16.

115 *al-Insān al-kāmil*, p. 6.

116 Ibid, p. 182.

117 Ibid, p. 7–8.

118 Ibid, p. 139.

119 K. A. Nizami, "The Naqshbandiyya Order," in *Islamic Spirituality: Manifestations*, edited S. H. Nasr, p. 173.

120 D. DeWeese has suggested that the early Kubrāwī shaykhs such as Najm al-Dīn Kubrā, Najm al-Dīn Rāzī and 'Alā' al-Dawla Simnānī ultimately rejected political connections and this policy may account as one reason why this order declined in Central Asia to be eclipsed by the Naqshbandiyya. See "The Eclipse of the Kubrāviyah in Central Asia," *Iranian Studies*, Vol 21, no. 1–2, 1988). Yet not all of the early Kubrāwī shaykhs were non-political. DeWeese himself cites the case of Sayf al-Dīn Bākharzī (d. 1261) who was involved in the *waqf* administration and was responsible for the education of the Mongol khān, Berke. In addition, it has been suggested that Sa'd al-Dīn Ḥammūya was collaborating with the Il-khān state. See J. J. Elias, "The Sufi Lords of Bahrabad," op. cit., p. 73.

121 *Kitāb-i tanzīl*, fol. 78b, lines 12–13.

122 Reference to the *ḥadīth*, "My Friends are under My domes and only I know them." Furūzānfar, op. cit., no. 131.

123 *Kashf al-ḥaqā'iq*, p. 28–29.

124 *Manāzil al-sā'irīn*, p. 454.

125 F. Daftary, *The Ismā'īlīs* (Cambridge University Press, 1990), p. 454.

Conclusion

The obvious question that arises after studying Nasafī's treatises is what contribution did he make to the existing Sufi beliefs in thirteenth century Central Asia and Iran? Nasafī was not an original mystic in the same way as Ibn 'Arabī or Najm al-Dīn Kubrā, for Ibn 'Arabī's esoteric interpretation of the Koran probably cannot be matched by any other Sufi,[1] and Najm al-Dīn Kubrā's explanation of the ascent of the soul through visionary experience was quite unique during his lifetime.[2] However, Nasafī's importance lies in his ability to both incorporate all the major elements of Sufi belief as discussed by others and also to present them in a coherent fashion for novices of the Sufi path. Thus many familiar themes appear in a summarised yet lucid fashion including God's incomparability and similarity, the ultimate station of bewilderment, the all-encompassing nature of Sufism *(hama ūst)*, spiritual creating through *himmat* and the perfection of man in the form of *walāyat*. This simple and clear version of Sufism is demonstrated in his systematisation and order of Sufi ontology and epistemology; proof of this is Nasafī's six spiritual stations and the four stages of mystical knowledge, from *dhikr* to *fikr*, and then to *ilhām* and finally to contemplation *('iyān)* which is the station of stability *(tamkīn)*.

It is highly probable that his treatises provided the foundation for many Sufi novices to progress to more profound works of other Sufi masters. That Nasafī was establishing a basis and foundation and addressing beginners on the Sufi path may explain why he did not elaborate on more "advanced" topics, such as Najm al-Dīn Kubrā's *shaykh al-ghayb* and the *wujudī* explanation of the nature of the soul in the grave. Whatever the reason for Nasafī's failure to discuss these topics in detail, he should be considered as a major figure in strengthening and developing Sufism in Central Asia and Iran. Yet his influence extended further than these two areas as the existence of numerous manuscripts of his treatises in Turkey, China, Egypt and India demonstrate. Regarding the last of these, it has been shown that the Indian Sufi Muḥammad Gīsūdirāz (d. 1422) cited and utilised Nasafī's *Kitāb-i tanzīl* and also called Nasafī a "wise man."[3]

The popularity of Nasafī's brand of Sufism may be a result of the following points.

(i) Nasafī's "orthodox" Sufi treatises continued the trend of presenting Sufism in the terminology of the *kalām* and of the Philosophers as well as utilising their logic to demonstrate the "Islamicity" of Sufism. He aimed to deliver the Sufi message to an audience who probably would have been familiar with the terminology of the Koran and *kalām*, and may even have had some knowledge of the language and ideas of the Philosophers. Had Nasafī composed his treatises in the fashion of Sa'd al-Dīn Ḥammūya's highly enigmatic and esoteric works, such as *Miṣbaḥ fī'l taṣawwuf*, it is unlikely that the audience which Nasafī desired would have understood very much.

(ii) One of the major concerns of speculative Sufism is the classification of the levels of existence, which for Nasafī meant *Mulk, Malakūt* and *Jabarūt*. The Sufi would have found Nasafī's classification and interpretation of these levels both simple and comprehensive.

(iii) Nasafī attempted to be impartial in portraying the discourses of the various Islamic beliefs, that is, the beliefs of the *'Ulamā'*, Philosophers, Transmigrationists and the Sufis (who included the People of Unity). This non-partisan perspective was assisted by his belief that everything is a self-disclosure of God, which meant that every belief was a genuine expression of reality. Such a non-biased standpoint may have appealed to an audience larger than that claimed by more dogmatic Islamic thinkers.

(iv) Nasafī's version of Sufi belief was not extreme and adherence to it probably would not have caused excessive difficulty to novices. The discussions on ascetic discipline and religious effort, renunciation and other Sufi practices, constantly advised moderation. Moreover, his Sufism was strictly personal, in other words, between the novice, the Shaykh and God. For example:

> O Dervish! Make your manifest dimension resemble [that] of other people. You should live in the same way that others live since this is the legacy of the Friends and the dome *(qubba)* of the Friend, and everyone is beneath this dome.

> O Dervish! If there is interaction *(mu'āmala)* for you with God, [then] these are the states *(aḥwāl)* of the heart and no one else is aware of them. The progress and ascent pertain to [one's] inside *(andarūn)*, and your advantage *(imtiyāz)* over others is at the inside not at the outside *(bīrūn)*. The advantage of the hypocrites over others is at the outside, not the inside.[4]

Such advice from Nasafī contained several layers of meaning. Firstly it was a warning against those who made claims and used Sufism for their own gain, for the true Sufi upheld values such as humility and selflessness. Secondly, it provided a way for preserving the teachings of Sufism should any danger arise from unsympathetic political rulers. The threats of secular rulers always hung over Sufism, as did the opposition from some members of the *'Ulamā'* who stressed the exoteric dimension of Islam. One is struck by Nasafī's refusal to discuss matters pertaining to the letter of the law, however, the *'Ulamā'* may have been reconciled to Nasafī's Sufism because of his belief that the dervishes must first attend the *madrasa* and then progress to the *khānaqāh*. Related to this issue of not antagonising the "established" powers in society is the problem surrounding Nasafī's Shī'-ism. While some Sufis (such as Ḥaydar Āmulī) may indeed have witnessed such a nexus between Sufism and Shī'-ism, Nasafī's own beliefs remain a highly contentious issue. It appears that the problem of Shī'-ism was really quite peripheral to his Sufi message of perfection through ascetic discipline and religious effort.

Nasafī's form of Sufism was able to thrive during one of the most traumatic periods of Islamic history. His greatest contribution to Sufism in Central Asia and Iran was an interpretation of Sufism which was acceptable to most groups in society. It did not alienate the Mongol rulers or the *'Ulamā'* and at the same time his uncomplicated and summarised version of themes explained by Ibn 'Arabī and Najm al-Dīn Kubrā found new audiences, ensuring the survival and spread of Sufism.

Notes

1 See M. Chodkiewicz, *An Ocean Without Shore: Ibn 'Arabī, The Book, and the Law*, translated D. Streight, (Albany: SUNY Press, 1993).
2 Najm al-Dīn Kubrā, *Fawā'ih al-jamāl wa fawāṭih al-jalāl.*
3 H. Landolt, "Azīz-e Nasafī Et La Monisme Ésoterique," p. 168.
4 *al-Insān al-kāmil*, p. 290–291.

Appendix

NASAFĪ'S KNOWN WORKS

(1) *Kitāb-i tanzīl* (Book of the Descent)

This work of twenty chapters was probably one of Nasafī's very first because he mentions that the first six chapters were composed in Nasaf.[1] The subsequent four chapters were written in Bukhārā,[2] and this must have been before the devastation of Abaqa's massacre in 1271. The remaining chapters were set out in Bahrabād[3] at the tomb of Sa'd al-Dīn Ḥammūya.

The contents of *Kitāb-i tanzīl* are in fact representative of all of Nasafī's subsequent works. The first and by far longest chapter, entitled "the gnosis of God," reflects his ontological pre-occupation. This is continued in the next chapters on the gnosis of the world, the angels and man. The fifth chapter is one of the most interesting because it focuses upon the differences between Prophets and Friends of God. In most of his works, Nasafī includes short passages that mention a distinction between the two, but chapters five through eight are more detailed and clear. The second half of the work is much shorter than the first half and concentrates mainly upon issues that are relevant to the practical dimension of Sufism (such as chapter fifteen, entitled "the gnosis of service, seclusion and love").

One last significant point about *Kitāb-i tanzīl* is that there are two Arabic translations.[4] This work was most likely composed in Persian and then translated at a later date into Arabic, and this indicates the extent to which Muslims held Nasafī's treatises in esteem.

(2) *Kashf al-ḥaqā'iq* (Unveiling of Realities)

This major work which was probably completed in 1281, is longer than *Kitāb-i tanzīl*, despite the fact that the last three chapters and conclusion that are mentioned in the introduction are missing. The seven chapters are entitled "existence," "man," "the journey," "unity," "man's return," "this world and the next world, the night of destiny and the day of resurrection, and life and death," and "which are the seven heavens and earths, what the transforming of the land and the folding up of the skies are, which is the land of resurrection, which is the land of *'Arafāt*, and what *Ḥajj* is an expression for and how many kinds there are." Fortunately, Nasafī gives the titles of the three missing chapters and the conclusion to the book and it is possible to find similar issues discussed in his other works.[5]

(3) *Bayān-i tanzīl* (Explanation of the Descent)

In the introduction to this treatise, Nasafī comments that the dervishes requested him to write a book which is longer than *Kitāb-i tanzīl* and shorter than *Kashf al-ḥaqā'iq*, which suggests that it was written after 1281. The dervishes found the former work was a summary in terms of words and they could not understand the meanings behind them. The latter was so long that the dervishes could not memorise all the meanings.[6] Despite the request to write a work longer than *Kitāb-i tanzīl*, *Bayān-i tanzīl* is in fact shorter than the latter treatise.[7]

Bayān-i tanzīl has ten chapters whereas *Kitāb-i tanzīl* has twenty. The content is similar although not the same. Of particular interest is the first chapter on God and the seventh and eighth chapters on the Book and Word of God.

(4) *Maqṣad-i aqṣā* (The Most Sublime Goal)

As mentioned in the introduction, this was one of the first Sufi works translated into Latin and was finally rendered into an English paraphrase by E.H. Palmer in 1867. Palmer's efforts should be recognised in the light of the nineteenth century when scholars did not have the benefit of a wider range of academic Orientalist studies which modern researchers have. However the truth of James Morris's statement that *Oriental Mysticism* is a "truncated, grossly inadequate summary,"[8] cannot be denied.

It is probable that *Maqṣad-i aqṣā* was completed by Nasafī prior to 1281. The reason for this assumption is that in the introduction to *Kashf al-ḥaqā'iq*, Nasafī gives the date of 1281 and he mentions *Maqṣad-i aqṣā* in the very same section.[9] He comments that his own opinions are not included in *Kashf al-ḥaqā'iq* but they are set out in *Maqṣad-i aqṣā*. Despite this, Nasafī own opinions are not explicitly revealed in *Maqṣad*. Typically, the views of the People of the Holy Law, the Philosophers, the Sufis and the People of Unity are given. He even explains that his own views are not set out so that others cannot accuse him of infidelity *(kufr)*.[10]

Maqṣad-i aqṣā is a relatively short work.[11] Its contents include a lengthy introduction followed by chapters on "the gnosis of God's essence," "God's attributes," "God's acts in the words of the Philosophers," "the knowledge of Prophecy and Friendship of God," "the beliefs of the People of Imitation, the People of Reasoning and the People of Unveiling," "the gnosis of man," "the Four Seas" and a conclusion. The emphasis is ontological, chapters seven and eight (which discuss the levels of existence) being the most detailed of all.

Within *Maqṣad* there are several passages which clearly reveal the "intellectual-spiritual" influences upon Nasafī. He mentions several Sufis including Sa'd al-Dīn Ḥammūya, Ibn 'Arabī and his *Fuṣūṣ al-ḥikām*,[12] Shihāb al-Dīn Suhrawardī and his *'Awārif al-ma'ārif* and Ṣadr al-Dīn Rūmī. The latter may have been Ṣadr al-Dīn Qūnawī who is thought to be the author of *Tabṣirat al-mubtadī'* and Nasafī quotes this work several times in *Maqṣad*.

The number of extant manuscripts of *Maqṣad-i aqṣā* suggest that it was a very popular work among the Islamic populace. Numerous copies have been found in regions of Iran, Turkey, Pakistan, India and China.[13] The lucid language and the clarity in explaining complex issues in a simple way may have made *Maqṣad-i aqṣā* an ideal book for Sufi novices.

(5) *al-Insān al-kāmil* (The Perfect Man)

This work is a collection of treatises containing an introduction and twenty two chapters. In the edited version by M. Molé, Nasafī comments in his introduction that he wrote twenty chapters, ten for beginners and ten for those more advanced in the Sufi path.[14] These chapters appear to been composed by Nasafī over a long period of time. The first chapter was written in Bukhārā in 660 (A.H.) before Abaqa's destruction of that city. The subsequent chapters were written in other cities, as Nasafī moved south-west into Iran. Thus chapter two was put to paper in Bahrabād, chapter three in Kirmān, chapters four through to seven in Shirāz and chapters eight through to ten in Isfahān. The introduction to the work (which was probably written after all the other chapters, was composed in Arbaqūh, a city between Shirāz and Isfahān.[15] The work may have been completed well into the 1280s because in chapter six there is a mention of *Kashf al-ḥaqā'iq* (which is known to have been completed in 1281).[16] Questions have been raised by both Molé and Morris concerning the title, order and number of the treatises.[17] It may indeed be true that the original work has been added to, or revised by Nasafī or others, but the style and content of all the chapters is the same as Nasafī's other works (except for *Kashf-i ṣirāṭ* which shall be commented upon later).

The contents, as one might expect, are discussions of the People of the Holy Law, the Philosophers and the People of Unity. They are predominantly of an ontological nature, such as the three chapters explaining the levels of existence (*Mulk*, *Malakūt* and *Jabarūt*). There are also several chapters of a practical nature such as chapter six on the rules of seclusion.

As mentioned in the introduction, *Kitāb al-insān al-kāmil* has been translated in to western languages several times. It was rendered into French by Isabelle de Gastines in 1984. W. M. Thackston also translated it into English although it has not been published and my own translation of this work was published in 1992.

(6) *Manāzil al-sā'īrīn* (The Waystations of the Travellers)[18]

In Molé's edition of this work there are eleven chapters, the most interesting of which is its opening chapter on the Friendship of God. The remaining chapters focus on ontological issues such as the origin and return, and real and imaginary existence. There are also chapters detailing the beliefs of the Transmigrationists, the People of Unity and the People of Gnosis. The first three chapters of this work were written in Isfahān,[19] probably before 1281 since *Manāzil al-sā'īrīn* is mentioned in *Maqṣad-i aqṣā*[20] (which was composed before this date).

(7) *Zubdat al-ḥaqā'iq* (Quintessence of Realities)[21]

This is a relatively shorter work, only seventy seven pages in Ḥaqqwardī Nāṣirī's edition. There are two main parts to this book; the first discusses the knowledge of the "big man" or macrocosm *('ālam-i kabīr)*, while the second covers the knowledge of the "small man" or microcosm *('ālam-i ṣaghīr)*. Once again, the discussion is presented in the form of the beliefs of the People of the Holy Law, the Philosophers and the People of Unity.

Zubdāt al-ḥaqā'iq contains the same discussions that appear in all of Nasafī's works. Despite this, he comments that his explanation of man and the levels of man cannot be found in any of his other treatises, moreover such explanations cannot be found even in the books written by different Sufis.[22] Perhaps the reason for such comments is that *Zubdāt al-ḥaqā'iq* is didactic, and he may have wanted his Sufi novices to fully comprehend this book before reading others.

In Nasafī's own introduction to *Zubdāt*, he says that he originally wrote a work at the dervishes' request which he called *Mabdā' wa ma'ād*. However when they saw *Mabdā' wa ma'ād*, they asked him to shorten it and the result was *Zubdāt al-ḥaqā'iq*.[23]

(8) *Mabdā' wa ma'ād* (The Origin and Place of Return)

Although I have not seen this work, there are extent copies in the Indian Subcontinent. The "Comprehensive Catalogue of Persian Manuscripts in Pakistan"[24] states that *Mabdā' wa ma'ād* contains five chapters. These are "the origin," "the intelligences and souls of the lower world," "the return," "the state of souls after separation from the body" and "advice." In addition, at the end of the fourth chapter, it is mentioned that the treatise was compiled at Shīrāz, which suggests a dating of around 1280.

F. Meier's article on Nasafī's manuscripts lists the five chapters as "the discourse of the People of the Holy Law;" "the discourse of the Philosophers," "the discourse of the People of Unity," "the levels of man" and "travelling and journeying."[25]

(9) *Kashf-i ṣirāṭ* (Unveiling of the Path)[26]

Kashf-i ṣirāṭ is the black sheep among works that are attributed to Nasafī. Before discussing whether or not Nasafī was the author, the contents are set out below. Following a lengthy introduction, there are two sections;

Section A

i) Explaining the natural soul, animal soul *(nafs-i ḥaywānī)* and human soul and explaining the inner and outer senses.

ii) Explaining the real human soul *(nafs-i ḥaqīqī-yi ādamī)* in an abridged way.
iii) Explaining the real human in a detailed way.
iv) Explaining the levels of names of the real soul in the terminology of the Sufis.

Section B

i) Explaining the person who is on the right path *(ṣirāṭ al-mustaqīm)*; the Righteous, the Gnostic, the Friend and the Prophet.
ii) The kinds of disciples *(murīdān)* and the right path of each one and explaining the school of free thinking and the school of compulsion.
iii) Explaining love, stations and states.
iv) The reality of submission *(islām)*, faith *(īmān)* friendship *(walāyat)* and prophecy *(nubuwwat)*.

The lengthy introduction[27] is concerned largely with the *ḥadīth* "whoever knows himself knows his lord," and "God created Adam in His form." In other words, it focuses upon the degree to which man can know God's essence and reflects the discussion in *Kashf al-ḥaqā'iq*.[28] This sets the tone for the second section of the work which describes the four types of individual and the limits to their knowledge. Individuals are classified into four groups, based upon the Koran which states: "And whosoever obeys God and the Messenger, shall be with those whom God has blessed; the Prophets *(al-nabīyīn)*, the truthful *(al-ṣiddīqīn)*, the martyrs *(al-shuhadā')* and the righteous *(al-ṣāliḥīn)*."[29]

The author of *Kashf-i ṣirāṭ* classifies the righteous in the station of submission *(islām)*, the martyr (also called the gnostic) in the station of faith *(īmān)*, the truthful man (also called the Friend of God) in the station of excellence *(iḥsān)* and the prophet in the station of witnessing *('iyān)*.[30] In *Kashf al-ḥaqā'iq*, Nasafī also makes the same classification in a section entitled discussing the beliefs of "some of the Sufis."[31] *Kashf al-ḥaqā'iq* differs from *Kashf-i ṣirāṭ* however, in that in the former work there are also sections which explain the esoteric meaning *(bāṭin)* of Friendship of God. In other words, Friendship of God is the level where the natures, qualities and realities of things are understood, whereas Prophecy is the level where only the natures and qualities are understood.[32]

The whole tone and emphasis of *Kashf-i ṣirāṭ* is the superiority of Prophecy over Friendship of God. This is one of the reasons that M.

Molé has raised doubts concerning Nasafī's authorship of this work. If Nasafī did not compose this work then it must have been written by someone who was very familiar with his treatises but perhaps did not favour an explicit revelation of the non-manifest dimension of Islam, or as Molé suggests, a position less sympathetic to Shī'-ism. It is interesting that the author of *Kashf-i ṣirāṭ* adopts a conciliatory approach on the issue of Shī'-ism by stating that although some Sufis say *walāyat* arose from Abū Bakr and others say that it arose from 'Alī, it is better to say that both Abū Bakr and 'Alī were in the station of *walāyat*.[33]

The second reason that Molé cites in doubting Nasafī's authorship is that the name of this work does not appear in any of his other treatises. The mentioning of one of his books within others was a practice often employed by Nasafī, for example, *Kashf al-ḥaqā'iq* is mentioned in both *al-Insān al-kāmil* and *Bayān-i tanzīl*; *Maqṣad al-aqṣā* in *Kashf al-ḥaqā'iq*; *Manāzil al-sā'irīn* in *Maqṣad-i aqṣā*; and *Mabdā' wa ma'ād* in *Zubdāt al-ḥaqā'iq*. This at least suggests that *Kashf-i ṣirāṭ* is a book that was composed after all the others, perhaps by someone other than Nasafī. In *Kashf-i ṣirāṭ* two other works are mentioned, the names of which do not appear in any of Nasafī's other books. The author of *Kashf-i ṣirāṭ* intended the work for intermediary Sufis *(mutawassiṭān)*, whereas "Courtesies of the Way," *(Ādāb-i ṭarīqat)* was composed for the beginners and "the Unveiling of Secrets" *(Kashf-i rumūz)* was written for the advanced Sufis. Unfortunately there are no known manuscripts of these works. If it is accepted that *Kashf-i ṣirāṭ* was indeed written for the intermediary Sufis, then this may explain why there is no mention of the esoteric dimension of the Friendship of God which is present in Nasafī's books such as *al-Insān al-kāmil*, *Manāzil al-sā'irīn* and *Maqṣad-i aqṣā*.

The final point that Molé makes regarding the authorship of *Kashf-i ṣirāṭ* is that the style is very different from all of Nasafī's other works. Having read all of Nasafī's works, one is indeed struck by the relatively long Persian sentences and also the frequent use of Arabic quotations from Sufis such as Shihāb al-Dīn Suhrawardī which are found in *Kashf al-ṣirāṭ* but not in other treatises.

Despite this, there are arguments for attributing this work to Nasafī. Firstly, in the introduction to this treatise, the author states that his name is 'Azīz ibn Muḥammad al-Nasafī al-Ṣūfī.[34] In addition, the style of the work is exceedingly reminiscent of Nasafī's treatises. Moreover the content (aside from the problems already mentioned) is remarkably similar to the issues that appear in Nasafī's other works. If

Kashf-i ṣirāṭ was not written by Nasafī it must have been composed by someone who was familiar with his works, perhaps even one of his followers. Even if it was not written by Nasafī, the fact that someone wrote under his name gives an indication of Nasafī's fame and importance.

Notes

1 *Kitāb-i tanzīl*, fol. 64a, line 4.
2 Ibid. fol. 71b, line 12–13.
3 Ibid. fol. 82b, line 1
4 See F. Coslovi, "Liste des Manuscits Arabe et Persans Microfilms (Fond Molé) de l'Insitut de Recherche et d'Histoire des Textes."
5 Chapter eight was to explain the Book of God and the Word of God. A chapter by the same name appears in *Bayān-i tanzīl* – (Oxford, Bodleian Library, Ms. Pers. e 35, fol. 25a–26b). Chapter nine was to be a discussion on the reality of submission *(ḥaqīqat-i islām)*, faith *(īmān)*, excellence *(iḥsān)* and contemplation *('iyān)*, which is a fourfold division of the *ḥadīth* of Gabriel that Nasafī associates with four kinds of individuals in other works. The tenth chapter was to explain the Possessor of the Holy Law and the author of the resurrection, and also how many religions and Holy Laws there are, and what is the abrogation of the Holy Law and why it takes place (several of these points appear in chapter five of *Kitāb-i tanzīl*). The conclusion to the book explains the Seal of Prophecy and the Seal of Friendship, which again is discussed in chapter five of *Kitāb-i tanzīl*.
6 *Bayān-i tanzīl*, fol. 1a. lines 5–8. *Kashf al-ḥaqā'iq* is indeed longer than *Kitāb-i tanzīl*, although not considerably. In the Veliyuddin no. 1767 collection of Nasafī's works, *Kashf al-ḥaqā'iq* contains seventy two folios while *Kitāb-i tanzīl* contains fifty.
7 In Veliyuddin no. 1767, *Bayān-i tanzīl* contains thirty four folios.
8 J.W. Morris, "Ibn 'Arabī and His Interpreters part II: Influences and Interpretations," p. 746.
9 *Kashf al-ḥaqā'iq*, p. 10.
10 *Maqṣad-i aqṣā*, p. 277.
11 This work is found in Rabbānī, op. cit., pp. 210–85.
12 *Maqṣad-i aqṣā*, p. 264.
13 For the copies found in Turkey and Iran see Coslovi, "Liste des Manuscrits Arabes et Persans Microfilmes (Fonds Molé) de l'Institut de Recherche et d'Histoire des Textes," for those in Pakistan see *Catalogue of the Persian Manuscripts in the National Museum of Pakistan at Karachi*, ed. S. Arif Naushānī, (Islamabad: Iran-Pakistan Institute of Persian Studies, 1983). For manuscripts of *Maqṣad-i aqṣā* in India see *Sufism in the Sub Continent: Papers presented in the Second Khudabakhsh South-Asian Regional Seminar on Tasawwuf Manuscripts*, (Patna: Khudabakhsh Oriental Public Library, 1985). A Persian manuscript of *Maqṣad-i aqṣā* has even been found in China, (Gansu province), see Mozafar Bakhtiyar's

article on China in *World Survey of Islamic Manuscripts*, Vol. IV, ed. G. Roper, (London: al-Furqān Islamic Heritage Foundation, 1994), p. 89. According to research on Islam in pre-modern China undertaken by S. Murata, only four Islamic texts were translated into Chinese. These were Najm al-Dīn Rāzī's *Mirsād al-'ibād*, Jāmī's *Lawā'ih* and *Ashi"at al-lama'āt,* and Nasafī's *Maqṣad-i aqṣā*. The Chinese translation was made in 1679 (see D. Leslie, *Islamic Literature in China* (Canberra, pp. 32–34)).

14 *al-Insān al-kāmil*, pp. 2–3.
15 *al-Insān al-kāmil*. For chapters 1–4 see p. 80; chapters 5–7 see p. 118; chapters 8–10 see p. 153; introduction see p. 14.
16 *al-Insān al-kāmil*, p. 110.
17 See J. Morris, "Ibn 'Arabī and his interpreters, Part II," p. 745.
18 This work is appended to M. Molé's edition of *al-Insān al-kāmil*, pp. 313–456.
19 *Manāzil al-sā'irīn*, p. 341.
20 *Maqṣad-i aqṣā*, p. 263.
21 *Zubdāt al-ḥaqā'iq*, ed. Ḥaqq-wardī Nāsirī (Tehran: Kitābkhāna-yi tahūrī, 1985).
22 Ibid. p. 94.
23 Ibid. pp. 41–42.
24 *Comprehensive Catalogue of Persian Manuscripts in Pakistan*, Vol II, compiled by Aḥmad Monzavī (Islamabad: Iran-Pakistan Institute of Persian Studies, 1984), p. 980.
25 F. Meier, "Die Schriften des 'Azīz Nasafī," p. 178.
26 *Kashf-i ṣirāṭ* Veliyuddin no. 1767, folios 204–244. Veliyuddin no. 1685, folios 79–103. The Centre National de la Recherche Scientifique hold microfilm of Veliyuddin no. 1765; the "pochette" number is 25587–25588. I was not able to locate a microfilm of Veliyuddin 1685, although there is a poor quality photocopy of the manuscript.
27 *Kashf-i ṣirāṭ*, Veliyuddin no. 1676, fol. 204a–210a.
28 *Kashf al-ḥaqā'iq*, pp. 123–125.
29 Koran 4:71.
30 *Kashf-i ṣirāṭ* Veliyuddin, no. 1767, folio 218–219.
31 *Kashf al-ḥaqā'iq*, p. 77.
32 Ibid. pp. 58–59. The discussion is examined in more detail in chapter six.
33 *Kashf-i ṣirāṭ*, Veliyuddin no. 1767, fol. 236a.
34 Ibid. fol. 204a.

Bibliography

I Works by Nasafī

Bayān-i tanzīl, Oxford: Bodleian Library, Ms. Pers. e 35.

al-Insān al-kāmil, ed. M. Molé. Tehran-Paris: Institut Franco-Iranien, 1962.

Kashf al-ḥaqā'iq, ed. A. Dāmghānī. Tehran: Bungāh-i tarjuma wa nashr-i kitāb, 1965.

Kashf-i ṣirāṭ, Istanbul: Veliyuddin no. 1767, folios 204–244.

Kitāb-i tanzīl, Manchester University: John Rylands Library, C112 folios 38–84.

Manāzil al-sā'īrīn, edited M. Molé. Tehran-Paris: Institut Franco-Iranien, 1962.

Maqṣad-i aqṣā, Appended to Jāmī's *Ashi"at al-lama'āt*, ed. H. Rabbānī, Tehran: Kitabkhāna-yi 'ilmīyya-yi hāmidī, 1973.

Zubdat al-ḥaqā'iq, edited Ḥaqq-wardī Nāsirī. Tehran: Kitābkhāna-yi tahūrī, 1985.

II Others

Addas, C. *Quest for the Red Sulphur*, translated P. Kingsley. Cambridge: Islamic Texts Society, 1994.

Affifi, A.E. "Ibn 'Arabi," in *A History of Muslim Philosophy*, Vol. I, ed. M.M. Sharif. Wiesbaden: Otto Harrassowitz, 1963.

Algar, H. "Some Observations on Religion in Safavid Persia," *Iranian Studies* 7 (1974)

Amulī, S.H. *Inner Secrets of the Path*, trans. Assadullah ad-Dhaakir Yate. Dorset: Zahra Trust, 1989.

Ansari, M. *Sufism and Shari'ah*. Leicester: The Islamic Foundation, 1986.

Arberry, A.J. *Fifty Poems of Hāfiz*. London: Cambridge University Press, 1947.

Arnold,T.W. *Painting in Islam*. New York: Dover Publications, 1965.

Ashtiyānī, J. *Rasā'il Qaysarī*. Tehran: Intishārāt-i anjuman-i islāmī-yi ḥikmat wa falsafa-yi Irān, 1975.

Austin, R. *Ibn al-'Arabī: The Bezels of Wisdom*. New York: Paulist Press, 1980.

'Ayn al-Quḍāt. *Tamhīdāt*, ed. 'Afīf 'Ussayrān. Tehran: Intishātāt manuchihrī, 1373/1994.
——*Nāmahā-yi 'Ayn al-Quḍāt*, ed. 'Afīf 'Ussayrān, Tehran: Intishārāt zawār, 1362/1983.
Baldick, J. *Mystical Islam*. London: I.B. Taurus, 1989.
Barthold, W. *Turkestan Down to the Mongol Invasion*. London: Luzac, 1928.
Bausani, A. "Religion under the Mongols," *Cambridge History of Iran*, Vol. V. Cambridge: Cambridge University Press, 1968.
Böwering, G. *The Mystical Vision of Existence in Classical Islam*. Berlin-New York: Walter De Gruyter, 1980.
Boyle, J.A. *'Ala al-Din 'Ata al-Malik Juvaini, The History of the World Conqueror.* Manchester: Manchester University Press, 1958.
——*The Mongol World Empire*, London: Valorium Reprints, 1977.
Butterworth, C.E. *The Political Aspects of Islamic Philosophy.* Harvard: Harvard University Press, 1992.
Chittick, W. "Rūmī and waḥdat al-wujūd," *The Heritage of Rūmī*, eds A. Banani and G. Sabagh. Cambridge: Cambridge University Press, 1994.
——*The Sufi Path of Knowledge*. Albany: SUNY Press, 1989.
——*The Sufi Path of Love*. Albany: SUNY Press, 1983.
——*Imaginal Worlds*. Albany: SUNY Press, 1994.
——*Faith and Practice*. Albany: SUNY Press, 1992.
——"The Five Divine Presences," *Muslim World* 72, (1982).
——"Death and the World of Imagination in Ibn 'Arabi's Eschatology." *Muslim World* 78, (1988)
Chodkiewicz, M. *Seal of the Saints*, translated L. Sherrard. Cambridge: The Islamic Texts Society, 1993.
——*An Ocean Without Shore*, translated D. Streight. Albany: SUNY Press, 1993.
Corbin, H. "De la Philosophie Prophétique en Islam Shī'ite," *Eranos Jahrbuch* 1962 (Zürich, 1963).
——*Creative Imagination in the Sufism of Ibn 'Arabî.* Princeton: Princeton University Press, 1969.
——*Spiritual Body and Celestial Earth*, translated N. Pearson. Princeton University Press, 1977.
——*The Man of Light in Iranian Sufism*, translated N. Pearson. London/Boulder: Shambhala, 1978.
——*History of Islamic Philosophy*, translated Liadain Sherrard. London: Kegan Paul International, 1993.
Coslovi, F. "Liste des Manuscits Arabe et Persans Microfilms (Fond Molé) de l'Insitut De Recherche et d'Histoire Des Textes," *Studia Iranica* 7 (1978).
——"Second Liste de Microfilms des Manuscrits Arabes et Persans du Fond Molé," *Studia Iranica* 14/2 (1985).
Dabashi, H. "The Sufi Doctrine of 'The Perfect Man' and a View of the Hierarchical Structure of Islamic Culture." The Islamic Quarterly, Vol. XXX, No. 2, 1986, pp. 118–130.
Davidson, H. *Alfarabi, Avicenna and Averroes on Intellect*. Oxford: Oxford University Press, 1992.
DeWeese, D. "The Eclipse of the Kubraviyah in Central Asia," *Iranian Studies*, Vol. 21, Nos. 1–2, 1988.

Elias, J.J. *The Throne Carrier of God: The Life and Thought of 'Ala ad-Dawla as- Simnani*. Albany: SUNY Press, 1995.

——"The Sufi Lords of Bahrabad: Sa'd al-Dīn and Sadr al-Dīn Ḥamuwayi," *Iranian Studies*, volunme 27, numbers 1–4, 1994.

——"A Kubrawi Treatise on Mystical Visions: the Risāla-yi Nūriyya of 'Alā' ad- Dawleh as-Simnānī," *The Muslim World*, Vol. 83, no. 1 (1993).

Ernst, C.W. *Words of Ecstacy in Sufism*. Albany: SUNY Press, 1985.

——*Rūzbihān Baqlī*. Richmond: Curzon, 1996.

Friedmann, Y. *Prophecy Continuous*. Berkeley: University of California Press, 1989.

Furūzānfar, B. *Aḥādīth mathnawī*. Tehran: Amir kabir, 1982.

Gairdner, W.H.T. *al-Ghazālī's "The Niche for Lights:" Mishkāt al-anwār*. London: Royal Asiatic Society, 1915; repr. Lahore: SH Muḥammad Ashraf, 1952.

Ghazālī (Abū Ḥāmid) *Kīmīyā-yi sa'ādat*, edited Husayn Khadīwjam. Tehran: Markaz-i intishārāt-i 'ilmī wa farhangī, 1361/1983.

Graham, W.A. *Divine Word and Prophetic Word in Early Islam*. The Hague: Mouton, 1977.

Goodman, L.E. *Avicenna*. London: Routledge, 1992.

Halm, H. *Shiism*, trans. Janet Watson. Edinburgh: Edinburgh University Press, 1991.

Ḥammūya, S. *Miṣbāḥ fī'l-taṣawwuf*. Tehran: Intishārāt mawlā, 1983.

Hodgson, M. *The Venture of Islam*. Chicago: University of Chicago, 1974–77.

Hujwīrī. *Kashf al-maḥjūb*, trans. R.A. Nicholson. London: Luzac, 1911; repr. London: 1976.

Huxley, A. *The Doors of Perception*. London: Chatto and Windus, 1954.

Irving, C. *Crossroads of Civilization*. London: Weidenfeld and Nicholson, 1979.

Izutsu, T. *Sufism and Taoism*. Berkeley: University of California Press, 1983.

——"The Theophanical Ego in Sufism," *Sophia Perennis*. Tehran: the Bulletin of the Imperial Iranian Academy of Philosophy, Vol. IV, no. 1. (1978).

——*Creation and the Timeless Order of Things: Essays in Islamic Mystical Philosophy*. Oregon: White Cloud Press, 1994.

Jones R.H. *Mysticism Examined*. Albany: SUNY Press, 1993.

Katz, S. *Mysticism and Religious Traditions*. Oxford: Oxford University Press, 1983.

——*Mysticism and Philosophical Analysis*. London: Sheldon Press, 1978.

Kubrā, Najm al-Dīn. *Fawā'iḥ al-Jamāl wa fawātiḥ al-Jalāl*, ed. F. Meier. Wiesbaden: Steiner, 1957.

——*al-Sā'ir al-ḥā'ir*. Tehran: Naqsh-i Jahān, 1361.

——*Ila' al-hā'im al-khā'if min lawmat al-lā'im*. Tehran: Sāzmān i intishārāt-i kayhān, 1364.

——*Risāla ādāb al-sulūk* (Persian translation by Ḥ. Qumsha'ī), in *Kīmiyā*, ed. A. Bihishtī Shīrāzī. Tehran, 1366.

Leaman, O. *An introduction to Medieval Islamic Philosophy*. Cambridge: Cambridge University Press, 1985.

Landolt, H. "Simnânî on waḥdat al-wujûd." *Wisdom of Persia: Collected Papers on Islamic Philosophy and Mysticism*. Edited by H. Landolt and

M. Mohaghegh. Tehran: La branche de Téhéran de l'institut des études islamique de l'Université McGill, 1971.

——"Le Paradoxe De La "Face De Dieu": 'Azīz-e Nasafī (VIIe/XIIIe) Et Le "Monisme Ésoterique" De L'Islam, "*Studia Iranica*, 25, 1996.

——"Two Types of Mystical Thought in Muslim Iran," *Muslim World*, Vol. 68 (1978).

——"Walāyah." *Encyclopedia of Religion*, Ed. M. Eliade, pp. 316–323.

——"Sa'd al-Dīn Ḥammū'ī," *Encyclopedia of Islam*[2], vol VIII.

Lewisohn, L. *Beyond Faith and Infidelity*. London: Curzon Press, 1995.

Meier, F. "Das problem der Natur im Esoterischen Monismus des Islams," *Eranos- Jahrbuch* 14 (1946). Translated into English as "The Problem of Nature in the Esoteric Monism of Islam," *Spirit and Nature: Papers from the Eranos Yearbook*, ed. J. Campbell. New York: 1954.

——"Die Schriften des 'Azīz-i Nasafī," *Wiener Zeitschrift für die Kunde des Morganlandes* 52 (1953).

Melville, C. "Pādishāh-i Islām: the Conversion of Sultan Maḥmūd Ghāzān Khān." *Pembroke Papers I: Persian and Islamic Studies in honour of Peter Avery*, ed. C. Melville. Cambridge: Cambridge University Press, 1990.

Michon, J.L. "Sacred Music and Dance" *Islamic Spirituality:Manifestations*, ed. S.H. Nasr. London: SCM Press, 1991.

Mohammad, O.N. *Averroes Doctrine of Immortality*. Ontario: Wilfrid Laurier University Press, 1984.

Molé, M. "Les Kubrawiya Entre Sunnisme et Shiisme Aux Huitieme et Neuvieme Siecles de l'Hégire," *Revue des Études Islamiques* 52 (1961).

Momen. M. *An Introduction to Shi'i Islam*. New Haven: Yale University Press, 1985.

Morewedge, P. *Islamic Philosophy and Mysticism*. Albany: SUNY Press, 1981.

——*Neoplatonism and Islamic Thought*, Albany, SUNY Press, 1992.

Monzavī, A. *Comprehensive Catalogue of Persian Manuscripts in Pakistan*, Vol II. Islamabad: Iran-Pakistan Institute of Persian Studies, 1984.

Morgan, D. *The Mongols*. Oxford: Blackwell, 1986.

Morris, J. "Ibn 'Arabī and His Interpreters," *Journal of the American Oriental Society* 106 (1986).

Mueller, A. *Excerpta Manuscripti Cujusdam Turcici*. Coloniae Brandenburgicae: 1665.

Murata, S. *The Tao of Islam*, Albany: SUNY Press, 1992.

Murata and Chittick. *The Vision of Islam*, New York: Paragon House, 1994.

Nakamura, K. "Imam Ghazali's Cosmology Reconsidered with Special Reference to the Concept of Jabarut," *Muslim World*, (1994).

Nasr, S. H. *Three Muslim Sages*. (Cambridge: Harvard University Press, 1964).

Naushānī, S.A. *Catalogue of the Persian Manuscipts in the National Museum of Pakistan at Karachi*. Islamabad: Iran-Pakistan Institute of Persian Studies, 1983.

Netton, I.R. *Allah Transcendent*. London: Routledge, 1989.

——*Al-Farabi and His School*. London: Routledge, 1992.

——*Muslim Neoplatonists*. London: Allen and Unwin, 1982.

Nicholson, R.A. *The Mystics of Islam*. London: G. Bell & Sons, 1914.

——*Selected Poems from the Diwan-i Shams Tabrizi*. Cambridge, Cambridge University Press, 1898; repr. Richmond: Curzon Press, 1994.
Nizami, K.A. "The Naqshbandiyyah Order." *Islamic Spirituality: Manifestations*, ed. S.H. Nasr. London, SCM Press, 1991.
Niẓāmī. *Makhzan al-asrār*: Tehran, Matba'a Armaghān, 1313/1895. For an English translation see Gholām Hosein Dārāb's *The Treasury of Mysteries*. London: Arthur Probsthain, 1945.
Palmer, E.H. *Oriental Mysticism: a Treatise on Sufiistic and Unitarian Theosophy of the Persians*. London: 1867; second edition, 1938.
Paul, J. "A Propos De Quelques Microfilms Du Fond Molé." *Studia Iranica* 18 (1989).
Petroshevsky, I.P. "The Socio-Economic Conditions of Iran under the Il-Khans," *Cambridge History of Iran*, Vol. V, Cambridge: Cambridge University Press, 1968.
Philips, D.E. *The Mongols*. New York: Frederick A. Praeger, 1969.
Pike, N. *Mystic Union*. London: Cornell University Press, 1992.
Plotinus. *Enneads*, translated Stephen MacKenna. London: Penguin, 1991.
Radtke, & O'Kane. *The Concept of Sainthood in Early Islamic Mysticism*, London: Curzon Press, 1996.
Rahman, F. *Avicenna's Psychology*. London: Oxford University Press, 1952.
Rāzī, Najm al-Dīn. *Mirṣad al-'ibād*, translated H. Algar: *The Path of God's Bondsmen from Origin to Return*. New York: Caravan Books, 1982.
Rice, C. *The Persian Sufis*. London: Allen and Unwin Ltd, 1964.
Ridgeon, L. "The Life and Times of 'Azīz Nasafī," *Sufi: A Journal of Sufism* XXII (1994): 31–35.
——"'Azīz Nasafī and Visionary Experience," *Sufi: A Journal of Sufism* XXIV, (1995): 22–28.
——"The Felicitous Life in Sufism," *Sufi: A Journal of Sufism* XXVIII (1996): 30–35.
——"'Azīz Nasafī's Six Ontological Faces," *Iran*, 1996, 85–99.
Roper, G. *World Survey of Islamic Manuscripts*, Vol IV, London: al-Furqān Islamic Heritage Foundation, 1994.
Rūzbihān Baqlī. *Sharḥ-i Shaṭḥiyyāt,* ed. H. Corbin. Tehran: Department D'Iranologie de l'Institute Franco-Iranien, 1966.
Sachedina, A.A. *Islamic Messianism*. Albany: SUNY Press, 1981.
Al-Sarrāj. *Kitāb al-luma' fī'l-taṣawwuf*, ed. R.A. Nicholson. Leiden and London: E.J. Brill, 1914.
Saunders, J.J. *The History of the Mongol Conquests*. London: Routledge & Kegan Paul, 1971.
Schimmel, A. *As Through a Veil*. New York: Columbia University Press, 1982.
——*And Muhammad is His Messenger*. Chapel Hill: The University of North Carolina Press, 1985.
——*Mystical Dimensions of Islam*. Chapel Hill: University of North Carolina Press, 1975.
Sells, M. *Early Islamic Mysticism*. New York: Paulist Press, 1996.
Simnānī. *Muṣannafāt-i fārsī*, ed. Najib Māyil Hirawī, Tehran: Shirkat-i intishārāt-i 'ilmī wa farhangī, 1990.
Smith, M. *al-Ghazālī the Mystic*. London: Luzac, 1944; repr. Lahore: Hijra International Publications, 1983.

——*Rābi'a the Mystic*. Cambridge: Cambridge University Press, 1928.

Stade, R.C. *al-Ghazālī's Maqṣad al-asnā, "The Ninety Name of God in Islam."* Ibadan, Nigeria: Caystar Press, 1970.

Suhrawardī, (Yaḥyā) *Ḥikmat al-ishrāq*, translated into Persian by Sayyid Ja'far Sajjādī, Tehran University Press, 1357/1978.

Ṭabāṭabā'ī, M.H. *Shi'ite Islam*, trans, S.H. Nasr, Albany: SUNY Press, 1977.

Takeshita, M. *Ibn 'Arabī's Theory of the Perfect Man and its Place in the History of Islamic Thought*. Tokyo: Institute for the Study of Languages and Cultures of Asia and Africa, Tokyo University of Foreign Studies, 1987.

Thackston, W.M. *Intimate Conversations*. New York: Paulist Press, 1978.

Tholuck, F.A.G. *Ssufismus Sive Theosophia Persarum Pantheistica*. Berlin: 1821.

Trimingham, J.S. *The Sufi Orders in Islam*. Oxford: Oxford University Press,1971.

Waley, M.I. "Contemplative Disciplines in Early Persian Sufism." *Classical Persian Sufism: from its Origins to Rūmī*., ed. L. Lewisohn. London: KNP, 1993.

Ware, T. *The Orthodox Church*. London: Penguin, 1987.

Watt, W.M. *The Faith and Practice of al-Ghazālī*, (al-munqidh min al-ḍalāl), London: G. Allen and Unwin, 1953.

Wensinck, A. J. "On the Relation Between Ghazālī's Cosmology and His Mysticism." *Mededeelingen der Koninklijke Akademie wan Wetenschappen*. Amsterdam: Noord-Hollandsche Uitgevers-Maatschappij, 1933.

Zaehner, R.C. *Hindu and Muslim Mysticism*, London: Athlone Press, 1960.

——*Mysticism, Sacred and Profane*. London: Oxford University Press, 1961.

Zarrīnkūb, A.H. *Justujū dar taṣawwuf-i Irān*. Tehran: Amir kabir, 1983.

Zhukorski, V. "The Idea of Man and Knowledge in the Conception of Persian Mystics," *Bulletin of the School of Oriental Studies*, Vol. VI, 1930–32.

Koranic and Ḥadīth Index

Koranic References

Ḥadīth References

Subject Index